RECORDS OF CIVILIZATION, SOURCES AND STUDIES

RECORDS OF CIVILIZATION
IN NORTON PAPERBACK EDITIONS

AN INTRODUCTION
TO DIVINE AND HUMAN
READINGS

BY CASSIODORUS SENATOR

TRANSLATED

WITH AN INTRODUCTION AND NOTES

BY LESLIE WEBBER JONES

W · W · NORTON & COMPANY · INC · *New York*

TO MY WIFE

RACHEL RAND JONES

Preface

━━━◆ ◆━━━

In its length and industry Cassiodorus' career as a statesman and scholar is almost without parallel. From A.D. 503 to 539, the period during which he held a succession of important political offices under four Ostrogothic rulers—Theodoric, the regent Amalasuentha, Theodahad, and Witigis—he strove to build a strong Italian state in which Gothic and Roman elements might work together in complementary and harmonious fashion. His dream was utterly shattered by the victories of Belisarius. From 539 to 575, the year in which he died, at the advanced age of ninety-five, he devoted an equal amount of energy to matters which ultimately proved of much more importance to the world: commenting on the Christian Scriptures, assembling an important collection of theological and of classical works, and teaching the monks of the two monasteries which he had founded precise rules for the copying and preservation of his precious manuscripts.

The two books of the present work belong to the monastic phase of his activities. The contents of the work are analyzed in detail in my Introduction. Here, however, it will be enough to state that Book I considers, among other things, the nature of the Bible; the importance of various ecclesiastical and secular works as keys to its understanding; and the procedure to be followed by the monks in copying, emending, and annotating manuscripts. Book II is a treatise on the seven liberal arts. Both books are also bibliographical guides and inspirations to librarians to collect sound copies of the works recommended.

Except in approximately a dozen instances in which I have preferred a different reading, I have based my translation upon the excellent Latin text of Mynors. To the best of my knowledge, my translation is the first in any language. The task has been difficult for reasons which I have pointed out in my Introduction. The wordy and elaborate style seems to cry out for simplification. In his translation of a more difficult work of Cassiodorus, the *Variae*, Hodgkin omitted half of the original contents and paraphrased the rest. My method has been much less radical: I have attempted to retain as much as possible of the original, even when the original is awkward and complicated. I hope that various readers, even some Latinists who may not be well acquainted with the syntax and style of the period, will find my rendering useful.

The index has been prepared by a professional indexer supplied by the Columbia University Press. Some scholars will desire to consult the three detailed Latin indices (_rerum, nominum,_ and _auctorum_) which appear in Mynors' critical text; the _index auctorum_ gives a provisional indication of the contents of the library at Vivarium.

I am grateful to Professor R. A. B. Mynors, of Cambridge University, for granting me permission to use his Latin text as the basis of my translation and for answering queries on the meanings of three or four of Cassiodorus' words; to Professor Martin R. P. McGuire, of the Catholic University of America, and to Sister Mary Gratia Ennis, of the College of Notre Dame of Maryland, for making the latter's doctoral dissertation available to me in page-proof form; to Professor Austin P. Evans, of Columbia University, editor of the series in which the present volume appears, Mr. Henry H. Wiggins, manager of the Publication Department of the Columbia University Press, and Miss Ida M. Lynn, an assistant editor of the same Press, for providing prompt and efficient guidance in the preparation of the manuscript for the printer; and, finally, to my wife for expressing patiently her reactions to my translation in its various stages.

LESLIE W. JONES

The City College, New York
February 15, 1946

Contents

Abbreviations

⸻❖⸻

THE READER will find immediately below a list of the books and articles cited most frequently in this volume together with the abbreviations by which they are indicated. References to the Bible normally relate to the Latin Vulgate and also to the Catholic (Douai-Rheims) English translation of 1609, both of which observe the same divisions for books, chapters, and verses. When the King James version observes different divisions, the necessary additional references are placed in parentheses after the references to the Latin Vulgate and the Douai-Rheims version.

Batiffol	Batiffol, Pierre. L'Abbaye de Rossano. Paris, 1891.
Beer, *Bemerkungen*	Beer, Rudolf. "Bemerkungen über den ältesten Handschriftenbestand des Klosters Bobbio," *Anzeiger der kaiserliche Akademie der Wissenschaft zu Wien, philologische-historische Klasse,* Vol. XLVIII (1911), No. XI.
Beer, *Monumenta*	—— ed. Monumenta palaeographica Vindobonensia, II (Leipzig, 1913), 15–26.
Bieter	Bieter, Frederic Arnold. The Syntax of the Cases and Prepositions in Cassiodorus' Historia ecclesiastica tripertita. Washington, D.C., The Catholic University of America, 1938. Dissertation.
Birt	Birt, Theodor. Das antike Buchwesen in seinem Verhaltniss zur Litteratur. Berlin, 1882.
Chapman, *Amiatinus*	Chapman, John. "The Amiatinus and Cassiodorus," *Revue bénédictine,* XXXVIII (1926), 139–150; XXXIX (1927), 12–32; XL (1928), 130–134.
Chapman, *Notes*	—— Notes on the Early History of the Vulgate Gospels. Oxford, 1908.
Chapman, *St. Benedict*	—— Saint Benedict and the Sixth Century. New York and London, 1929.
Comm. Psalt.	Cassiodorus Senator, Flavius Magnus Aurelius. *Expositio in Psalterium,* in Migne, *Pat. Lat.,* Vol. LXX.

De orthographia	—— "De orthographia," in Heinrich Keil, ed., *Grammatici latini,* Vol. VII (Leipzig, 1880).
Donat.	Donatus, Aelius. "Artes grammaticae," in Heinrich Keil, ed., *Grammatici latini,* IV, 355–403. Leipzig, 1864.
Ennis	Ennis, Mary Gratia. The Vocabulary of the Institutiones of Cassiodorus; with special advertence to the technical terminology and its sources. Washington, D.C., The Catholic University of America, 1939.
Fortun.	Fortunatianus. "Ars rhetorica," in C. F. Halm, *Rhetores latini minores,* Leipzig, 1863, p. 79.
Franz	Franz, A. M. Aurelius Cassiodorus Senator. Breslau, 1872.
Garet	*Cassiodori opera omnia,* ed. by Johannes Garetius (originally published in 1679); as reprinted in *Pat. Lat.,* Vol. LXX (1865).
Heath	The Thirteen Books of Euclid's Elements; translated from the text of Heiberg . . . by T. L. Heath. Cambridge (Eng.), 1908.
Hermann	Hermann, T. "Die Schule von Nisibis," in *Zeitschrift für neutestamentliche Wissenschaft,* XXV (1926), 89–122.
Hodgkin	The Letters of Cassiodorus . . . with an introduction by Thomas Hodgkin. London, 1886.
Hörle	Hörle, G. H. Frühmittelalterliche Mönchs- und Klerikerbildung in Italien. Freiburg im Breisgau, 1914.
Howell	The Rhetoric of Alcuin & Charlemagne; a translation . . . by Wilbur Samuel Howell. Princeton, 1941.
Inst.	Cassiodorus Senator, Flavius Magnus Aurelius. Institutiones. See Mynors also.
Isid.	Isidore. Etymologiae.
Jones, *Cologne*	Jones, Leslie Webber. The Script of Cologne from Hildebald to Hermann. Cambridge, Mass., The Mediaeval Academy of America, 1932.

Lehmann	Lehmann, Paul. "Cassiodorstudien," *Philologus,* LXXI (1912), 278–279; LXXII (1913), 503–517; LXXIII (1914), 253–273; LXXIV (1917), 351–383.
Löfstedt	Löfstedt, Einar. Syntactica; Studien und Beiträge zur historischen Syntax des Lateins. 2 vols. Lund, 1928–1933.
Manitius	Manitius, Max. Geschichte der lateinischen Litteratur des Mittelalters. I, 36–52. Munich, 1911.
Mart.	Martianus Capella. De nuptiis Philologiae et Mercurii.
Mercati	Mercati, Giovanni. M. Tulli Ciceronis De re publica libri e codice rescripto Vaticano latina 5757 phototypice expressi; codices e Vaticanis selecti quam simillime expressi iussa Pii XI. P. M. consilio et opera curatorum Bibliothecae Apostolicae Vaticanae, Vol. XXIII. Bibliotheca Apostolica Vaticana, 1934.
Migne, *Pat. Lat.*	Migne, Jacques Paul, ed. Patrologia cursus completus; series latina. 221 vols. Paris, 1844–1864.
Minasi	Minasi, G. M. A. Cassiodoro Senatore . . . ricerche storico-critiche. Naples, 1895.
Mommsen, *Variae*	Mommsen, Theodor, ed. Cassiodorus, Variae, in *M.G., Auct. ant.* (see the item immediately below), Vol. XII (1894).
M.G.	Pertz, Georg Heinrich, Theodor Mommsen, and others, eds. Monumenta Germaniae historica (500–1500). Berlin, folio series, 1826–1896. Quarto series, 1876 ff.
M.G., Auct. ant.	—— Auctores antiqui.
M.G., Conc.	—— Conciliae.
M.G., Ep.	—— Epistulae.
M.G., SS.	—— Scriptores.
Mynors	Mynors, Roger Aubrey Baskerville. Cassiodori Senatoris Institutiones Edited from the MSS. Oxford, 1937.
Nelz	Nelz, R. Die theologische Schulen der morgenländischen Kirchen während den 7sten Jahrhundert. Bonn, 1916.

Notitia	Seeck, Otto, ed. Notitia dignitatum. Berlin, 1876. (See also Eduard Böcking, ed., Notitia dignitatum et administrationum omnium tam civilium quam militarium in partibus Orientis et Occidentis. 2 vols. Bonn, 1839–1853.
Pfeilschifter	Pfeilschifter, Georg. Theodorich der Grosse. Mainz, 1910.
Pliny	Pliny. Naturalis historia.
Quentin, *Essais*	Quentin, Henri. Essais de critique textuelle. Paris, 1926.
Quentin, *Mémoire*	—— Mémoire sur l'établissement du texte de la Vulgate. *Collectanea Biblica Latina.* Rome and Paris, 1922. Vol. VI.
Quint.	Quintilian. Institutio oratoria.
Rabanus	Rabanus Maurus.
Rand, *Founders*	Rand, Edward Kennard. Founders of the Middle Ages. Cambridge, Mass., 1928. Chapter VII.
Rand, *New Cassiodorus*	—— "The New Cassiodorus," *Speculum,* XIII (1938), 433–447.
Roger	Roger, Maurice. L'Enseignement des lettres classiques d'Ausone à Alcuin. Paris, 1905.
Rohlfs	Rohlfs, Gerhard. Griechen und Romanen in Unteritalien. Geneva, 1924.
Sandys	Sandys, John Edwin. A History of Classical Scholarship. 3d ed. Cambridge (Eng.), I (1921), 258–270.
Schanz	Schanz, Martin. Geschichte der römischen Literatur . . . Vol. IV, Part 2 (Leipzig, 1920).
Skahill	Skahill, Bernard Henry. The Syntax of the Variae of Cassiodorus. Washington, D.C., The Catholic University of America, 1934. Dissertation.
Suelzer	Suelzer, Mary Josephine. The Clausulae in Cassiodorus. Washington, D.C., The Catholic University of America, 1944. Dissertation.
Teuffel	W. S. Teuffel's Geschichte der römischen Literatur . . . neu bearbeitet von Wilhelm Kroll und Franz Skutsch. Leipzig, 1913–1920. 3 vols.

Thiele   Thiele, Hans. "Cassiodor, seine Kloster-gründung Vivarium und sein Nachwirkung im Mittelalter," in Studien and Mitteilungen zur Geschichte des Benediktiner-Ordens und seiner Zweige, III (1932), 378–419.

Thorbecke   Thorbecke, August. Cassiodorus Senator. Heidelberg, 1867.

Usener   Usener, Hermann Karl. Anecdoton Holderi; ein Beitrag zur Geschichte Roms in ostgothischer Zeit. Bonn, 1877.

van de Vyver   van de Vyver, A. "Cassiodore et son œuvre," *Speculum,* VI (1931), 244–292.

van de Vyver, *Vivarium*   —— "Les *Institutiones* de Cassiodore et sa fondation à Vivarium," *Revue bénédictine,* LXIII (1941), 59–88.

Var.   Varro. De lingua latina.

Variae   See above under Mommsen, *Variae.*

Zimmermann   Zimmermann, Odo John. The Late Latin Vocabulary of the *Variae* of Cassiodorus; with special advertence to the technical terminology of administration. Washington, D.C., The Catholic University of America, 1944. Dissertation.

Introduction

Introduction

❖

I. THE ANCESTRY, BIRTHPLACE, AND EDUCATION
OF CASSIODORUS

His ancestors   Flavius Magnus Aurelius Cassiodorus Senator
was born *ca.* 480 [1] at Scyllacium in southern
Italy. His ancestors for at least three generations had been most
distinguished.[2] His great grandfather Cassiodorus (390?–460?),
who held the rank of *illustris,* defended the coast of Brutii (where
his domains were situated) and Sicily (of which he was governor) from the incursions of the Vandals in 455. His grandfather
(420?–490?), who bore the same name, not only was a *tribunus*
and a *notarius* under Valentinian III, but as a friend of the great
statesman Aetius was sent with the latter's son, probably between
440 and 450, on an embassy to the Hun Attila, on whom he ex-
erted an extraordinary influence. His father, the third Cassiodorus, rose to even greater eminence under Odovacar (476–492)
and Theodoric. Under the first ruler his father was the chief financial officer of the empire; in his capacity as *comes privatarum rerum* and later as *comes sacrarum largitionum* he acted as overseer
of the domains and private charities of his sovereign. Under Theodoric he successively occupied the offices of governor (*consu-
laris*) [3] of Sicily, administrator (*corrector*) [4] of his native province, Brutii and Lucania combined,[5] and from 503 to 507, as a

---

[1] John Trithemius, *De scriptoribus ecclesiasticis,* § 212, ed. by J. A. Fabricius, in
Bibliotheca ecclesiastica (Hamburg, 1718), III, 58: *Claruit temporibus Iustini se-
nioris* [518–527] *usque ad imperii Iustini iunioris paene finem* [565–578], *annos
habens aetatis plus quam 95, anno Domini 575.* T. Mommsen proposes 490 as the
date of C.'s birth. Cf. J. Sundwall, *Abhandlungen zur Geschichte des ausgehenden
Römertums* (Helsingfors, 1919), p. 154; *Sandys,* p. 258, gives the date of birth as
between 480 and 490 and the date of death as between 575 and 585; L. Schmidt,
in *Mitteilungen des Instituts für österreichisches Geschichtsforschung,* XLI (1920),
321 ff., and in *Historisches Jahrbuch,* XLVII (1926), 728, gives the date of C.'s
birth as *ca.* 481.

[2] Mommsen *Variae* I. iii–iv.

[3] For the title see the early fifth-century gazetteer of the empire, the *Notitia.*

[4] *Ibid.*

[5] According to a letter of Pope Gelasius "Philippo et Cassiodoro." The office
was held between 493 and 496 according to Usener, p. 76.

reward for his tact and skill, praetorian prefect. The prefecture
conferred a semi-regal splendor upon its holder and may have involved an extensive participation in the actual work of reigning.
After three or four years of holding this office our author's father
retired from the court at Ravenna to his beloved Brutii [6] and received the high honor of the patriciate. The circumstances under
which his son was first introduced to public life were surely aus-
picious.

His name The last three of our author's names require
brief comment. The gentile name Aurelius denotes a large gens, of which Quintus Aurelius Memmius Symmachus was one of the most illustrious members. The cognomen
is correctly written Cassiodorus, not Cassiodorius.[7] That the word
Senator, moreover, is a real name rather than a title of honor
may be concluded from the titles of letters written by Cassiodorus,[8] from his punning allusions to his own name, from references
in Jordanes [9] and Pope Vigilius,[10] and from instances of the use
of this word as a proper name in the case of other individuals.[11]

His birthplace According to Cassiodorus [12] his birthplace,
Scyllacium, was the first, either in age or im-
portance, of the cities of Brutii. It is situated at the head of the
gulf of the same name, in the southeastern part of Italy, in the
narrowest part of the peninsula, upon one of the lower depend-
encies of the Apennine chain. Before the town there is a slight
promontory, whose possible dangers to mariners pass unnoticed
by Cassiodorus despite Virgil's ominous "navifragum Scyla-
ceum" [13] and the supposed allusion in the early Greek name

---

[6] Mommsen *Variae* III. xxviii.

[7] Among the various arguments in favor of the former see Alcuin's poetic line
(Migne, *Pat. Lat.* CI, 843),

"Cassiodorus item Chrysostomus atque Iohannes,"

which seems to indicate that -*rus* was the form accepted as early as the eighth
century. Cf. T. Stettner in *Philologus*, LXXVI (1926), 233–236.

[8] Most of the letters in *Variae*, Bks. XI and XII, bear the words "Senator Praefectus Praetorio."

[9] "Duodecim Senatoris volumina de origine actibusque Getarum," Preface to the
Getica, p. 53, in Theodor Mommsen, *Iordanis Romana et Getica* (1882), *M.G.,
Auct. ant.*, vol. V, Part I.

[10] "Religiosum virum filium nostrum Senatorem," *Epistola XIV ad Rusticum et
Sebastianum*, in Migne, *Pat. Lat.*, LXIX, 49.

[11] Thorbecke, p. 34. Cf. Patricius as the name of St. Patrick.

[12] *Variae* XII. xv.   [13] *Aeneid* III. 553.

Scylletion to dangers like those of the nearby coast of Scylla of the barking dogs.

The Greek city

According to Strabo [14] the city was founded by Menestheus, and according to Cassiodorus by Ulysses, whose traditional energy after the destruction of Troy is well known. Though the form of the name seems to indicate a probable Ionian descent for the colonists, in later times Scylletion was actually subject to the Achaean city of Crotona, from whom it was taken in 389 B.C. by the elder Dionysius. As a result of the wars of Dionysius and Agathocles there was then a general decay of the towns in this part of Magna Graecia. Scylletion, like Crotona, may possibly have been taken and destroyed by the Brutian banditti in the Second Punic War. In any case, during the latter part of this war Hannibal seems to have occupied a position near the already ruined city, and its port was known long afterwards as Castra Hannibalis.[15]

The Roman colony

In 123 B.C., on the rogation of Caius Gracchus, a colony of Roman citizens was sent to a site near that on which the old Greek town had existed. This colony was designated as Colonia Minervia Scolacium,[16] a name similar to Colonia Neptunia Tarentum and to Colonia Junonia Karthago, which were decided on at the same time. It was an important city from its earliest days and remained so until the end of the empire. Pomponius Mela, Strabo, Pliny, and Ptolemy all refer to it as one of the chief cities of Brutii. A new settlement of veterans added to its population in the reign of Nero, when the city's name became Colonia Minervia Nervia Augusta Scolacium.[17]

Cassiodorus himself provides us with a description of this Roman colony in the sixth century.[18]

[14] Bk. VI. i. 10 (H. L. Jones, ed. and trans., *The Geography of Strabo,* London, 1924, Loeb Library).

[15] Pliny III. x.

[16] This old Latin form of the name is used in Velleius Paterculus and in an extant Latin inscription of the time of Antoninus Pius. *Scyllacium* (or *Scylacium*), first used by writers of the first century A.D., is apparently a literary form influenced by the Greek *Scylletion.*

[17] This is the form in an inscription (discovered in 1762 at a distance of 1800 meters from the modern Squillace) which mentions the construction of an aqueduct bringing water to the town in A.D. 143 at the expense of the Emperor Antoninus.

[18] *Variae* XII. xv. The translation is that of Hodgkin, pp. 503–505. For a dis-

Appearance of the city in Cassiodorus' time

The city of Scyllacium, which is so placed as to look down upon the Hadriatic Gulf, hangs upon the hills like a cluster of grapes: not that it may pride itself upon their difficult ascent [*i.e.,* the ascent of the hills], but that it may voluptuously gaze on verdant plains and the blue black of the sea. The city beholds the rising sun from its very cradle, when the day that is about to be born sends forward no heralding Aurora; but as soon as it begins to rise, the quivering brightness displays its torch. It beholds Phoebus in his joy; it is bathed in the brightness of that luminary, so that it might be thought to be itself the native land of the sun, the claims of Rhodes to that honor being outdone.

It enjoys a translucent air, but withal so temperate that its winters are sunny, and its summers cool; and life passes there without sorrow, since hostile seasons are feared by none. Hence, too, man himself is here freer of soul than elsewhere, for this temperateness of the climate prevails in all things.

. . .

Scyllacium has also an abundant share of the delicacies of the sea, possessing near it those gates of Neptune which we ourselves constructed. At the foot of the Moscian Mount we hollowed out the bowels of the rock, and tastefully introduced therein the eddying waves of Nereus. Here a troop of fishes, sporting in free captivity, refreshes all minds with delight, and charms all eyes with admiration. They run greedily to the hand of man, and before they become his food seek dainties from him. Man feeds his own dainty morsels, and while he has that which can bring them into his power, it often happens that being already replete he lets them all go again.

The spectacle moreover of men engaged in honorable labor is not denied to those who are sitting tranquilly in the city. Plenteous vineyards are beheld in abundance. The fruitful toil of the threshing-floor is seen. The face of the green olive is disclosed. No one need sigh for the pleasures of the country, when it is given him to see them all from the town.

And inasmuch as it has now no walls, you believe Scyllacium to be a rural city, though you might judge it to be an urban villa; and thus placed between the two worlds of town and country, it is lavishly praised by both.

Education

The evidence of Cassiodorus' own works indicates that he received the usual instruction in philosophy and rhetoric which was given the young noble who aspired to governmental office. There are also signs that he had

---

cussion of the exact site of the Roman Scyllacium and C.'s monastic foundations there and for an account of the later history of these foundations see F. Lenormant, *La Grand Grèce; paysages et histoire* (Paris, 1882), II, 329 ff., especially pp. 360-369; Evans in Hodgkin, pp. 8-9 and 68-72; Minasi, pp. 145 ff.; G. Gissing, *By the Ionian Sea* (London, 1905; 2d ed., 1921), pp. 155 ff.; and P. Courcelle, "Le Site du monastère de Cassiodore," in *Mélanges d'archéologie et d'histoire*, École française de Rome, LV (1938), 259-307.

an unusual interest in natural history, though his statements on the subject are frequently strange or ridiculous.

II. HIS PUBLIC LIFE

Consiliarius

In 503 Senator's father, just made praetorian prefect, appointed his son to be *consiliarius,* or assessor, in his court,[1] a position normally held by some young jurist fresh from studies. Our author thus exercised functions somewhat similar to those exercised by Procopius in the camp of Belisarius, but probably required a more thorough legal training.[2] Father and son continued to hold office until 507.[3]

Quaestor

On some public occasion after 503 Senator was asked to deliver an oration in praise of Theodoric.[4] The panegyric was so genuine in its enthusiasm and so admirable according to the taste of the times that the emperor at once gave the youthful and relatively obscure assessor the extremely important office of quaestor.[5] This appointment placed him among the ten or eleven highest-ranking royal ministers (*illustres*).[6]

The duties of the quaestor were threefold.[7] First, he gave a final revision to the laws signed by the emperor, saw that they were consistent with one another and with previous enactments, and clothed them in suitable language. Second, he replied in the emperor's name to the petitions presented to the latter. Third, he had audiences with foreign ambassadors and in the emperor's name delivered fitting and dignified harangues to them or forwarded them written replies to the letters which they had brought.

---

[1] As this and other specific references suggest, the present account of Cassiodorus' career (pp. 7–25 in particular) is heavily indebted to the summary in Hodgkin.

[2] For further details concerning the post of *consiliarius* see Hodgkin, pp. 12–13.

[3] Van de Vyver, pp. 247–248.

[4] Usener, p. 4. Cf. van de Vyver, p. 248 and note 5.

[5] In 507: van de Vyver, pp. 245–247.

[6] The ministers actually in office at this time were probably the following: *praefectus praetorio Italiae* (= Senator's father), *praefectus urbis Romae,* two *magistri militum in praesenti, praepositus sacri cubiculi, magister officiorum, quaestor, comes sacrarum largitionum, comes rerum privatarum,* and two *comites domesticorum equitum et peditum.*

[7] According to the *Notitia* (Occidentis I): "Sub dispositione viri illustri quaestoris / leges dictandae / preces. / Officium non habet sed adiutores de scriniis quos voluerit."

He had no large official staff himself, but he could summon clerks
at will from the four great governmental bureaux (*scrinia*) for
copying letters, filing correspondence, and other manual labor.

The quaestor beyond all other ministers was the mouthpiece of
the emperor. For this reason a quaestor as fluent and learned in
law and rhetoric as Cassiodorus was a fortunate acquisition for a
ruler like Theodoric, who, though anxious to make a good im-
pression upon his Roman as well as his Gothic subjects, could not
himself speak or write Latin with any ease.[8]

Variae

The *Variae*, or "diverse letters," of Cassiodorus are the chief monument of his official ca-
reer. This work, edited by him in the closing years of his public
life,[9] contains, apparently without substantial change,[10] the correspondence written during a period of more than thirty years in
the names of Theodoric (Books I–V), Athalaric (VIII [11]–IX),
Amalasuentha (X), Theodahad (X), Theodahad's wife Gude-
lina (X), and Witigis (X), as well as formulae for the granting
of all the dignities of the state [12] (VI–VII) and letters written by
Cassiodorus in his own name as praetorian prefect (XI [13]–XII).
The work is thus a source not merely for the reigns of the various
sovereigns but also for our author's life.

Style

The style [14] of the letters is verbose, flaccid,
and devoid of humor. Not only is it often dif-
ficult for a modern reader to discover the central thought of the

[8] According to tradition he never could learn to write, but had to stencil his
signature.

[9] At the end of 537: van de Vyver, p. 252 and note 4.

[10] In many of the letters which were meant to serve as credentials to ambassadors or commissions to civil servants no personal names are inserted. This phe-
nomenon may be due to the fact that C. based his *Variae* upon rough drafts in
his own possession. It seems unlikely that copies in the public archives did not
bear the names, as Hodgkin (p. 53) thinks.

[11] Except letter 11, written in the name of the patrician Tulum, Cassiodorus'
fellow minister of state.

[12] The consulship, the patriciate, the praetorian prefecture, and so forth.

[13] Letter 13 is written on behalf of the Roman senate.

[14] The vocabulary of the *Variae* is treated in Zimmermann, who attempts to
determine the meanings of words used arbitrarily, of Late Latin words not yet ade-
quately discussed in our lexica, of neologisms, and of technical administrative
terms. His section on administrative terms (an adequate compilation and interpretation) is probably the most valuable part of his work. Cf. my review of Zimmermann in *Classical Philology*, XLI (1946), 55–57.

The clausulae in the *Variae* and in four other important works of Cassiodorus
are treated in Suelzer. For the details and a notice of my review of this dissertation see below, p. 39.

sentences, but if he succeeds he is likely to find that this thought is an obvious commonplace. One rather remarkable example will suffice. Theodoric desired to complain to Faustus, the praetorian prefect, of the latter's delay in the execution of an order which he had received for the shipment of crops from Calabria and Apulia to Rome. The complaint is voiced as follows by our literary quaestor.[15]

Why is there such great delay in sending your swift ships to traverse the tranquil seas? Though the south wind blows and the rowers are bending to their oars, has the sucking-fish (*echeneis*) fixed its teeth into the hulls through the liquid waves; or have the shells of the Indian Sea, whose quiet touch is said to hold so firmly that the angry billows cannot loosen it, with like power fixed their lips into your keels? Idle stands the bark though winged by swelling sails; the wind favours her but she makes no way; she is fixed without an anchor, she is bound without a cable; and these tiny animals hinder more than all such prospering circumstances can help. Thus, though the loyal wave may be hastening its course, we are informed that the ship stands fixed on the surface of the sea, and by a strange paradox the swimmer [the ship] is made to remain immovable while the wave is hurried along by movements numberless. Or, to describe the nature of another kind of fish, perchance the sailors in the aforesaid ships have grown dull and torpid by the touch of the torpedo, by which such a deadly chill is struck into the right hand of him who attacks it, that even through the spear by which it is itself wounded it gives a shock which causes the hand of the striker to remain, though still a living substance, senseless and immovable. I think some such misfortune as these must have happened to men who are unable to move their own bodies. But I know that in their case the echeneis is corruption trading on delays; the bite of the Indian shell-fish is insatiable cupidity; the torpedo is fraudulent pretence. With perverted ingenuity they manufacture delays that they may seem to have met with a run of ill-luck. Wherefore let your Greatness, whom it specially concerns to look after such men as these, by a speedy rebuke bring them to a better mind. Else the famine which we fear will be imputed not to the barrenness of the times but to official negligence, whose true child it will manifestly appear.

*Cassiodorus'
foresight in
aiding Theodoric's
policy of civili-
tas and religious
tolerance*

One must not assume that Cassiodorus' inflated rhetorical style is a proper index of his character. To be sure, he overestimated the power of mere words and was inclined to humble himself before rank and power.[16] On the other

---

[15] *Variae* I. xxxv. The translation is from the introduction of Hodgkin, pp. 18-19; on p. 163, however, Hodgkin reduces this translation to a little more than one half its original bulk, in accordance with his usual practice.

[16] Thiele, however, points out (p. 399) that C.'s bombastic style, a product of his age, underwent a complete change when he later interested himself in religious

hand, he was a strenuous and successful administrator and a far-sighted statesman.[17] He was therefore prompt to recognize the soundness of Theodoric's desire to rule Goth and Roman in peace. For more than a hundred years there had been wars: Alaric, Attila, and Gaiseric in turn had ravaged Italy, while she had exhausted herself trying to preserve dominion over Gaul, Spain, and Africa and had smarted under the insults of the *foederati* who served under Ricimer and Odovacar. Theodoric brought peace and a strong government and *civilitas,* which is variously translated as "good order," "civilization," and "the character of a law-abiding citizen." Of course his theory of a warrior caste of Goths and a trading and laboring caste of Romans hardly flattered the national vanity of the latter, but Cassiodorus was wise enough to see that in this government lay Rome's only hope. An attempt to restore the Roman Empire would probably have resulted in subjection by Byzantium, and an attempt to arouse the religious passions of the orthodox Romans against the heretical Arian intruders would probably have benefited no one but the Franks. With *civilitas,* finally, came religious tolerance. Except during the last few years of his life Theodoric, himself an Arian, was eminently fair toward both orthodox Christians and Arians [18] and even toward the generally proscribed Jews. And Cassiodorus, an orthodox believer, thoroughly commended this tolerance: "We cannot order a religion, because no one is forced to believe against his will." [19]

End of Cassiodorus' office as quaestor The letters contained in the *Variae* are not arranged in a strict chronological order and are not in most cases datable.[20] Some scholars have accordingly found it difficult to determine the close of Senator's incumbency as quaestor, though since Mommsen's time there has been fairly general agreement that the incumbency ended in 512.[21]

---

affairs and that he was actually trying to save what he could of Roman civilization in a time of barbarian conquest.

[17] Van de Vyver, pp. 244–259, cautions us against exaggerating his political role in the Italo-Gothic kingdom.

[18] There is a tradition that Theodoric beheaded an orthodox deacon who was very dear to him, because the deacon had professed the Arian faith to win his sovereign's favor: Theodorus Lector (*ca.* 550), *Ecclesiastica historia,* II. xviii.

[19] *Variae* II. xxvii (King Theodoric to all the Jews living in Genoa).

[20] On the dates of certain letters see Hodgkin, pp. 23–24, 50, and van de Vyver, *passim.*   [21] Van de Vyver, p. 245.

Throughout his term of service Senator must have held his sovereign's confidence and must have continued to have a large share in the direction of the affairs of state. He himself says in a letter supposed to be addressed to himself after Theodoric's death:[22] "For under your administration no dignity kept its exact limits; anything that was to be honestly done by all the chiefs of the state together, you considered to be entrusted to your conscience for its performance."

Consulship

In the year 514 Senator became *consul ordinarius,* thus acquiring an honor much sought by Roman nobles despite its lack of real authority at this time. For some reason, possibly because Constantinople was then threatened by the insurrection of Vitalian, he had no colleague in the East. During his term of office he was able to persuade the nobles, the clergy, and the people to lay aside the dissensions which had arisen from the contested papal election of Symmachus and Laurentius in 498 and to unite in choosing Hormisdas as undoubted pope. He was also highly successful in carrying out Theodoric's policy of soothing the wounded pride of the Roman senate and of flattering its vanity: the senators were treated with every outward show of respect and deference; every nomination of importance was communicated to them; there was always a pretense of consulting them in regard to peace or war; the appeals to their loyalty were real enough.

Patriciate and governorship of Lucania and Brutii

Cassiodorus received the dignity of patrician, possibly upon the expiration of his term as consul. If this was the correct date, he received the honor at an earlier age than had his father, to whom Cassiodorus had written a letter announcing the bestowal of the honor only ten or eleven years before. The title, of course, conferred neither wealth nor power, but às one borne by Ricimer, Odovacar, and Theodoric, it must have been exceptionally desirable. It was perhaps also at this time that our author became, as his father had been, governor of his native Lucania and Brutii.[23]

The Chronicon

For a period of ten years (512–522), the apogee of Theodoric's reign, he held no official position. In 519, however, the year of the consulship of the

---

[22] *Variae* IX. xxiv.   [23] The precise date is unknown.

Emperor Justin and of Theodoric's son-in-law Eutharic, Cassiodorus attracted attention by writing a *Chronicon,* an abstract of
the history of the world from the flood right down to his own day.
For the most part this chronicle consists of borrowings, often incorrectly executed, from the well-known works of Eusebius and
Prosper. It adds so little to Cassiodorus' reputation as an author
that he himself does not include it in the list of his writings. It
contains, among other unfortunate features, a reckless combination of two modes of reckoning—by consular years and by years
of emperors. Its treatment of the fourth and fifth centuries is not
without interest, though there is a definite tendency to praise the
virtues of the Goths and to extenuate their faults. Thus, the battle
of Pollentia (402) is claimed as a Gothic victory, Alaric's clemency at the capture of Rome (410) is magnified, Attila's defeat
on the Catalaunian plains (451) is represented as due to the valor
of the Goths, and the name of Eutharic the Goth precedes that
of Justin the Byzantine in the consular list.

The Gothic   No doubt shortly after the composition of the
History   *Chronicon* [24] Cassiodorus began a much more
important work—the *Gothic History,* arranged in twelve books.
This work was by no means an impartial history. It aimed, first,
to vindicate the claim of the Goths to rank among the historic
nations of antiquity by bringing them into connection with the
Greeks and the Romans, and, second, to exalt the Amal line, to
which Theodoric himself belonged. The aims were really lofty
ones, for in showing the nobility of the northern nations they had
in view the reconciliation of the decadent Latin race with that of
the more vigorous Goths. As Cassiodorus himself says, in a letter
written as a purported address by the young Athalaric to the senate on Cassiodorus' elevation to the prefecture: [25]

He extended his labours even to our remote ancestry, learning by his reading that which the hoar memories of our forefathers retained. He drew
forth from their hiding place the Kings of the Goths, hidden by long forget-

[24] The work could not have been begun in its present form before 516 (the
date of Athalaric's birth according to Jordanes) or 518 (the date according to Procopius), since Athalaric's birth is mentioned in it; nor could it have been begun
after 521 (the date of the *Anecdoton Holderi,* in which it is mentioned: see Usener,
p. 74). Van de Vyver, p. 249, holds that it was begun before 523–527 and completed during 527–533.
[25] *Variae* IX. xxv; Hodgkin, pp. 29–30.

fulness. He restored the Amals to their proper place with the lustre of their [26] lineage, evidently proving that up to the seventeenth generation we have had kings for our ancestors. He made the origin of the Goths a part of Roman history, collecting as it were into one wreath all the flowery growth which had before been scattered through the plains of many books.

Getae and Scythians represented as Goths

In his attempt to connect Gothic history with that of Greece and Rome, Cassiodorus was considerably aided by the current confusion between Goths and Getae, on one hand, and between Goths and Scythians, on the other. The use of the word Getae for Goths is at least as old as the triumphal arch of Arcadius and Honorius; it occurs regularly in the poems of Claudian and the works of his contemporaries. The term Scythian, moreover, is applied freely by Greek historians to any barbarian nation living beyond the Danube and the Cimmerian Bosporus. Cassiodorus, though not himself responsible for the confusion and though not conscious of it, was accordingly able to cull stories from a considerable part of the borderland of classical antiquity. The uncertain interval between the migration of the Goths from the Baltic to the Black Sea and their appearance around A.D. 250 as conquerors in the eastern half of the Roman Empire was filled in by such stories as the battles between the Scythians and the Egyptians, the tale of the Amazons, the account of Telephus, son of Hercules and nephew of Priam, the defeat of Cyrus by Tomyris, the unsuccessful expedition of Darius, and the war of Sitalces the Thracian against Perdiccas of Macedon. Of course, these stories from Herodotus and Trogus have little value in a scientific history of the Goths.

The truly Gothic element

The *Gothic History* did, however, contain a truly Gothic element: it obviously possessed information drawn from the songs and sagas known to the Goths who had followed Theodoric. This information, despite its legendary character, is important to the historian.

The Amals

The Amal line of descent was presented in the form used for pedigrees in the Saxon Chronicle. There is no reason to suppose that Cassiodorus' account, whether or not it dealt with real historical personages or events,

---

[26] Hodgkin's first version is "his own lineage." "Their," which seems to me correct, appears in a note.

was not current and accepted among the people over whom Theodoric ruled.[27] The account began, not with men, but with demigods, the Anses,[28] the first of whom, Gaut, was obviously the eponymous hero of the Goths. Though many of the later names —Amal, Ostrogotha, Athal, for example—are similarly suspect, the names of the immediate ancestors of Theodoric are undoubtedly historical. Noteworthy is the fact that Cassiodorus makes no attempt to include in the Amal line the names of many distinguished Gothic kings who do not really belong there.

Jordanes'
abstract

Unfortunately for us, the *Gothic History* is no longer extant. The knowledge of its contents as outlined above is derived from Jordanes' résumé (551),[29] an inferior work to be sure, but one which still obviously preserves many of the features of the original. Jordanes' statement that he was loaned Cassiodorus' work by the latter's steward for only three days is manifestly false, since the purpose which he himself indicates would have required several months. His further statement that he has added some suitable passages from the Greek and Latin historians may be accepted as true, if one bears in mind that these additions were probably exceedingly few.

Master of
the Offices

Unquestionably Cassiodorus' glorification of the Goths in his works had much to do with his elevation by Theodoric in 523 to the high position of master of the offices—a post which he continued to hold until 527.[30] In this capacity he was in charge of the civil service of the Ostrogothic state. The master of the offices, according to Priscus, "is a partaker of all the counsels of the emperor, inasmuch as the messengers and interpreters and the soldiers employed on the

---

[27] But some scholars suspect the zeal of this fanciful genealogy: van de Vyver, p. 249, and the authors quoted in note 4.

[28] Jordanes, *De rebus Geticis* XIII (in Theodor Mommsen, *Iordanis Romana et Getica* [1882], *M.G., Auct. ant.*, Vol. V, Part 1).

[29] The title is given variously as *De rebus Geticis, De Gothorum origine,* and *Getica.*

[30] So van de Vyver, p. 247. In *Variae* IX. xxiv, C. implies that he has held this position for some time before Theodoric's death in 526. Hodgkin, p. 35, thinks that C. was not actively engaged in the service of the state during the terrible years 524 and 525, in which the failing intellect of Theodoric, goaded almost to madness by Justin's persecutions of his Arian coreligionists, sought ignoble measures of retaliation, which brought him into collision with the senate and the pope and resulted in the execution of Boethius and Symmachus. Hodgkin thinks that C. may have been enjoying a period of literary retirement at Squillace.

guard are ranged under him." The *Notitia Occidentis* [31] gives us even more precise details: the master was in charge of five *scholae* of the ruler's household troops, the great *schola* of the king's "messengers" (the *agentes in rebus* and their assistants), the four great bureaux whose duty it was to conduct the ruler's correspondence with foreign powers and to answer petitions from his subjects (the *scrinium memoriae,* the *scrinium dispositionum,* the *scrinium epistolarum,* and the *scrinium libellorum*), the six great arsenals of Italy (Concordia, Verona, Mantua, Cremona, Ticinum, and Lucca), and, finally, the *cursus publicus,*[32] which provided relays of post horses to properly authorized persons for travel between the capital and the provinces.

Athalaric and   Upon the death of Theodoric his grandson
Amalasuentha   Athalaric, then a boy of only eight or ten, was named king, and supreme power was vested in the boy's mother, Amalasuentha. The various difficulties which beset the new reign are clearly indicated in the letters which appear in the eighth book of the *Variae.* These difficulties were due in large measure to Amalasuentha's extreme impulsiveness in trying to carry out Cassiodorus' scheme of Romanizing the Goths.

The various services of Cassiodorus to the new regent are best described in his own words: [33]

In the early days of our reign what labour he gave to the settling of our affairs! He was alone sufficient for all. The duty of making public harangues, our own private counsels, required him. He laboured that the Empire might rest.

We found him Magister; but he discharged the duties of Quaestor, and willingly bestowed on us, the heir, the experience which he had gained in the counsels of our grandfather.

And not only so, he helped the beginning of the reign both with his arms and his pen. For when the care of our shores [34] occupied our royal meditation, he suddenly emerged from the seclusion of his cabinet, boldly, like his ancestors, assumed the office of General, and triumphed by his character when there was no enemy to overcome. For he maintained the Gothic war-

[31] Chapter ix.

[32] Charge of the *cursus publicus* was later transferred to the praetorian prefect; cf. Hodgkin, p. 37 and note 1.

[33] *Variae* IX. xxv (Hodgkin, pp. 412–413): King Athalaric to the senate of the city of Rome on the promotion of Cassiodorus Senator to the praetorian prefecture.

[34] Probably from some expected descent of the Vandals (in connection with the murder of Theodoric's sister Amalafrida by the Vandal king, Hilderic) or possibly from a descent of the Franks.

riors at his own charges, so that there should be no robbery of the Provincials on the one hand, no too heavy burden on the exchequer on the other. Thus was the soldier what he ought to be, the true defender, not the ravager of his country. Then when the time for victualling the ships was over, and the war was laid aside, he shone as an administrator rather than a warrior, healing, without injury to the litigants, the various suits which arose out of the sudden cessation of the contracts.

Praetorian prefect For the next six years of Amalasuentha's regency Cassiodorus held no official position. Then, on September 1, 533, at the age of fifty-three, he was chosen praetorian prefect. As a friend and possibly the tutor of the regent Cassiodorus must have made the most of this high office, which, according to Joannes Lydus,[35] "is like the ocean, encircling all other offices and ministering to all their needs." The praetorian prefect had four chief functions:[36] (1) he promulgated the imperial laws and issued edicts which had the force of laws; (2) he proclaimed the general tax ordered by the emperor for the year and took part in its levy; (3) he proposed the names of the provincial governors, had general oversight of them—could inflict punishments upon them as their ordinary judge, could depose them from their offices, and could temporarily nominate substitutes; and (4) he was the highest judge of appeal. Cassiodorus held his prefecture until 537.[37]

Amalasuentha and Theodahad The cultivated, but self-willed, Amalasuentha eventually met with considerable opposition from her Gothic subjects and set in motion a train of events which

[35] *De dignitatibus* II. vii, viii, ix, xiii, xiv. He goes on to say: "The Consulate is indeed higher in rank than the Praefecture, but less in power. The Praefect wears a *mandye,* or woolen cloak, dyed with the purple of Cos, and differing from the Emperor's only in the fact that it reaches not to the feet but to the knees. Girt with his sword he takes his seat as President of the Senate. When that body has assembled, the chiefs of the army fall prostrate before the Praefect, who raises them and kisses each in turn, in order to express his desire to be on good terms with the military power. Nay, even when the Emperor himself walks (or till lately used to walk), he goes on foot from his palace to meet the Praefect as he [the latter] moves slowly towards him [the Emperor] at the head of the Senate. The insignia of the Praefect's office are his lofty chariot, his golden reed-case [pen-holder], weighing one hundred pounds, his massive silver inkstand, and silver bowl on a tripod of the same metal to receive the petitions of the suitors. Three official yachts wait upon his orders, and convey him from the capital to the neighbouring provinces."—(Hodgkin, pp. 40–41.)

[36] Hodgkin, p. 41 and notes 1 and 2.

[37] So van de Vyver, p. 247. Although C.'s *Variae* gives an interesting picture of internal administration during this period, it fails to give much information about the course of public events. Procopius and Jordanes fill in this gap.

had tragic consequences. She was compelled, first of all, to remove the young Athalaric from the bookish influence of his teachers and to allow him to get acquainted with the spear and the sword. Resentful of this compulsion, she banished three of the most powerful nobles involved to opposite ends of Italy, and then, finding that they were still communicating with one another, she had them secretly assassinated. The *coup* was successful, and she had no need of the asylum which she had requested at Justinian's court. But, still fearing for her own life because of this deed and worrying over what might happen upon the death of the feeble and licentious Athalaric, she again negotiated secretly with Justinian for an assurance of shelter and maintenance at Byzantium in return for the surrender of Italy into his hands. Athalaric died in 534. Since the principle of female sovereignty had not been accepted by the Goths, Amalasuentha now sought to strengthen her position by associating with herself, not by matrimony—for he was already married—but by a regal partnership, her cousin Theodahad, the nearest male heir of Theodoric. This desperate expedient had unfortunate results. Theodahad, who had previously been restrained by Amalasuentha from various acts of land robbery, soon found it convenient to forget his tremendous oaths that he would be satisfied with the mere name of royalty. After first slaying many of her supporters, he put the queen in prison and finally encouraged the kinsmen of the three previously assassinated nobles to murder her in her bath. The rhetorician and exconsul Peter, who came to Italy from Constantinople at this juncture with instructions to accept the surrender of Italy from Amalasuentha, could do little but declare a war of vengeance.

Cassiodorus in Theodahad's service It is remarkable that Cassiodorus continued in the service of the man who had brought about this murder. Who can say whether our author was motivated by private or by public gain? He may well have been reluctant to lay down the high dignity of his prefecture. On the other hand, he may have felt it his duty to continue in the service of the government at a time when war with Justinian was imminent, or perhaps he was merely trying to use his high office to bring about the downfall of the king.[38]

---

[38] Thiele, pp. 399–401, points out that, although Cassiodorus did serve many masters, he was trying to save what he could of Roman culture in a time of bar-

Theodahad's vacillation

In his relations with Justinian, Theodahad was continually wavering between arrogance and timidity.[39] Whenever Belisarius won a victory, Theodahad was inclined to resume the old negotiations with the emperor and to secure peace either by allowing his kingdom to become a tributary or by selling it outright for high position and financial security. Whenever the Gothic generals triumphed, however, he was elated. Indeed, upon the defeat and death of the Byzantine general Mundus in Dalmatia, Theodahad broke off negotiations altogether and imprisoned the envoy Peter and his colleague Athanasius.

Witigis

In July, 536, a little more than a year after the death of Amalasuentha and the beginning of the war, Belisarius captured Naples and began to threaten Rome. The Gothic warriors, disgusted at the incapacity of their king and, no doubt, suspecting his treachery, met in August, deposed Theodahad, and elected Witigis as his successor. Witigis at once ordered the execution of Theodahad and, in order to strengthen his title to the crown, married Matasuentha, Theodoric's granddaughter and only surviving descendant. Cassiodorus approved the change in rulers enthusiastically and remained in the new king's service.

Cassiodorus' retirement from public life

It seems unlikely that Cassiodorus was present at the siege of Rome (March, 537, to March, 538) or that, as an elderly civilian, he took part in the military operations which followed. As praetorian prefect he was no doubt endeavoring to the utmost to preserve the normal functioning of the civil administration. But Belisarius, with the emperor's consent, appointed Fidelis to the office of prefect in 537, and it is probable that Cassiodorus retired from public life soon afterwards.[40] Ravenna was finally captured in 540, and Witigis was imprisoned.

---

barian ascendancy and that he deserves more credit for this attitude than does Boethius for his unbending opposition to barbarism.

[39] Cassiodorus apparently expunged from his *Variae* all letters which reflected too great discredit upon his king. Procopius (*De bello Gothico* I. vi, in H. B. Dewing's edition in the Loeb Library, London and New York, 1914–1928) gives a more accurate account.

[40] So van de Vyver, p. 253, and Hodgkin, pp. 50–51. The dates of the latest letters (one, *Variae* XII. xx, of the year 536; five, *Variae* XII. xxii, xxiii, xxiv, xxvii, xxviii, of the year 537; and one, *Variae* XII. xxv, possibly of the year 538) allow this conclusion. Moreover, Procopius' failure to mention Cassiodorus at all in his *De bello*

His treatise
On the Soul

During the closing years of his busy official career [41] Cassiodorus turned, as Cicero and many other Romans had done, not merely to the collecting and editing of his letters but also to the composition of a short philosophic treatise, *On the Soul*. In this treatise his inspiration came chiefly from various works of St. Augustine and from the *De statu animae* of Claudianus Mamertus. Our author pointed out that it was absurd to treat the very center of our being as an unknown quantity and proceeded to investigate the matter in the following twelve chapters: (1) Why is the soul called *anima*? (2) What is the definition of the soul? (3) What is its substantial quality? (4) Has it any shape? (5) What moral virtues has it which contribute to its glory and adornment? (6) What are its natural virtues [or powers] given to enable it to hold together the framework of the body? (7) Concerning the origin of the soul; (8) What is its special seat, since it appears to be in a certain sense diffused over the whole body? (9) Concerning the form and composition of the body itself; (10) Sufficient signs by which we may discern what properties the souls of sinners possess; (11) Similar signs by which we may distinguish the souls of righteous men, since we cannot see them with our bodily eyes; (12) Concerning the soul's state after death and the manner in which it will be affected by the general resurrection. The work is clearly consolation literature. It marks a turning not so much to abstract philosophy as to religion.

III. HIS LATER CAREER

Cassiodorus'
devotion
to religious
affairs

One is not therefore surprised at Cassiodorus' subsequent announcement of his intention to devote the rest of his life to religious affairs.[1] He had served various rulers wisely and well. His dream of building a strong Italian state with Gothic and Roman

---

Gothico may be partially explained by assuming that the late prefect was not in Ravenna in 540 when Procopius entered in the train of the victorious Belisarius.— Thiele, pp. 380–381, gives 538–546 as the date of C.'s "conversio."

[41] Very soon after the editing of the *Variae* in 537 according to van de Vyver, p. 253. Cf., however, Mommsen, *Variae*, p. xxxi, and Schanz, p. 101.

[1] Thiele, pp. 398–399, objects to van de Vyver's apparent tendency to represent Cassiodorus as a rhetorician and asserts (rightly, I think, at least in C.'s later life) that religion was a determining force in Cassiodorus' life.

elements working in complementary and harmonious fashion had been utterly shattered by the victories of Belisarius. He now accepted the decision of fate and planned to spend his old age in religious meditation and in commenting on the Christian Scriptures, not forgetting entirely his previous hope of founding a theological school and of preserving the Scriptures and the great works of classical antiquity through the pens of monastic copyists. This phase of his activities ultimately proved much more important to the world than his political labors.

Commentary on Senator first began to write a very long and
the Psalms diffuse *Commentary on the Psalms* [2] based upon St. Augustine and other authors. The work contains, among other things, refutations of all the heresies which have ever existed and rudiments of all the sciences which the world has ever seen. It is a marvel of erudition, though much of the effort involved seems to a modern reader misdirected. Our author, for example, maintains that all of the one hundred fifty Psalms were written by David, that Asaph, Heman, and Jeduthun have only a mystical meaning, that the first seventy Psalms represent the Old Testament and the last eighty the New, because we celebrate Christ's resurrection on the eighth day of the week.

Cassiodorus at Belisarius' defeat of Witigis had not brought
Constantinople peace to Italy, for in 542 and 543 the usurper Totila extended his domination as far as Brutii and Calabria. In 547 Belisarius tried in vain to install himself in these provinces. Moreover, the Gothic king proceeded to take Rome a second time, to occupy Tarentum, and even to go on to Sicily (550). For some time before Totila's first capture of Rome (546) Sicily had become the rallying point for *émigrés*. Now upon his approach they fled *en masse* to Constantinople and besought the emperor to do all in his power to reconquer Italy. Among the *émigrés* who made this plea we find not merely their leaders Liberius and Cethegus and Pope Vigilius but also Cassiodorus.[3]

The emperor, stung by the defeats of his army in Italy, at once charged Liberius, ex-praetorian prefect under Odovacar and

---

[2] Numerous bibliographical notes were added later: van de Vyver, pp. 271–275. See p. 39–40 below.

[3] That Cassiodorus favored Byzantine reconquest of Italy is proved by his support of Pope Vigilius at this time: van de Vyver, pp. 255–256.

Theodoric and ex-praetor of the Gauls (*i.e.*, Provence) and Egypt, with the reconquest and directed him to begin with Sicily. A little later (mid-June, 550) he appointed his cousin Germanus generalissimo of the army which, raised in Thrace, was given the task of reconquering Italy by the route used by Theodoric. To facilitate his campaign Germanus immediately married Matasuentha, the widow of Witigis, and hoped by this union to secure the fealty of the Goths in Italy and to end Totila's usurpation. Upon the Byzantine's unexpected decease in September, 550, his son-in-law John and his son Germanus were at first put in charge of the campaign, but before they had had a chance to fight they were relieved (in April, 551) by the eunuch Narses, who was then seventy-five years old. After another year of delay Narses proceeded to reconquer Italy.

Cassiodorus'
decision
to found
a monastery

Cassiodorus may well have profited by his stay in Constantinople to get as much information as possible about the Jewish theological school at Nisibis in Syria, a counterpart of which he had previously desired, in connection with Pope Agapetus, to create at Rome.[4] During his residence our author undoubtedly met the quaestor Junilius, who among other tasks edited the notes which he had taken during his pursuit of a course given by one of the professors of this school,[5] and also Bishop Primasius of Hadrumetum, author of a commentary on the *Apocalypse*,[6] on whose account the notes were edited. It is likely that these experiences caused Cassiodorus to make a definite decision to found a monastery in the West for profound study of the Scriptures.[7] The founding of a monastery by a member of the laity was not extraordinary at this time. The patrician Liberius, for example, founded a monastery at Alatri in Campania before 534, the patrician Venantius (consul in 508?) had established a similar foundation on his property at Fondi (Samnium), and the general Belisarius himself had founded and endowed a convent near Orta on the Flaminian Way.

[4] *Inst.* praef. 1.
[5] C. refers to Junilius' treatise, *Instituta regularia divinae legis*, in *Inst.* I. x. 1. Cf. van de Vyver, *Vivarium*, p. 85.
[6] *Inst.* I. ix. 4.
[7] Van de Vyver, p. 260.

The double
monastery at
Scyllacium

Upon his return to Italy, or possibly several years afterwards,[8] Cassiodorus founded a double monastery at his ancestral Scyllacium, between the mountains of Aspromonte and the sea. One section, for the solitary hermit, was situated among the "sweet recesses of Mount Castellum"; the other, for the less austere cenobite, contained well-watered gardens and was named Vivarium [9] after the fish ponds which Cassiodorus had constructed there in connection with the River Pellena. There were also baths built on the banks of the stream for the use of the sick.[10] The monastic life was thus simple, but not without comfort.

Relationship
to Benedict

The rule of the order—insofar as there was a formal rule—was founded upon the recommendations of Cassian,[11] who had died about a hundred years earlier; the great Benedict and his famous rule pass unmentioned in any of Cassiodorus' writings.[12] The pleas of Dom Garet [13] and of Mgr. Amelli [14] (Dom-Abbé of Monte Cassino) to establish the fact that our author was influenced by the founder of the great monastic order have not been generally accepted by scholars. Moreover, Dom Chapman's apparent discovery of traces of the influence of the famous Benedictine Rule in Cassiodorus' works and his conclusion that the founder of Vivarium actually adopted this rule [15] cannot be proved definitively until some scholar has examined more carefully the sources common to the

[8] *Ca.* 552? Usener fixes the foundation of Vivarium *ca.* 540. According to Thiele, p. 381, C.'s mention in his *Commentary on the Psalms* of "legentes fratres," who translated Josephus' *Antiquitates,* indicates that the founding of Vivarium preceded the writing of the commentary, and van de Vyver's objection (pp. 271–272) that these items are later additions may be explained by a break in the continuity of C.'s writing of this work: Thiele sets the founding of Vivarium toward the beginning of the period 538–546. Van de Vyver, pp. 260 and 290, on the contrary, argues for a date after 550. See also van de Vyver, *Vivarium,* p. 80, on a pertinent passage in *Inst.* I. iv.

[9] Vivarium today is the town of Staletti, three quarters of an hour from Squillace, a Calabrian town of four thousand inhabitants and seat of a bishopric. For the exact site and later history of the monastery see p. 5, note 18, above.

[10] On these details see *Inst.* I. xxix.

[11] Cassiodorus warns his monks to choose the good in Cassian's writings and to avoid the evil caused by his semi-Pelagian bias.

[12] On this whole subject see Thiele, pp. 388–391.

[13] Migne, *Pat. Lat.,* LXIX, 483 ff. Cf. R. Coens, in *Analecta Bollandiana,* XLII (1923), 188. This and the two following references are from van de Vyver, p. 280.

[14] "Cassiodoro e S. Benedetto," *Rivista storia benedettino,* XI (1920), 168–172.

[15] Chapman, *St. Benedict,* pp. 93–110. Cf. also van de Vyver, p. 262, note 1, end.

works of both of these great figures.[16] In any case, there is no doubt whatever that the pains taken by Cassiodorus for the instruction of his monks distinguish his monastery quite clearly from Benedictine foundations.

Did Cassiodorus ever become a monk? It is doubtful whether Cassiodorus ever entered either of his monasteries as monk or abbot. Though van de Vyver [17] originally stated that, were it not for an obscure text in the *Commentary on the Psalms,* he would be fully convinced that our author entered as neither; he now feels that this text has no importance. To be sure, this commentary speaks of the delights of the monastic life, but it makes no allusion to the Vivarian monastery. Since it begs the indulgence of competent masters ("Vos autem, magistri, qui caelestium litterarum copiosa lectione pinguescitis, parcite rudi, dimitte confitenti, estote benevoli"), Cassiodorus had apparently not yet collected his vast library or begun his annotation of sacred authors.[18] The touching reference to the monk Dionysius Exiguus in the *Institutiones* [19] seems to reveal that this well-known canonist and chronologist passed the last years of his life at Vivarium, but it is not enough to prove that Cassiodorus belonged to the same profession. Otherwise it would be rather odd for our author, immediately after having stated that the monks should look after their convent, to remind them that he has annotated certain Scriptural accounts "quantum aut senex aut longa peregrinatione fatigatus relegere praevalui." [20] Nevertheless it is a fact that he did give up the practice of mentioning at the begin-

[16] Hodgkin, p. 59, even goes so far as to hold that literary work among the Benedictines may have been influenced by the Vivarian monastery.

[17] Pages 261 (and note 4), 262 (and notes); 263 (and notes). The obscure text comes at the conclusion of C.'s treatment of Psalm 100: "Pudet enim dicere, peccatis obnoxium centenarii numeri fecunditate provectum et quod sanctorum diximus meritis applicatum, indigno mihi fuisse collatum." The question to be decided is whether the clause "quod . . . applicatum" refers to the crown reserved for martyrs and virgins and hence to the crown-shaped tonsure of a monk or merely to the observation that the author succeeded in commenting upon Psalms to the number of one hundred, the coefficient applied by the Lord to the merits of saints. Van de Vyver, *Vivarium,* p. 83, states that van de Vyver originally attached excessive importance to the obscure text, and that he now believes, if "crown" is the proper interpretation, that a pious member of the laity had a tonsure during this epoch.

[18] This is also the reason why most of the bibliographical information in the commentary is inserted later by C.; van de Vyver, p. 262, note 3.

[19] I. xxiii. 2.

[20] *Inst.* I. xxvi. Cf. van de Vyver, *Vivarium,* p. 87.

ning of his works his titles of *patricius* and *illustrissimus* and the names of the governmental offices which he had held.[21] The term *conversio* applied by Cassiodorus to himself [22] and the epithet *religiosus vir* applied to him by Pope Vigilius [23] indicate merely that our author was living a pious but secular life. The supposition that he was neither monk nor abbot seems to be strengthened by his mention of the actual abbots of his double monastery [24] and by the fact that he never includes himself among the members of the foundations, but always refers to *his* monks or *his* monastery.[25]

Thiele, however, objects strenuously to van de Vyver's exposition of the "obscure text" [26] and to his interpretation of the terms *conversio* and *religiosus vir*. The "obscure text," in Thiele's opinion,[27] undoubtedly refers to Cassiodorus' tonsure. The exact connotation of the term *conversio* cannot be fixed beyond a reasonable doubt by Schanz's mention of its use in Jordanes,[28] for of Jordanes' life we know practically nothing. The *Thesaurus linguae Latinae*,[29] moreover, gives only the following for its metaphorical meanings as applied to persons: a movement toward belief (and hence conversion to Christianity; baptism), or the completely spiritual act of penitence, or the entrance into the status of cleric or monk. St. Benedict, Caesarius of Arles, and

[21] Van de Vyver, p. 263, and notes 2–4.

[22] *De orthographia*, praef., p. 144 (= Migne, *Pat. Lat.*, LXX, 1240C): "post commenta psalterii, ubi conversionis meae tempore primum studium laboris impendi." This remark is a later bibliographical addition: van de Vyver, *Vivarium*, pp. 78–79. For the different meanings of *conversio* see Schanz, § 1058 (Jordanes), p. 118; and the authors quoted in van de Vyver, p. 257, note 5. For further examples of Cassiodorus' usage of such words as "conversio" and for the expert opinion of Father Galtier see van de Vyver, *Vivarium*, pp. 81–82. Cf. also *ibid.*, pp. 83–84.

[23] Van de Vyver, pp. 255–256, gives other examples. Cf. van de Vyver, *Vivarium*, pp. 82–83.

[24] Chalcedonius and Geruntius: *Inst.* I. xxxii. 1. Thiele, p. 382, calls C. "Altmeister" (senior master), who instructs the monks and gives them information. As van de Vyver, p. 263, note 5, points out, St. Gregory the Great found himself no longer at the head of the monastery which he had founded in his paternal abode, but the role of the future pope in his foundation was different from that of the exminister Cassiodorus.

[25] *Inst.* I. xxxii; chapter xxix; *De orthographia*, p. 210, 3 (= Migne, *Pat. Lat.*, LXX, 1270B 13); and *ibid.*, pp. 143, 2 and 145, 25 (= Migne, *Pat. Lat.*, LXX, 1239C 3 and 1242A 2). See van de Vyver, p. 263, notes 6 and 7. Cf. van de Vyver, *Vivarium*, pp. 85–88.

[26] Mentioned in the paragraph above, sentence 2, and the corresponding note.

[27] Thiele, pp. 379–380. Cf. also Franz, pp. 12–13.

[28] See p. 24, note 22, above; Thiele, p. 379.   [29] IV, 855. Thiele, *loc. cit.*

Gregory the Great all use *conversio* in the sense of becoming a monk. And, finally, Thiele takes exception [30] to van de Vyver's use of the patrician Theodore as an example of one who retired from the worldly life, since Theodore was never called *religiosus vir*.

Whatever the truth of the matter may be, the founder of the monasteries was a busy man, attempting to accomplish at Vivarium the purpose previously projected (in 535 or 536), in company with Pope Agapetus, for Rome—to establish a school of theology and Christian literature similar to the schools at Alexandria and Nisibis (the latter in Syria).[31] Though the Roman project had gone no farther than the creation of a Christian library by Pope Agapetus,[32] our author's two foundations were not only successfully completed but also had a very useful career.

The merit of Cassiodorus' monastic work The great merit of Cassiodorus' monastic work lay in his determination to utilize the vast leisure of the convent for the preservation of divine and human learning and for its transmission to posterity. While a critical and complete study of teaching during the first centuries of monasticism is yet to be written, Cassiodorus must not, however, be considered the first man to have introduced into monasteries either the copying of manuscripts or the study of the Scriptures. The rule of St. Pacomius (who died in 346) had already prescribed knowledge of reading and writing and the study of lessons to this end thrice daily,[33] and in his foundations there had also existed a body of monastic copyists.[34] The younger monks alone were copyists in the monastery of St. Martin's at Tours.[35] St. Jerome, in his cell at Bethlehem, had not only shown what great results a single recluse could obtain

[30] *Ibid.* Thiele, however, overlooks the fact that van de Vyver, p. 256, cites two other laymen to whom the term *religiosus vir* was applied: the patrician Albinus (in 519) and a count Narses (590–597).

[31] *Inst.* praef. 1. Van de Vyver, p. 252, thinks that the initiative came from the pope.

[32] According to van de Vyver, p. 252, note 1, this library on the hill of Scaurus (*ad clivum Scauri*) was still in existence in the time of Gregory the Great, a descendant of Agapetus, whereas the library of Rome (*bibliotheca Romae*), whose possible pillaging during the capture of Rome in 546 had been envisaged by Cassiodorus, designated the public library and not this private collection.

[33] Lucas Holstenius, *Codex regularum monasticarum*, I (Rome, 1661), 83, §§ 139–140; cf. § 25. I owe this note and notes 34–37, below, to van de Vyver, pp. 279–280.

[34] Cf. Lenain de Tillemont, *Mémoires*, VII (Paris, 1700), 179–180.

[35] Sulpicius Severus *Vita S. Martini* vii.

from patient literary toil but also had taught grammar to the monks resident there.[36] In Gaul, moreover, there had been famous schools, such as those at Lérins,[37] and in the rules laid down *ca.* 550 by Ferreolus reading and copying were considered suitable for monks who were too weak for harder work.[38] At the same time Cassian and Gregory the Great had rejected the liberal arts as being unnecessary for the study of the Scriptures.[39] It remained for Cassiodorus to make of the monastery a theological school and a *scriptorium* for the multiplication of copies of the Scriptures, of the Fathers of the Church and the commentators, and of the great secular writers of antiquity.[40] His work was more systematic than that of his predecessors, and it had more important results. He showed deep insight into the needs of his time. The quality of theological study had seriously declined, the best works of classical literature were no longer being copied, and every movement of the Ostrogothic armies or of the still more savage imperial hordes against a city or even a villa resulted in the destruction of priceless codices.

Cassiodorus' attitude toward the liberal arts — Despite his constant praise of the liberal arts,[41] Cassiodorus was after all a product of his age. For him, as for the Fathers of the Church and St. Augustine in particular,[42] these arts were simply aids to the study of theology; all literary culture, all profane science were thought of as contained in the Scriptures and derived from them. To be sure, our author sometimes cites Virgil and does not give up entirely the habits of a scholar,[43] but nowhere

[36] *Apologia adversus Rufinum* I. xxx–xxxi (Migne, *Pat. Lat.,* XXIII, 421–424), cited by Rand, *Founders,* p. 120.

[37] Cf. P. Lahargou, *De schola Lerinensi* (Paris, 1892).

[38] Chap. xxviii: "paginam pingat digito, qui terram non praescribit aratro" (Franz, p. 56).

[39] Cf. Roger, pp. 131–143; 175–187; Rand, *Founders,* pp. 234 ff. Cf. also A. Hauck, *Kirchengeschichte Deutschlands,* II (2d ed., 1912), 61 ff.; Erna Patzelt, *Die Karolingische Renaissance* (Vienna, 1924), pp. 41 ff.; and Chapman, *St. Benedict,* pp. 90–91.

[40] Copies of the works of many of these secular writers belonged to the private library of Cassiodorus rather than to the library of Vivarium according to van de Vyver, p. 283 and note 5.

[41] Cf. *De orthographia,* p. 143 (= Migne, *Pat. Lat.* LXX, col. 1239C 11): "labor nobis antiquorum omnino servandus est, ne nos auctores earum rerum mentiamur qui sequaces esse cognoscimur." In general, however, C.'s expressions are somewhat more reserved: "scripturae saeculares non debent respui," and the like.

[42] In the *De doctrina Christiana.*

[43] Van de Vyver, p. 279 and note 2, where he states that M. Bacherler, "Cassiodors

does he urge—or forbid, it must be admitted—the study of the poets.[44] One must keep in mind that even while he was a minister at court he read his Bible fervently [45] and that shortly after quitting public life he planned his theological school and published his *De anima* and his *Commentary on the Psalms*. For such a devout individual to busy his monks in a systematic study of the Bible was in itself a remarkable accomplishment. As van de Vyver declares,[46] "Nous ne connaissons personne qui à cette date l'ait réalisée en Occident avec autant de méthode et en faisant largement appel aux sciences profanes."

Literary activity elsewhere in Italy confined to revisions of theological works

The greatness of our author's accomplishment becomes apparent when we survey the literary activity in Italy at the end of the fifth century.[47] The first half of this century had seen revisions of the works of numerous secular authors—Virgil, Horace, Caesar (*De bello Gallico*), Pomponius Mela, Valerius Maximus, Macrobius (commentary on the *Somnium Scipionis*), Martianus Capella (*De nuptiis Mercurii et Philologiae*), and Sedulius—revisions which were made by the noble Christian descendants of such great pagan literary figures as the Symmachi, the Nicomachi, and the Praetextati. The second half of the century, however, was characterized by the dislocation of the senatorial class and a consequent decline in the cultivation of secular letters: [48] there was interest in little except the revision of theological works.[49] Thus, in 559 an anonymous writer "in territorio Cumano in possessione nostra Ascheruscio" corrected a *De trinitate* of St. Augustine; in 582, during the siege of Naples by the Lombards, "Petrus notarius ecclesiae catholicae Neapolitanae" corrected a selection of extracts from the works of St. Augustine (*Paris, lat. 11642* [Corbie], *s.* ix); [50] presumably before 590

Dichterkenntnisse und Dichterzitate," *Bayerische Blätter für das Gymnasial-Schulwesen*, LIX (1923), 215–224, establishes the fact that many of C.'s citations of authors do not presuppose a direct knowledge of their works.

[44] Cf. van de Vyver, p. 279, note 3, and the references there quoted.

[45] *Variae* IX. xxv: "hos igitur mores lectio divina solidavit."

[46] Page 279.

[47] This paragraph is based on van de Vyver, pp. 280–283.

[48] Cf. C. Jullian, *Histoire de la Gaule*, VIII (Paris, 1926), 242 ff.

[49] All the revisions come from southern Italy because Rome had not yet recovered from the Gothic War and northern Italy was subjected to invasion by the Lombards.

[50] Eugippius had dedicated this selection to the famous virgin, Proba, Cassiodorus'

the grammarian Dulcitius corrected, punctuated, and annotated in Cassiodorian fashion a papyrus copy of the *De trinitate* by St. Hilary of Poitiers (*Vienna, 2160, s.* vi). The monastery of Lucullanum (at Naples) [51] was especially prominent at this time: apparently one of its manuscripts of Jerome's text was used in 558 by Cassiodorus himself for the revision which appeared in the seventh volume of his nine-volume Bible; [52] another—an epistolary of St. Augustine—was used in 560 by a certain Facistus (Faustus?) as a model for a copy (*Paris, n. acq. lat. 1143* [Cluniac.], *s.* ix); and in 569 a "presbyter Donatus . . . infirmus" corrected his own manuscript of Rufinus' translation of Origen's commentary on the *Epistle to the Romans* (*Monte Cassino, 150* [346], *s.* vi), as well as two other works by Rufinus—the *De adulteratione librorum Origenis* and his translation of Origen's Περὶ ἀρχῶν (*Metz, 225, s.* xi).

Revisions, trans-
lations, and
commentaries

The first few years after the founding of the double monastery were employed in scholarly labors of a varied sort.[53] Cassiodorus surrounded himself with a small but capable group of translators and grammarians and with their help proceeded to prepare the manuscripts which were needed. This group aided him in his collation of the complete body of the Scriptures—a delicate and important labor—and, since the ordinary monks were none too expert even at the time of his death, undertook independently the revision of other works.[54] One of the most distinguished members of this group was the "vir disertissimus Epiphanius scholasticus," who translated the exposition of the *Song of Songs* written by Philo Carpasius,[55] the commentaries of Didymus on Proverbs, and those on the seven canonical letters which Cassio-

kinswoman, at the beginning of the sixth century before becoming abbot of the monastery of St. Severinus in the Lucullan castle (*in castello Lucullano:* Castel dell' ovo at Naples).

[51] See the preceding note.

[52] Cf. below, p. 29, note 69. Van de Vyver, p. 283, thinks that the MS used was obtained by Eugippius from the library of Proba, C.'s illustrious kinswoman, whose ancestors had been in touch with Jerome.

[53] The account of the labors contained in this paragraph and the two which follow is based to a large extent upon the description of van de Vyver, pp. 264–271.

[54] *Inst.* praef. 8.

[55] Not Epiphanius of Cyprus, as Cassiodorus states, *Inst.* I. v. 4.

dorus attributes to the same author, but which actually constitute a collection of homilies by different Fathers of the Church,[56]
the *codex encyclius* containing letters in favor of the council of
Chalcedon by the bishops consulted by Emperor Leo,[57] and the
ecclesiastical histories of Socrates, Sozomenus, and Theodoretus,
which were fused into a single narrative—the *Historia tripartita* [58]—to continue the translation and extension of Eusebius'
work by Rufinus. A second member of the little group, the "vir
disertissimus Mutianus," turned into Latin the thirty-four homilies of St. John Chrysostom on the Epistle to the Hebrews [59] as
well as Gaudentius' treatise on music.[60] The diversity of his work
indicates that he was employed to fill in gaps in the library. A
third member, the priest Bellator, undoubtedly the almoner at
Vivarium,[61] produced an important series of commentaries on
Ruth,[62] Wisdom,[63] Tobias, Esther, Judith, and Maccabees,[64] and
translated Origen's homilies on Ezra.[65] Though Cassiodorus fails
to give proper credit, Bellator also translated into Latin, after a
suitable purging, the commentaries of Clement of Alexandria on
the canonical epistles.[66] Unnamed scholars, finally, designated
merely as "friends," were (no doubt, collectively) responsible
for two vast enterprises—the translation of Josephus' *Jewish
Antiquities* [67] and the translation of the fifty-five homilies of St.
John Chrysostom on the Acts of the Apostles.[68]

The codex grandior   Though his scholarly friends had helped him
of the Bible   somewhat in his collations, Cassiodorus was
himself responsible for the assembling of a text of Jerome's version of the Scriptures—a "codex grandior littera clariore con-
scriptus"—and for its division into nine volumes and its complete revision.[69] Contrary to general opinion,[70] however, Cassio-

---

[56] *Inst.* I. v. 2; and viii. 6.   [57] *Ibid.* xi. 2.
[58] *Ibid.* xvii. 1. The work is apparently full of mistranslations from the Greek.
On the similar work by Theodore, reader of St. Sophia, see van de Vyver, p. 265, and
the references cited by him in note 1.
[59] *Ibid.* viii. 3.   [60] *Ibid.* II. v. 1 (and § 10 in ΦΔ).
[61] Cf. U. Berlière, *Revue bénédictine*, XXXIX (1927), 228.
[62] *Inst.* I. i. 9.   [63] *Ibid.* v. 5.   [64] *Ibid.* vi. 4.
[65] *Ibid.* § 6.   [66] *Ibid.* viii. 4.   [67] *Ibid.* xvii. 1.
[68] *Ibid.* ix. 1.
[69] See below, p. 33. As van de Vyver, p. 282 and note 5, points out, the seventh
volume apparently contained a revision by Cassiodorus of a MS from the library

dorus did not extend to the entire Vulgate the arrangement *per cola et commata* [71] (the use of unequal lines whose length depended upon the sense). This arrangement, used previously in certain editions of Jerome's version, or those supposed to be such,[72] caused our author to make certain general remarks which have been misinterpreted.[73] He did state, to be sure, that he would not be so presumptuous as to desire to modify the method adopted by the great master, but at the same time he supposed that this method was used only for monks unfamiliar with the punctuation of the grammarians.[74] Moreover, he employed punctuation in all the parts of the Scriptures not translated by Jerome [75] and added punctuation to the one volume of his nine which contained the Psalms.[76] He was firm in his insistence upon using the methods of the liberal arts to aid the study of sacred works.

Further work of revision and annotation

Among his other accomplishments, he divided the books of the Bible into chapters, provided the chapters with titles,[77] and placed summaries of the chapters at the head of each book. At some time after the publication of the *Institutiones* [78] he united these sum-

---

of Eugippius: Chapman, *Notes,* pp. 23 ff., and *Revue bénédictine,* XXIII (1911), 283-295. Cf., however, E. von Dobschütz, *Berliner philologische Wochenschrift,* XXIX (1909), 617–621, and Dom Donatien de Bruyne, *Revue bénédictine,* XXI (1909), 112. Cf. also p. 28, note 52, above.

[70] Cf., e.g., Dom D. de Bruyne, *Revue bénédictine,* XLI (1929), 102–103.

[71] Van de Vyver, pp. 267–269, provides many interesting proofs in addition to those cited here.

[72] Van de Vyver, p. 267, note 5, points out that we are probably ignorant of many editions of the Bible in the sixth century and (note 6) mentions Dom D. de Bruyne's apparent proof (*Revue biblique,* XXIII [1915], 358 ff.) that of the books of the New Testament St. Jerome revised only the Gospels.

[73] Van de Vyver, p. 269 and note 2, believes that it was at Jarrow that the arrangement "per cola et commata" was extended to the entire *Amiatinus* (see below, p. 34) because of a misinterpretation of the *Inst.*

[74] In the preface to his translation of Isaiah Jerome himself says simply "utilitati legentium."

[75] *Inst.* I. xv. 12.   [76] *Ibid.*

[77] In some of the books of the Bible, at least in the edition which he used, there had been no titles.

[78] And apparently after even his final revision of his *corpus* of grammar (cf. p. 40, below), for this *corpus* is mentioned—though after its last revision—before the *Liber titulorum* (and the *Complexiones*) in the list of works (composed after his *conversio*) which Cassiodorus placed at the beginning of his edition of the *De orthographia:* van de Vyver, p. 278, note 2, and p. 271, note 4. On the date of the *Institutiones* see p. 32, below.

maries and published them as a separate work—the *Liber titulorum sive memorialis*. Not long before the composition of the *Institutiones* he provided a copy of the Prophets with marginal notes drawn from a brief exposition (*annotationes*) which he attributed to St. Jerome.[79] He purged of their Pelagian errors the annotations on the Epistle to the Romans which were written by an author whose identity he did not know, but who was actually Pelagius himself.[80] By this purging and by returning to the ideas of St. Augustine and St. Jerome and those expressed in the *De statu animae* by Claudianus Mamertus [81] he completely altered the heretical work. Some of his monks—three at most—corrected the other epistles of St. Paul without, however, introducing proper considerations.[82] Cassiodorus himself marked with the sign ἄχρηστον unorthodox passages in the works of Origen and in the commentary on Revelation by the Donatist Tychonius. He likewise pruned troublesome passages from his specially prepared translation of the treatise on the canonical letters by Clement of Alexandria.[83] Moreover, he read through certain commentaries written by the Fathers of the Church and noted in red letters, wherever necessary, the particular volume of his nine volumes of the Scriptures to which each passage in the texts referred.[84] And, finally, after the manner of the correctors of old (*more maiorum*), he placed in the margins of his *Commentary on the Psalms* various signs to indicate definitions, locutions proper to the Scriptures, matters which belonged to the different liberal arts, and the like.[85]

[79] Cf. van de Vyver, p. 270 and note 1.

[80] *Inst.* I. viii. 1. On the relative date of this purging see below, p. 32, the end of note 87. C.'s work is extant under Primasius' name (A. Souter, note 82, below).

[81] C. also used this work as one of the inspirations for his own *De anima;* see above, p. 19.

[82] *De orthographia*, p. 144, l. 5; cf. *Inst.* I. viii. 1. See A. Souter, "Pelagius' Exposition on the Thirteenth Epistle of St. Paul," *Texts and Studies*, edited by Armitage Robinson, Vol. IX, Parts 1–3 (Cambridge, 1922–31), especially Vol. IX, Part 1, pp. 318 ff. The activity described above caused Cassiodorus to state in his *Inst.* praef. 8 that of all the parts of the Scriptures he was particularly concerned with the Psalms, the Prophets, and the Epistles.

[83] *Inst.* I. viii. 4   [84] *Ibid.* xxvi. 1.

[85] These signs have been edited by A. Reifferscheid, *Sitzungsberichte der kaiserliche Akademie der Wissenschaft zu Wien*, LVI (1867), 507, who does well to point out, however (*Rheinisches Museum*, XXIII [1868], 133), that C.'s notes are different from the critical signs employed by grammarians (cf. A. Reifferscheid, *Suetonii reliquiae* [Leipzig, 1860], pp. 139 ff.; Heinrich Keil, *Grammatici latini*, VII [1880],

Cassiodorus'
Institutiones

The *Institutiones divinarum et humanarum lectionum*,[86] written for the instruction of his monks at some time after 551,[87] is undoubtedly Senator's best work. It begins with a description of his unsuccessful effort (already mentioned) to found a theological school at Rome in conjunction with Pope Agapetus and continues as follows:

But although my ardent desire could in no way have been fulfilled . . . I was driven by divine charity to this device, namely, in the place of a teacher to prepare for you under the Lord's guidance these introductory books; through which, in my opinion, the unbroken line of the Divine Scriptures and the compendious knowledge of secular letters might with the Lord's beneficence be related.

Book I:
contents

In the first of the two books of which the treatise is composed Cassiodorus describes briefly the contents of the nine codices [88] which make up the Old

---

533) in that they have to do with the background, the matter, the content, and do not serve to correct the text. As van de Vyver, p. 271, note 2, points out, the Irish made a similar use of these signs during the epoch of Sedulius Scottus. Cf. H. Hagen, in *Verhandlungen der 39. Versammlung deutscher Philologer und Schulmänner zu Zürich* (1888), p. 247, and his edition of *MS Bernensis 363 (Codices . . . photographice editi,* II [Leyden, 1897], xxix) ; and on this MS cf. Ludwig Traube, *Abhandlungen der bayerische Akademie,* Vol. XIX, Part 2 (1892), p. 346.

86 On the title see Mynors, pp. lii–liii, and Rand, *New Cassiodorus,* pp. 434–435.

87 Since the introduction mentions the treatise of Junilius composed in this year (Lehmann, LXXI [1912], 290). As van de Vyver points out, pp. 271–272, the traditional date for the founding of Vivarium (540) is due to an erroneous interpretation of C.'s statement that his *Commentary on the Psalms* was his first work after his "conversio" (which means merely entering upon a pious life and not actually becoming a monk: see above, pp. 23–25) ; and the mention in the preface of this commentary of the tripartite division of a copy of the work for the use of his monks is revealed by the context to be a later addition to the text (cf. also van de Vyver, *Vivarium,* pp. 78–79). Lehmann's (pp. 290 ff.) *terminus ante quem* (562) for the *Inst.* is based on the fact that certain extracts from the *Argumenta paschalia* of Dionysius Exiguus, edited in 562, have been annexed to the *Inst.,* but van de Vyver, pp. 289–290, holds that the date of these extracts is uncertain since chronological evaluations in computistical treatises are usually copied from previous MSS without being brought up to date; van de Vyver pushes the date of the *Inst.* as far as 560 in order to allow time for the completion of the vast scholarly work described therein (cf. also van de Vyver, *Vivarium,* pp. 77–78).

C. placed a list of the works which he had composed after his *conversio* at the beginning of his edition of the *De orthographia.* As van de Vyver, p. 271, note 4, points out, the chronological order of the list (questioned by Lehmann, LXXI [1912], 285) is at fault only in the case of the *Inst.;* apparently because the *Inst.* is important and because it contains a résumé of practically all the work accomplished between his commentary on the Psalms and his revision of Pelagius' commentary on the Epistle to the Romans, C. has placed it between these two items, although strictly speaking it ought to follow the second (cf. *Inst.* i. viii).

88 (1) Octateuch, (2) Kings (Samuel, Kings, and Chronicles), (3) Prophets (four

and New Testaments and lists the names of the chief commentators. He proceeds to describe the various methods of understanding the Scriptures. Then, after giving an account of the four accepted synods, he carefully cautions scribes and editors to preserve the purity of the sacred text and to abstain from making plausible emendations.[89] He points out the value of the Scriptures; lists the historians whose works are of value in interpreting them—Eusebius, Rufinus, Socrates, Sozomenus, Theodoritus, Orosius, Marcellinus, Prosper, and several others—and gives brief character sketches of some of the chief Fathers of the Church—Hilary, Cyprian, Ambrose, Jerome, Augustine, and Eugippius. He mentions incidentally as a colleague and literary helper the monk Dionysius Exiguus, who settled the date of our present era.[90] After a recapitulation he provides one chapter on cosmographers and a second on the system of notes which he has used in his manuscripts of the various ecclesiastical commentators. He urges his monks to cultivate learning, not as an end in itself, but as a means toward the better knowledge of the Scriptures.[91] After dealing with secular literature and recommending the study of the classics, he exhorts those of his readers who are not inclined toward literature to spend their time in farming and gardening and to read the manuscripts of the ancient authors on this subject which he has left for their perusal —Gargilius Martialis, Columella, and Aemilianus Macer.[92]

He tells us that he sought out and bought manuscripts from northern Africa and other parts of the world,[93] and encouraged his monks to copy them with care. He mentions a fact already noted above [94]—that he had assembled a text of Jerome's ver-

---

major, including Daniel, and twelve minor), (4) Psalms, (5) Solomon (Proverbs, Ecclesiastes, Canticles, Wisdom, Ecclesiasticus), (6) Hagiographa (Tobias, Esther, Judith, Maccabees, Esdras), (7) Gospels, (8) Epistles of the Apostles (including that to the Hebrews), (9) Acts of the Apostles and Apocalypse. The various methods of dividing the Scriptures—those employed by Jerome, Augustine, and the writers of the Septuagint—are discussed in chapters xii–xiv.

[89] *Inst.* I. xv. Only scholars of the highest standing in both sacred and secular literature are to be allowed to correct sacred texts. Other texts are to be revised only after study of the works of the ancients and after consultation with men proficient in secular literature.

[90] Its earliest use occurs in 562 A.D. (*Computus paschalis* in Migne, *Pat. Lat.*, LXIX, 1249, first ascribed to Cassiodorus by Pithoeus).

[91] *Inst.* I. xxvii.   [92] *Ibid.*, chap. xxviii.

[93] *Ibid.*, chap. viii.   [94] Page 29.

sion of the Scriptures into nine volumes completely revised by himself.[95] This text seems to have been preserved in the first and oldest quaternion [96] of the best manuscript of the Vulgate, the *codex Amiatinus*,[97] which was written at Jarrow (perhaps under the direction of Bede), temporarily lost sight of in 716 after the death of the abbot Ceolfrid (who was taking it to the pope at Rome), and rediscovered at the monastery of Monte Amiata in southern Tuscany, whence it passed into the Laurentian Library at Florence. The frontispiece of the *codex Amiatinus* represents the prophet Ezra correcting the Scriptures, seated before a press containing the nine volumes mentioned above.[98] Presses of this sort (*armaria*) were used in the monastic library at Vivarium: nine of them contained the Scriptures and works which bore on their study, while a single press (the eighth) was enough for the few Greek manuscripts. The arrangement was in general, not by authors, but by subjects. Thus the biographical works of St. Jerome and Gennadius were combined in one codex, and certain rhetorical works of Cicero, Quintilian, and Fortunatianus in another.[99]

The work of the scribe   Senator was especially interested in the copying of manuscripts. His opinion of the nobil-

[95] Chapman, *Amiatinus*, 1927, p. 12, is wrong in thinking that the nine volumes contain the text of the Scriptures exclusively, for Cassiodorus expressly declares that he has placed homilies of different authors after the book of Kings, and it is also likely that in the one volume (of the nine) which contained the Prophets Cassiodorus set down the marginal notes which he had taken from St. Jerome (*Inst.* I. iii): cf. van de Vyver, p. 267, note 4, and p. 270, note 1.

[96] In 678 Ceolfrid acquired the *codex grandior* in Rome and had the first quaternion reproduced at the beginning of the *Amiatinus*.

[97] Cf. Chapman, *Amiatinus;* Quentin, *Mémoire,* I, 438–450, 496–497, and Dom D. de Bruyne, *Revue bénédictine*, XL (1928), 261–266, think that the *Amiatinus* depends upon the *codex grandior*. Nevertheless, Quentin, *Essais,* p. 16, makes allusion to a revision of the Vulgate by Cassiodorus. Cf. also Chapman, *Amiatinus*, 1927, pp. 15 and 32, who envisages the possibility that the *Amiatinus* depends upon the *Pandects,* Cassiodorus' "bible hiéronymmienne." H. Glutz, *Britannien und Bibeltext* (Leipzig, 1930), pp. 94–95, speaks of the Vivarian Bibles with little precision. For the references in this note I am indebted to van de Vyver, p. 266, note 5.

[98] Chapman, *Amiatinus*, 1927, p. 30, believes that the *codex grandior* originally contained a portrait of Cassiodorus represented as a monk correcting the Scriptures and that his portrait was changed into that of Ezra at Jarrow. Cf. also van de Vyver, p. 261, note 4. The design in question is given (as van de Vyver, p. 266, note 3, points out) by Pfeilschifter, p. 126 (after R. Garrucci, *Storia del arte christiano*, III, 1876, tavola 126[?]), and by A. Hessel, *Geschichte der Bibliothek* (Göttingen, 1925), Abbildung 2 (after J. W. Clark, *The Care of Books,* Cambridge, 1901, frontispiece).   [99] *Inst.* I. viii; chap. xvii; II. ii.

ity of the scribe's work is well shown in the following description.[100]

I admit that among those of your tasks which require physical effort that of the scribe, if he writes correctly, appeals most to me. . . . Happy his design, praiseworthy his zeal, to preach to men with the hand alone, to open tongues with fingers, to give salvation silently to mortals, and to fight against the illicit temptations of the devil with pen and ink. Every word of the Lord written by the scribe is a wound inflicted on Satan. And so, though seated in one spot, with the dissemination of his work he travels through different provinces. . . . O sight glorious to those who contemplate it carefully!

One must not infer from the passage above that Cassiodorus was interested merely in sacred literature. The greater part of chapter xxviii of the first book of the *Institutiones,* for example, is devoted to an argument against neglecting secular writers.

Orthographical rules   Book I of the *Institutiones* contains, among other things, certain rules of spelling. Thus, for the sake of euphony, Cassiodorus apparently favors assimilation of the prefix *in* [101] and prefers *quicquam* to *quidquam.* In order that he may avoid errors the copyist is instructed to read the works of ancient authors on orthography [102]—Velius Longus, Curtius Valerianus, Papyrianus, "Adamantius Martyrius" on V and B and other subjects, Eutyches on the rough breathing, and Phocas on genders—works which Cassiodorus had himself collected to the best of his ability.

Bookbinding   Senator now goes on to describe the care which he has taken to bind the sacred codices in covers worthy of their contents, as the householder in the parable provided fitting garments for all who came to his son's wedding feast.[103] He states that he has prepared a single volume containing samples of various sorts of binding and directs anyone interested in bindings to choose that which seems best to him.

Mechanical devices   Senator continues with an account of the various mechanical devices provided for the convenience of the copyists. For use at night there were mechanical

---

[100] *Ibid.* I. xxx.
[101] *Ibid.,* chap. xv: *illuminatio, irrisio, immutabilis, impius, improbus.*
[102] *Ibid.* xxx. 2.   [103] *Ibid.,* § 3.

lamps, cleverly constructed so as to trim themselves and to provide themselves with a steady supply of oil.[104] There were also water clocks for nights and cloudy days, and sundials for bright weather.[105]

After a brief discourse on medical works Book I ends with an admonition of the abbot to the community of monks and a prayer.

Institutiones: Book II contains a brief account of the seven
Book II liberal arts—grammar, rhetoric, dialectic, arithmetic, geometry, music, and astronomy. A complete investigation of the sources of Senator's information on all these subjects is yet to be made. The extremely short chapter on grammar lists various grammarians and quotes a number of definitions from Donatus. The treatment of rhetoric is based chiefly upon Cicero's *De inventione* and to a lesser extent upon Fortunatianus; Quintilian is used twice, and the author of the *Rhetorica ad Herennium* once. The long chapter on dialectic [106] depends upon several sources: Aristotle's *Categories;* Pseudo-Apuleius' *De interpretatione* (or Martianus Capella); three works by Marius Victorinus—the *De syllogismis hypotheticis,* the *De definitionibus,* and the commentary [107] on Cicero's *Topica;* and two works by Boethius—his translation of Porphyry's *Introduction* and his commentary on Aristotle's *De interpretatione.* The source of most of Senator's treatment of arithmetic remains to be found; Boethius' *De arithmetica* seems to supply a few lines at the beginning, while Eucherius' *Formulae* certainly furnishes a page at the end on the importance of numbers in the Scriptures. The chapter on music lists several works and especially recommends Mutianus' Latin translation of Gaudentius; Varro or Censorinus may be the authority used in the first part of section 9. Little is known of the sources of the chapters on geometry [108] and on astronomy.[109]

---

[104] *Ibid.,* § 4. [105] *Ibid.,* § 5.

[106] Martianus Capella is the source of almost all of Appendix A (commonplaces); Boethius' *De differentiis topicis* is used once.

[107] A possible source only.

[108] Boethius' *De geometria* is the source of the first two sentences. Varro and Censorinus are mentioned incidentally. Boethius' *Euclid* is the source of Appendix C (on geometry).

[109] The source of Appendix B (on the four elements) is unknown.

The *Institutiones* is not written for the learned. Instead of the *affectata eloquentia* which Cassiodorus employs in the official correspondence in his *Variae*,[110] we find "more utility than ornament." [111] The change, however, is only relative; the style is still wordy and elaborate, often to the point of obscurity.[112] Superlatives whose force has been lost either partly or completely are common. In less than two pages of text (I. pref. 5–6) we find the following: "most ready masters" (*magistros . . . paratissimos*), "very delicate strength" (*tenuissimas vires*), "most wisely" (*prudentissime*), "a very obscure passage" (*obscurissimo loco*), "a very frequent prayer" (*oratione creberrima*), "most difficult matters" (*res difficillimas*), and "an exceedingly sweet gift" (*suavissimum donum*). Of equally frequent occurrence are two other types of exaggeration—the application of *nimis* ("exceedingly") to the positive or superlative form of an adjective or an adverb without the addition of any emphasis and the use of stronger words than the context seems to require. Examples follow: "unusually eloquent sermons" (*eloquentissimae nimis omeliae*, I. i. 8), "a name exceptionally pleasant" (*dictio nimis suavissima*, I. v. 5), "remarkably profound books" (*libri . . . mirabili profunditate*, I. xvi. 3, "anything unsightly" (literally "base": *quicquam turpe*, I. xv. 15), and "the gravest heresy" (literally "most violent," "most furious": *saevissimi erroris*, I. xxiv. 1).

Without question the influence of years of official correspondence has caused Cassiodorus not merely to exaggerate but also to cultivate abstract expressions at the expense of concrete and to fall naturally into complicated and unnecessary periphrases. Heaven is described literally as "that sweetness of fatherland" (*in illa suavitate patriae*, I. xxviii. 5). For the single words "substance" and "reckoning" we have *substantiae ratio* (II. iii. 9) and *calculi . . . quantitatem* (II. xiv. 7). Most troublesome of all, perhaps, is the type of periphrasis in which two verbs are used instead of one—*probor esse compulsus* for the aorist perfect

---

[110] The language of the *Variae* is so turgid and bombastic that Hodgkin felt under no compulsion to reproduce it in its entirety; his translation of each letter is only half as long as C.'s original and considerably simpler.

[111] This is C.'s own characterization in *De orthographia*, p. 144.

[112] For a more extended consideration of C.'s style see Ennis, pp. 147–154.

compulsus sum ("I was driven," I. pref. 1) and *reliquisse cog-noscor* for the present perfect *reliqui* ("I was driven," II. ii. 10) ; *monstro, nosco, cerno,* and other verbs are commonly used in these expressions.

Despite these shortcomings Cassiodorus has a genuine feeling for style. His numerous parenthetical expressions, for example, show an endless variety. Thus, "as most people hold" (*ut usus habet,* I. v. 5) becomes first "as it seemed to our Fathers" (*sicut et Patribus nostris visum est,* I. xxvii. 1), and then "as it has been said (*sicut dictum est,* I. xxxii. 4), and finally "according to the ancients" (*sicut antiqui voluerunt,* II. v. 1). His desire for balance often causes him to prefer two adverbs or two adjectives at a time instead of one; such combinations as "with caution and wisdom" (*caute sapienterque,* I. i. 8) and "very subtle and very concise words" (*suptilissimas . . . ac brevissimas dictiones,* I. xiii. 2) are carefully chosen and not at all redundant. His characterizations of authors are concise and effective: Ambrose is called "a clear and very delightful interpreter" (*planus atque suavissimus doctor,* I. i. 3) and Augustine "a fluent and extremely wary disputant" (*disertus atque cautissimus disputator,* I. i. 4). His poetic figures are often as pleasing as the two which follow: contemplation, "the mother of understanding" (*mater . . . intelligentiae,* I. pref. 7) ; and the marks of punctuation, "the paths for thoughts and the beacon-lights for words" (*viae . . . sensuum et lumina dictionum,* I. xv. 12).

Vocabulary and syntax   The archaic and artificial quality of his rich vocabulary is impressive; *Ennis* [113] treats its important aspects. Highly specialized technical terms abound, particularly in the discussion of the seven liberal arts. Ecclesiastical expressions are varied. The late Latin words include fifty-

---

[113] This invaluable but not infallible work has to be consulted with care. I have often deviated from it in my translation. The more important deviations, listed and discussed in my article, "Notes on the Style and Vocabulary of Cassiodorus' *Institutiones,*" *Classical Philology,* XL (1945), 24–31, concern the following words: "contropabilis" (Mynors, p. 75, lines 21–23), "linealiter" (*ibid.,* p. 139, lines 9–12), "clima" (*ibid.,* p. 156, lines 4–15), "extrinsecus" (*ibid.,* p. 127, lines 10–11), "qualitas" (*ibid.,* p. 43, lines 7–15), "ab adiunctis [argumentum]" (*ibid.,* p. 125, lines 13–19), "praemium" (*ibid.,* p. 100, lines 11–12), "secundae substantiae" (*ibid.,* p. 113, lines 23–25), "tempus" (*ibid.,* p. 95, lines 18–20), "diapason simul et diatessaron symphonia" (*ibid.,* p. 145, lines 13–15), and "temperamentum" (*ibid.,* p. 144, line 21, to p. 145, line 2).

three [114] apparent neologisms, none very daring. The translator is often at a loss to determine whether a word is being employed in its classical or late Latin sense. He is likely to have a similar difficulty in deciding between classical and late Latin syntax.[115]

The clausulae in five of the chief works of Cassiodorus (the *Variae*, the *Institutiones*, the *De anima*, the *Expositio in psalterium*, and the *Complexiones in epistulis Sancti Pauli*) are treated in Suelzer. There is a detailed study of the clausulae of the *Variae*, a work less typical of Cassiodorus' ordinary productions than is the *Institutiones*. Cassiodorus seems to have been guided primarily by a feeling for accent and secondarily by a feeling for meter. His five favorite metrical forms—the cretic spondee, $\smile\!\!\smile \,\smile\, \smile\!\!\smile$ followed by the dichoree, the double cretic, the cretic tribrach, and $\smile\!\!\smile \,\smile\, \smile\!\!\smile$ followed by the double spondee— satisfy the demands of the four chief forms of the universally recognized medieval cursus: the planus, the velox, the tardus, and the trispondaicus. He uses the metrical cretic spondee more frequently than do most of the Latin prose writers from the first century B.C. to the sixth century A.D.; he uses the four forms of the accentual cursus more frequently than any of the writers except Ammianus Marcellinus, Leo the Great, and Pomerius.

I cannot agree with Suelzer's feeling that a study of the clausulae is helpful in determining the authenticity of one of several textual variants. Though the mathematical incidence of preferred types may be calculated exactly, an editor cannot always be sure which of several preferred types a writer has used in a particular instance. As a matter of fact, quantitative statistical data in general are of little value in deciding the correctness of a particular textual reading: see my review of this dissertation in *Classical Philology*, XLI (1946), 118-121.

Later bibliographical notes   Even before the composition of the *Institutiones* Cassiodorus had already begun to add later bibliographical notes in the margins of his commentary on the Psalms. In this way he was able to keep his treatise constantly up-to-date, adding references to new manuscripts as he

---

[114] J. L. Heller, in his review of Ennis in the *Classical Weekly*, XXXIII (1939), 58, points out that "panaretus" is not a neologism but a word quoted from Jerome.

[115] There has been no special study of the syntax of the *Institutiones*, but Löfstedt, Bieter, and Skahill are extremely useful in this connection.

acquired them, created them, or had time to become acquainted with them. These references eventually became incorporated into the text.[116] He employed a similar system of marginal additions in the *Institutiones*.[117] The modern reader will do well to keep these facts in mind in his interpretation of various passages in both works.

The gathering of closely related works into a single MS

The general substitution in the early centuries of our era of the relatively large unit—the codex—for the *volumen,* which ordinarily contained only one "book" of one work, allowed the assembling of several complete works on one subject in a single manuscript.[118] This practice must have been known to others at least as early as the fifth and sixth centuries, but Cassiodorus applied it so systematically that he made it one of the most salient characteristics of his scholarly work.[119] He was thus responsible for individual codices containing respectively a *corpus* of rhetoric,[120] a *corpus* of introductions to the study of the Scriptures,[121] a *corpus* of manuals on grammar (which he later revised),[122] and similar collections of extracts from orthographical works [123] and

---

[116] See van de Vyver, pp. 271–275, for the details.

[117] *Ibid.,* pp. 275–277.

[118] *Ibid.,* p. 276, note 2, cites the following references: Birt, pp. 95 ff., and T. Birt, *Kritik und Hermeneutik* (*Handbuch* of Iwan von Müller, Vol. I, Part 3), 1913, pp. 293 ff. and pp. 344 ff., where Birt speaks of the substitution of the codex as occurring in the fourth century; and W. Schubart, *Das Buch bei den Griechen und Römern* (Berlin, 1907), pp. 101–112, who speaks against the tendency to date the employment of the codex too late. As van de Vyver states (*loc. cit.*), its employment must have been fairly extensive in the second century, though the *corpus* (*i.e.,* the assembling of several related works in a single MS) is a particular method of using the codex and is surely more recent (cf. Birt, p. 41).

[119] Van de Vyver, p. 276, note 3, points out that "In hoc corpore continentur" is one of C.'s favorite expressions, but that it is usually synonymous with "in hoc codice continentur" and is not at all peculiar to our author. He also cites Ludwig Traube, in *Theodosiani libri XVI* (edited by T. Mommsen and P. Meyer) . . . *tabulae sex* (Berlin, 1905), p. ii, and Dom G. Morin, *Revue bénédictine,* XXVI (1914), 239, note 1. See p. 46 and note 36, below.

[120] Van de Vyver, p. 275.

[121] *Ibid.,* pp. 272, note 2; 275.

[122] *Ibid.,* pp. 276–277. The plan at first envisaged merely Donatus' *Grammar,* possibly followed by the commentaries of Servius. Somewhat later orthographical extracts (which Cassiodorus had originally taken from different authors to form a distinct work) and a selection of etymologies were added, as well as the *De schematibus* of Sacerdos, which is no longer extant. Cassiodorus also placed four additional chapters at the beginning and end of these extracts at the time when he edited his *De orthographia*.

[123] *Loc. cit.*

from textbooks on logic.[124] These truly important achievements speak eloquently of Cassiodorus' desire not merely to provide his library with a revised text of the Bible and a very complete collection of Scriptural treatises but also to promote and facilitate the study of the liberal arts.

The commentary on the Epistles and the De orthographia   Two works written by Cassiodorus remain— the comparatively short commentary entitled *Complexiones in epistolas apostolorum* and the *De orthographia*. The former requires no special comment.[125] The latter was written for his beloved monks when the author was ninety-three years old. According to his account the monks suddenly exclaimed: "What doth it profit us to study either those works which the ancients have composed or those which your wisdom has caused to be added to the list if we are altogether ignorant how we ought to write these things and on the other hand cannot understand and accurately represent in speech the words which we find written?" Cassiodorus naturally felt called upon to supply a treatise on spelling.[126] He therefore compiled from twelve grammarians[127] a list of rules to be observed by those who would avoid the usual faults. One of the greatest sources of error, the confusion between *b* and *v*, is treated with nice discrimination in no less than four chapters. Though the work was undoubtedly little more than a compilation, it must have been exceedingly useful.

Death of Cassiodorus   Cassiodorus died at the age of ninety-five,[128] after a long and industrious career as statesman and scholar. As Hodgkin states:[129]

The period covered by his life had been one of vast changes. Born when the kingdom of Odovacar was only four years old, he had as a young man

---

[124] Van de Vyver, pp. 288–289.

[125] On its date (after the *Inst.*) see above, p. 30, note 78.

[126] In the *Inst.* I. xv, Cassiodorus points out that assimilation of prefixes in compound words had been introduced, but was not yet universal; and that the monks required instruction in the writing of "qui*c*quam" for euphony instead of "quidquam."

[127] Donatus, Cnaeus Cornutus, Velius Longus, Curtius Valerianus, Papirianus, Adamantius Martyrius, Eutyches, Caesellius, Lucius Caecilius, Priscian, and two writers whose names are apparently omitted by Cassiodorus.

[128] The date of his death depends, of course, upon the date of his birth. See above, p. 1, note 1.

[129] Pages 66–67.

seen that kingdom overthrown by the arms of Theodoric; he had sat by
the cradle of the Ostrogothic monarchy, and had mourned over its grave;
had seen the eunuch Narses supreme viceregent of the emperor; had heard
the avalanche of the Lombard invasion thunder over Italy, and had out-
lived even the Lombard invader Alboin. Pope Leo, the tamer of Attila
and the hero of Chalcedon, had not been dead twenty years when Cassiodorus was born. Pope Gregory the Great, the converter of England, was
within fifteen years of his accession to the pontificate when Cassiodorus
died. The first great schism between the Eastern and Western Churches
was begun in his boyhood and ended before he had reached old age. He
saw the irretrievable ruin of Rome, such as Augustus and Trajan had
known her; the extinction of the Roman senate; the practical abolition
of the Consulate; the close of the schools of philosophy at Athens.

In him, as in few other men, the ancient and the medieval world
were closely united. In his striving to bind together the culture
of Rome and the vigor of Germany he played a most important
part in history.

IV. THE FATE OF VIVARIUM AND ITS BOOKS

Vivarium rela-
tively peaceful Very little is known about the history of Vivarium after Cassiodorus' death. While the
Lombards were ravishing the northern section of southern Italy,
the southwestern tip (including Squillace and Vivarium) remained until 1060 in Byzantine control and enjoyed relative
peace.[1] Until 594 the monastery was a place of refuge for the
archdeacon and clerics of the church of Myria.[2]

Bishop John
in 598 In 598 the monks of Vivarium must have com-
plained to Gregory I about Bishop John, who
had been driven by the enemy from his bishopric of Alessio, near
Durazzo, and had since 592 administered the now destitute district of Scyllacium.[3] It appears that John desired to take privi-
leges away from them, promulgated unjust taxes, and made no
attempt to collect the taxes owed the monastery by the inhabitants of Squillace. He had, moreover, taken more land from the
monks than had been given him for the building of a church. He
was eventually rebuked by Gregory and forced to make full resti-
tution.[4]

[1] Batiffol, p. ii.   [2] *M.G., Ep.*, I, 290.   [3] *Ibid.*, p. 132.
[4] *M.G., Ep.*, II, 33.

Vivarium and an associated cloister in Taormina

In the same year, 598, Gregory I empowered Bishop Secundinus of Taormina to defend the monks of Vivarium (*monachi Castellienses*) against the encroachments of a layman in a cloister that was connected with Vivarium.[5] Minasi believes that the bishop of Taormina was addressed because the bishop of Scyllacium was a usurper.[6] Thiele, however, points out that this is hardly the real reason, since Bishop John of Scyllacium was addressed by Gregory after the previously mentioned complaint of the monks; the cloister connected with Vivarium (*Castelliense*) must have been situated at some distance, in the diocese of Taormina, in which Secundinus had jurisdiction.[7]

The growth of Greek influence

At the end of the sixth century and the beginning of the seventh the influence of the Greek Church continued to grow in southern Italy at the expense of the Roman. One must recall that even before this time the use of the Greek language had not ceased in this area, especially in the country parishes.[8] In 591 Gregory I, still recognized as metropolitan in southern Italy, recalled his imposition of celibacy upon subdeacons three years before and enjoined it anew,[9] though this regulation was never observed by the Greek Church. That this injunction was not obeyed in 594 is shown clearly by his letter to Bishop Leo of Catania [10] and by his even sharper letter to Bishop Boniface of Reggio.[11] These letters signalized the beginning of a long conflict. Moreover, Greek influences came to southern Italy from Egypt [12] and from Syria, whence Greek monks fled to Italy after the destruction of Antioch and Alexandria.[13]

In 668 Bishop Gregory of Syracuse introduced *troparia* (liturgical hymn-like songs of the Greek Church) into the liturgy of Christmas and of the Epiphany.[14] His successors introduced these songs in 680 into the vespers celebrated on days of fasting. Leo the Isaurian confiscated the property of the Roman Church in Sicily and Calabria, and in 731 assigned Sicily, Calabria, and Apulia to the Patriarch of Constantinople. In 732 the

---

[5] *Ibid.*, p. 32. [6] Minasi, p. 193. [7] Pages 393–394.
[8] Witness Greek inscriptions: Rohlfs, pp. 81, 83.
[9] *M.G., Ep.*, I, 67. [10] *Ibid.*, p. 269. [11] *Ibid.*, p. 237.
[12] Batiffol, pp. v–vi. In Palermo (and Rome as well), for example, there was an Alexandrian brotherhood "unter den Namen des heiligen Mennas": Thiele, p. 394.
[13] Thiele, *loc. cit.* [14] Minasi, p. 196.

Greek rite was prescribed as obligatory.[15] Greek monks fleeing before the Saracens found asylum in Sicily and, when this island too was plundered in the ninth century, in Calabria.[16] In the seventh and eighth centuries Greeks even became popes. In 968 the emperor Nicephoros Phocas prescribed the Greek liturgy for the areas which had been taken from the Normans.[17]

Norman rule and the end of the monastery of Vivarium From the ninth century to the thirteenth the cloisters of Sicily and Calabria were continually robbed by Saracen plunderers. In 1060 the Normans too robbed all of Calabria, including Squillace and Reggio. From this time on Byzantine control ceased, and Norman power made itself supreme. New monasteries, such as that of Rossano (twelfth century), were founded and some of the older monasteries were given a new lease on life.[18] Vivarium's fate, however, was not so fortunate. Its establishment for hermits had long since disappeared, and its cenobitic monastery, dedicated in the thirteenth century to St. Gregory Thaumaturgos, was placed directly under the control of the bishop. This action destroyed all trace of monastic life.[19] The market town Staletti arose on the site of Vivarium.[20]

The fate of the library The fate of the excellent library [21] which Cassiodorus had assembled at Vivarium is a matter yet to be discovered. Thiele points out that this monastery must have used the Roman liturgy; that Cassiodorus was constantly exhorting his monks to spread Roman culture (not Greek).[22] We do not know whether the monastery kept its Roman character after the death of its founder or whether it succumbed to the increasing pressure of the Greek influences which surrounded it. Some of its books were doubtless destroyed by plunderers; others may have remained long in their places, or, if the monastery was now predominantly Greek in character, they may have wandered rather rapidly to other centers.

Beer's hypothesis: Bobbio and Verona In the absence of definite evidence Rudolf Beer in 1911 published the remarkable hy-

---

[15] *Ibid.,* p. 201.   [16] Rohlfs, p. 89.   [17] Minasi, p. 207.
[18] Batiffol, p. 6. The influence of the Greek Church remained undisturbed.
[19] Minasi, p. 223.   [20] *Ibid.,* p. 145.
[21] That is, the monastery library and C.'s personal library as well. On the latter cf. van de Vyver, p. 283 and note 5.   [22] Pages 392–393.

pothesis that the books of Vivarium were transported to Bobbio (and, in some cases, to Verona) not long after Bobbio was founded in 612.[23] Finding that no opponent had arisen to combat his startling views,[24] he repeated and amplified them in 1913.[25] It is astonishing what currency they gained,[26] even among such careful students of Cassiodorus as van de Vyver [27] and Thiele.[28] The first, apparently, to speak up against Beer's theory was Dom A. Wilmart.[29] Other scholars followed cautiously. As E. K. Rand says,[30] "the general tendency at the time of Beer's publications was not to deny; today it is not to believe."

Beer's hypothesis completely unfounded Beer held that the probabilities point toward Rome as the source of the pre-Columban manuscripts of Bobbio.[31] After having eliminated the pope's library (completely destroyed in the time of Pope Agapetus) and Eugippius' library, he selected Cassiodorus' library ("one of the richest collections of books of the early Middle Ages, without doubt the greatest library assembled by a single collector in that time") as the probable source of the early books of Bobbio. He then proceeded to identify Vivarian manuscripts with those of Bobbio on the basis of their contents. The fact remains, however, that the available descriptions of the Vivarian manuscripts are far too vague to allow any degree of certainty in these analogies. Moreover, scholars as yet simply do not know what hap-

[23] Beer, *Bemerkungen.*

[24] As Rand, *New Cassiodorus*, p. 437, points out. I quote Rand's note 2 on this page: "In 1912, when I had the pleasure of meeting this eminent scholar in Vienna, Beer told me that before publishing he had written to a number of librarians and palaeographers for their criticisms, but that no one had any to offer."

[25] Beer, *Monumenta*, pp. 15–16.

[26] Cf., *e.g.*, Hörle, pp. 9–12. Olga Dobias-Rozdestvenskaïa, in *Histoire de l'atelier graphique de Corbie de 651 à 830* (Leningrad, 1934), pp. 109 and 112–114, apparently subscribes to Beer's views in pointing out that *Leningrad MS Q. v. I. 6–10 (Patrum opuscula)* was probably used by Cassiodorus and that it went from his possession to Bobbio, thence to St. Germain, and thence to Leningrad. A recent attempt to defend Beer's theory has been made by H. Gomoll, "Zu Cassiodors Bibliothek und ihrem Verhältnis zu Bobbio," *Zentralblatt für Bibliothekswesen*, LII (1936), 185–189.

[27] Page 283.   [28] Pages 394–396, 417.

[29] In *Recherches de science religieuse*, IX (1910), 65, note 4.

[30] Rand, *New Cassiodorus*, p. 437.

[31] Cf. the subscriptions to the MSS; the MSS of Fronto, Gargilius Martial, Pelagonius, and others, whose archetypes probably came from Rome; the *fasti consulares*, whose origin was probably the same; Galen's writings, which had recently been illuminated at Rome by Alexander of Tralles; etc.: Beer, *Monumenta*, especially pp. 16–26.

pened to the Vivarian books when they left Vivarium in the seventh century.[32] Until a fresh investigation of this whole important matter has been made [33] one must dismiss Beer's views as attractive, but fanciful.

MSS ascribed to archetypes of Vivarium or at least of Cassiodorus' time

Though we do not know the exact course of the wanderings of Cassiodorus' manuscripts,[34] we may be fairly sure that some of them at least served as models for copies made in the Carolingian period. Traube [35] holds that certain of these copies or their descendants may be associated with archetypes belonging to Cassiodorus or at least to his period if they begin with the inscription "In hoc corpore continentur" [36] followed by a table of contents. Among such books he lists the following: the manuscript of the *Lex Romana Visigothorum* (breviary); the *codex Amiatinus* of the Bible; [37] Eusebius' *Chronicon;* Jerome and Prosper (in *codex Lemovicensis 1*); eight books of Gregory of Nazianzus (*codex Atrebatensis 621*); Hegesippius' *History* (formerly *Floriacensis* and *Miciacensis,* but now *Bernensis 180* and *Lugdunensis Batavorum 21*); the *Historia tripartita* (*Petropolitanus F.I.11*); the commentary of John Chrysostom on the *Epistle to the Hebrews*

[32] Of course, as His Eminence Giovanni Cardinal Mercati states in his history of Bobbio (Mercati, *Prolegomena,* p. 18), Cassiodorus' *Institutiones* may well have served the early librarians of Bobbio—and of other centers—as a bibliographical guide and an incentive to look for good old copies of the works therein mentioned.

[33] I hope at some later date to be able to take up Beer's hypothesis in somewhat greater detail.

[34] W. M. Lindsay, in "Primary MSS of Probus' *Instituta artium,*" *American Journal of Philology,* XLVIII (1927), 231-234, has conclusively shown that the Vatican Probus reverts to Cassiodorus.

[35] L. Traube, *Vorlesungen und Abhandlungen,* Vol. II (posthumous ed. of F. Boll, Munich, 1909), 130: "Diese ganz seltsame Ausdrucksweise erklärt sich aus dem Sprachgebrauch Cassiodors und seiner Zeit. Offenbar sind diese Inhaltsangaben Überreste eines Brauches in der Bibliothek des Cassiodor." Cf. van de Vyver, p. 276 and note 3. Cf. Dom G. Morin, *Revue bénédictine,* XXVI (1914), 239, note 1.

[36] Cf. p. 40, note 119, above. This formula (or a similar one) placed before a table of contents is fairly common in MSS of Cologne: cf. Jones, *Cologne,* p. 30 ("In hoc corpore continetur . . .": *Cologne 76*), p. 31 ("In hoc codice continentur . . .": *Cologne 54*), p. 41 ("In huius codicelli corpore continentur": *Cologne 106*), p. 55 ("In hoc corpore continentur . . .": *Cologne 65*), etc. The whole matter needs further study.

[37] Quentin, *Mémoire,* pp. 484 ff., gives reasons *against* the view that the first gathering of the *codex Amiatinus* (Florence, Mediceo-Laurentian Library, *saec.* vii) was once actually a part of a MS from Cassiodorus' own library, although in the judgment of Professor C. R. Morey of Princeton University the character of the illumination still furnishes ground for such a belief. For the views of Dom Chapman and of Dom de Bruyne and a further account of the views of Dom Quentin see p. 34 and notes 97 and 98, above.

(*Vindobonensis 961* and *Cameracensis 464*); a cosmography (*Parisinus lat. 2769, saec.* vi); Boethius' commentary on Cicero's *Topica* (*Vossianus F. LXX*); a manuscript containing *De opificio Dei epitomae Firmiani Lactanti, De fine saeculi,* etc. (formerly *Bobiensis,* but now *Taurinensis I.b.VI.28*); *Libri Vigilii episcopi contra Nestorium* (*Petropolitanus F.I.10*); the work by Filaster of Brescia *De omnibus heresibus* and St. Ambrose's *De Ioseph* (formerly *Goerresianus,* but now *Berolinensis* and *Vindobonensis 1080*); a Pentateuch (formerly *Ashburnhamianus,* but now *Parisinus*); *Synodus Ephesena cum epistolis suis* (*Veronensis 57*); and Jerome's *Commentary on the Psalms* (*Sangallensis 108*). To this list Beer [38] adds the *codex Mediceus* (*Laurentianus XXXIX.1 + Vatic. 3225*) as a Vivarian product and Traube [39] also claims the same provenience for *Bambergensis B.IV.21* (containing Jerome and Gennadius' *De viris illustribus* as well as Augustine's two works, the *De haeresibus* and the *Enchiridion*). To be sure, these ascriptions are all made upon slender evidence. The later history of Vivarium's manuscripts— a rich and profitable study—yet remains to be undertaken.

V. THE INFLUENCE OF CASSIODORUS ON THE CULTURE OF THE MIDDLE AGES

Cassiodorus made monastery a theological school and a scriptorium

As has been pointed out above,[1] Cassiodorus was not the first man to introduce into the monastery either the copying of manuscripts or the study of the Scriptures. He did, however, perform a remarkable service in transforming the monastery into a theological school and a *scriptorium* for the multiplication of copies of the Scriptures, of the Fathers of the Church and the commentators, and of the great secular writers of antiquity. His work was more systematic than that of his predecessors, and it had more important results.

---

[38] Beer, *Bemerkungen,* p. 86.   [39] *Loc. cit.*

[1] Pages 25–26. The contents of the present chapter were originally published, in somewhat different form, in my article, "The Influence of Cassiodorus on Mediaeval Culture," *Speculum,* XX (1945), 433–442. Late corrections and additions for the present chapter appear in my forthcoming, *Speculum* article, "Further Notes on C.'s Influence on Mediaeval Culture."

Cassiodorus sup-
plied a biblio-
graphical guide &
a schoolbook & pre-
served theological
& classical works

A critical and complete investigation of the culture of Italy and of Europe in general in the seventh and eighth centuries—a difficult but exceedingly important task—is yet to be made. It is therefore impossible to trace at present the direct routes by which knowledge of Cassiodorus' monastic program and of his books [2] arrived at other centers. For this reason, moreover, it is impossible to evaluate accurately the extent—probably considerable—to which Cassiodorus' cultural program was a model for monastic use.[3] One would like to know, for example, whether the Irish and the Anglo-Saxons of this period were familiar with the entire contents of the *Institutiones*.[4] When and by whom were the cultural views of the Irish and the Anglo-Saxons established and to what extent, if any, were these views modified by this contact? How did Cassiodorus' ideas and books move into central and northern Italy and into France? Countless questions of this type are bound to occur. On three points, however, there can be no doubt. At the very least the *Institutiones* must have served in many centers as a bibliographical guide and an inspiration to the librarians to look around for good old copies of the works recommended.[5] Second, Book II of the *Institutiones* took a place along with the works of Martianus Capella, Boethius, Priscian, and Donatus, as one of the important schoolbooks of the early Middle Ages. Third, and most important, the manuscripts of Vivarium and of Cassiodorus preserved in sound form for generations to come both the Fathers of the Church and the ancient Latin authors; this twofold

---

[2] Both those at Vivarium and those in his own personal library.

[3] Thiele, pp. 401–417, opposes various exaggerated claims of C.'s influence and holds that C. did not write *the* schoolbook of the Middle Ages and that Vivarium was not *the* model cloister. In his opinion C.'s works were used largely as sources of information, not as inspirations for a plan of monastic cultural training. Even Thiele, however (pp. 415–417), admits the considerable importance of Vivarium as a disseminator of historical and classical works.

[4] This is uncertain according to Lehmann, LXXII (1913), 503–517.

[5] See above, p. 46 and note 32. Mercati says, p. 18: "Anzi nei primi secoli che seguirono fino al X, presso i bibliofili che non mancarono nemmeno allora, le *Istituzioni* di Cassiodoro avranno servito, come una guida bibliografica, a farle apprezzare e cercare datorno." See also Lehmann, LXXI (1912), 281: "Mit Recht hat das M.A. deren erstes Buch [of the *Inst.*] als eine literarhistorische Quelle betrachtet und es mehrfach mit Hieronymus, Gennadius u. a. zu einem Corpus vereinigt." Cf. Lehmann, LXXII (1913), 507, and LXXIII (1914), 253.

culture might of course have survived somehow without the aid of Cassiodorus, but, as it is, the credit should go primarily to him.

The mere list of the more important manuscripts of the *Institutiones* described by Mynors (pp. x–xlix; see also pp. 58–63 of this introduction) bears eloquent testimony to the wide dissemination of this particular work. A complete account of all the manuscripts of all of Cassiodorus' works would be impressive. In the absence of such an account, however, we shall find it interesting and instructive to consider the detailed evidence which is presented by items other than manuscripts. Let us restrict our survey of Cassiodorus' influence to the period which runs from the time of his death to the end of the thirteenth century [6] and let us begin with the most general references.

Mention of Cassiodorus, but of no particular work

In some instances Cassiodorus is mentioned by subsequent writers without reference to any of his works in particular. Thus, Bede states that our author changed from a senator (*sic!*) into a "doctor" of the Church.[7] Sigebert, a monk at Gembloux in the eleventh century, gives Senator's dates briefly, but nothing else.[8] In the following century the anonymous writer of a *De scriptoribus ecclesiasticis* mentions our author in his preface without making further use of him,[9] while a library catalogue [10] compiled at Hirsau bears the simple entry "libri Cassiodori Senatoris" without specifying what work or works are meant.[11] Dur-

---

[6] The thirteenth century is arbitrarily selected here as a terminus to keep the investigation within reasonable bounds. As any student of the period knows, the number of MSS belonging to the next two centuries is great. Even for the period selected the evidence presented here is decidedly incomplete. Thus Manitius, our chief authority, himself incomplete, goes through the twelfth century only. The evidence assembled in Thiele, pp. 407–417, does not even cite all the material available in Manitius; one must also keep Thiele's bias in mind. A complete study of C.'s influence—an obvious *desideratum*—is apparently planned by Mary Stanley, notice of whose projected Oxford University thesis, *The Monastery of Vivarium and Its Historical Importance*, appeared in the *Revue d'histoire ecclésiastique*, XXXV (1939), 674.

[7] Thiele, p. 411.   [8] *M.G., SS.*, Vol. VI.   [9] Manitius, III, 313–314.

[10] All the information on medieval library catalogues contained in this entire chapter is based upon G. Becker, *Catalogi bibliothecarum antiqui* (Bonn, 1885; with additions by G. Meier, *ibid.*, II [1885], 239–241), and P. Lehmann, *Mittelalterliche Bibliothekskataloge Deutschlands und der Schweiz* (2 vols., Munich, 1918 and 1928). To save space more exact references are not given here.

[11] This catalogue is presumably, though not certainly, of the twelfth century.

ing the very same period the *Historia regum Francorum* of the cloister of St.-Denis reveals that Cassiodorus Senator and Bishop Dionysius were famous men who lived in the vicinity of Rome,[12] and the *Historia pontificalis* offers the somewhat misleading information that our author changed from a heathen into a Christian, from a senator into a monk, and from a rhetorician into an ecclesiastical teacher.[13] Around 1241 the *Chronicon* of the monk Alberic of Troisfontaines refers to Cassiodorus as the chancellor of Theodoric.[14] The so-called "interpolator Hoiensis" who appears in manuscripts of the *Gesta episcoporum Leodiensium* by Aegidius of Orval inserts Cassiodorus' dates from Sigebert's work of two hundred years before.[15]

A particular work used, but not identified by modern authorities

There is another group of instances in which subsequent writers have used particular books written by Cassiodorus, but in which the particular work or portion of the work is not mentioned by our modern authorities and cannot therefore be discovered without considerable research—research which is beyond the province of this introduction.[16] In this group we find as our earliest representatives Aeneas of Paris, in his ninth-century publication *Adversus Graecos*,[17] and an anonymous ecclesiastic, in a letter written between 1074 and 1079 under the name of Bishop Udalricus of Augsburg.[18] The twelfth century provides our remaining examples: Placidus of Nonantula, in his *De honore ecclesiae;*[19] Petrus Cantor, in his ethical work, the *Verbum abbreviatum;*[20] William of Malmesbury, in the *De dictis et factis memoralibus philosophorum;*[21] Alexander Neckam, in the description of waters and springs in his *De naturis rerum;*[22] and, finally, Alain de Lille, in his *Distinctiones.*

Institutiones: Book I

Let us now consider the particular works for which we have more precise and definite information. The two books of the *Institutiones* may be consid-

---

[12] *M.G., SS.,* Vol. IX.   [13] *Ibid.,* Vol. XX.

[14] *Ibid.,* Vol. XXIII.   [15] *Ibid.,* Vol. XXV.

[16] A single error may also be mentioned here: Manitius, III, 1097 (index) lists under C. "bei Petrus von Cluni . . . 140," but p. 140 contains no mention of C.

[17] Manitius, I, 416.   [18] *Ibid.,* III, 25.   [19] *Ibid.,* p. 50.

[20] *Ibid.,* p. 160.   [21] *Ibid.,* p. 469.

[22] *Ibid.,* p. 784. The work was written at the end of the twelfth or the beginning of the thirteenth century.

ered separately in view of the separate tradition of their manuscripts. Book I is cited in a ninth-century library catalogue of
Reichenau, in a later catalogue of St. Gall, which lists only manuscripts that can be identified with extant books of the ninth
century, in an eleventh-century catalogue of Pompuse, and in
twelfth-century catalogues of Michelsberg (near Bamberg) [23]
and of Reading.[24] There is at least the possibility that the twofold division of Cassiodorus' *Institutiones* may have influenced a
statement made by Virgilius Maro in the seventh century.[25] Lu-
pus of Ferrières mentions the first chapter of Book I in connection with a work written by Jerome.[26] In a letter to Haistulph,
archbishop of Mainz, Rabanus Maurus lists Cassiodorus among
the authorities whom he has used for his book *De ecclesiasticis
ordinibus*.[27] In another letter, written between 835 and 840 to
Otgar, also archbishop of Mainz, he quotes chapter v on the
difference between Ecclesiastes and Ecclesiasticus.[28] In a third
letter to the same correspondent he cites from chapter v again
a remark of Jerome's on the Book of Wisdom.[29] In still another letter (840–842), directed to the Emperor Lothaire, he
refers to chapter iii in connection with one of Jerome's works.[30]
In his *Institutio clericorum,* moreover, he also apparently makes
use among other sources of the important chapter xxviii, which
treats profane science as the basis of study of the Scriptures.[31]
Alcuin's use of Book I is not certain; Alcuin does, however, mention Cassiodorus in his *Versus de sanctis Euboracensis ecclesiae*
as being among the authors whose works were present at the
school of York.[32] Hildemar, in his *Expositio regulae* (a treatise

[23] It must be borne in mind that only tangible evidence is admitted throughout
the present account. Failure to be listed in a library catalogue (of which there are
only a few extant belonging to the earlier Middle Ages) and failure to be quoted
in recognizable form or by name are not necessarily proof that a work was either
unknown or without influence.

[24] Mynors, p. xlv and the reference there cited.

[25] Manitius, I, 125, note 3: "hoc consultissime statuerunt, ut duabus librariis con-
positis una fidelium philosophorum libros et altera gentilium scripta contineret."

[26] *M.G., Ep.,* VI, 62.   [27] *Ibid.,* V, 386.   [28] *Ibid.,* p. 427.

[29] *Ibid.,* p. 425.   [30] *Ibid.,* p. 443.

[31] Franz, p. 124. As it happens, Rabanus' chapter (III. xxvi) may also come directly from Augustine, as Thiele believes (p. 413), since C. is quoting Augustine
(but only in part).

[32] Thiele, p. 412. Thiele argues that since C. is mentioned together with Chrysostom
and Johannes Damascenus the reference is more probably to C.'s commentary on the

on Benedict's Rule) quotes chapter xv in its entirety.[33] Sedulius
Scottus knows Book I and cites part of a sentence from the preface.[34] An anonymous author who may belong to the ninth century wrote a handbook of Biblical and patrological knowledge
based entirely on this same book.[35] In the eleventh century Berno
of Reichenau cites chapter xxix in his letter 11, which criticizes
Cassian's *Institutiones* harshly;[36] while Gerard, bishop of Cza-
nád in Hungary, who came from Venice and was trained in Bologna and Chartres, uses chapter xvi in his *Deliberatio supra hym-
num trium puerorum*.[37] In the following century Hugo of St.
Victor employs Cassiodorus' treatment of theology as a model
for Books IV-VI of his *Didascalicon;*[38] Sigebert of Gembloux
cites chapter v (in his *De viris illustribus*) on Bellator's exposition of the Wisdom of Solomon;[39] and Ralph Diceto quotes from
chapter xvii in his *Abbreviationes chronicorum*.[40]

Institutiones: Book II of the *Institutiones,* Cassiodorus' trea-
Book II   tise on the seven liberal arts, is somewhat more
widely disseminated. Two copies of it appear in the previously mentioned ninth-century library catalogue of Reichenau; one copy each
in a catalogue of the same date from Fulda, in the previously mentioned eleventh-century catalogue of Pompuse, and in four catalogues of the twelfth century—those of St. Amand, Anchin, St.
Bertin, and Chartres.[41] Isidore of Seville makes a most extensive
use of Book II for all the disciplines treated in his *Etymologies,*
quoting great sections of the text verbatim.[42] It is likely that

---

Psalms and that in any event Alcuin shows little in his work that seems to be influenced by Book I.

[33] Thiele, p. 414.

[34] S. Hellmann, ed., *Sedulius Scotus, Liber de rectoribus christianis,* in *Quellen
und Untersuchungen zur lateinische Philologie des Mittelalters,* Vol. I, Part 1 (Munich, 1920), 31, 109.

[35] Manitius, II, 793. See also Lehmann, LXXIII (1914), 253–273. Lehmann points
out that *Inst.* I is not used in Rabanus' *Institutio clericorum,* in Notker's *Notatio,* or
in Hugo of St. Victor's *Libri VII eruditionis didascaliae,* each of which is an important handbook of ecclesiastical instruction. One should note, however, that Manitius,
III, 114, indicates Hugo's debt to C. and that Rabanus does use *Inst.* II as one of his
chief sources (see below, p. 53).   [36] Manitius, II, 62, 65.

[37] *Ibid.,* pp. 77, 79, 81.   [38] *Ibid.,* III, 114.

[39] *Ibid.,* p. 347.   [40] *M.G., SS.,* Vol. XXVII.

[41] Thiele points out (p. 408) that Book II occurs in library catalogues much less
frequently than Isidore's *Etymologies* or even Martianus Capella's work.

[42] For the details see the apparatus in Mynors or the notes in the present translation (*passim*). See also Lehmann, LXXII (1913), 504–517.

Alcuin brought this book from England to the continent; in any case, he uses it for his discussion of grammar, his discussion of rhetoric, and the chapter "De topicis" of his *Dialogus de dialectica*.[43] Rabanus Maurus employs Cassiodorus' second book as one of the chief sources for his work, the *Institutio clericorum*:[44] he appropriates a sentence on grammar from chapter i, the definition of rhetoric from chapter ii, the definition of arithmetic and a further large section from chapter iii, the definition of music and another large section from chapter v, a part of chapter vi as the only source for his treatment of geometry, and chapter vii, finally, as the main source for his treatment of astronomy. In the ninth century at least four authors base their works in part upon Book II: Aurelian of Moutier St. Jean (or of Reomé), in his *Musica disciplina;*[45] Regino of Prüm, in his *De armonice institutione;*[46] Erchanbert of Freising, in his commentary on *Donatus* (*minor* and *maior*);[47] and the author of the *Quaestiones grammaticae* (a work, apparently dictated by a teacher of grammar, which appears in part of *codex Bernensis 83*).[48] Finally, in the same century or the next, the author of an *Ars geometrica* borrows freely from Cassiodorus' chapter vi.[49]

Commentary on the Psalms   Cassiodorus' *Commentary on the Psalms*[50] is mentioned in no less than thirteen medieval library catalogues: four of the ninth century—those at Reichenau, St. Gall, Fontanelles, and St. Riquier; two of the tenth—those at Lorsch and Bobbio; two of the eleventh—those at Liège and Toul (the latter a fragment); and five of the twelfth—those at St. Bertin (a fragment), Chartres (also a fragment), Bec, Corbie, and Michelsberg (near Bamberg). Bede, the first man to mention our author by name, makes considerable use of

[43] Thiele, p. 412. Among other things, Thiele quotes Lehmann concerning the sporadic character of Alcuin's use (in his *Rhetoric*) of C.'s *Inst.* or of some work dependent upon C. For the details see Howell, pp. 14, 23–25, 159, 160, and my review of Howell's book in the *American Historical Review*, XLVIII (1943), 305–306.

[44] See Mynors' apparatus or the notes in the present translation (*passim*). Cf. Thiele, p. 413.

[45] Manitius, I, 446.   [46] *Ibid.*, p. 698.

[47] *Ibid.*, p. 492.   [48] *Ibid.*, p. 477.

[49] *Ibid.*, II, 741. Thiele's statement (p. 416) and his reference (note 110) are both incorrect.

[50] A listing of the actual MSS of this work and of the remaining works which are described below in this chapter, though bound to be illuminating, is beyond the province of this introduction.

the commentary in his own *De schematibus et tropis*.[51] Alcuin, who characterizes Cassiodorus as "eximius interpres psalmorum," is also apparently familiar with it.[52] The monk Hildemar makes frequent citations from it in his own *Expositio regulae* [53] and also mentions it in a letter sent between 841 and 846 to Pacificus, archdeacon of Verona.[54] Their contemporary, Angelomus of Luxeuil, employs the commentary as one of the sources for his own *Enarrationes in libros Regum*.[55] Flodoard of Reims mentions it in one of his great poetical achievements of the following century, the *De triumphis Christi sanctorumque apud Italos*.[56] Notker Labeo, who translated the Psalms, Terence's *Andria*, Virgil's *Eclogues*, and several other classical and early medieval works into German *ca.* A.D. 1000, finds it secondary only to Augustine's commentary in usefulness.[57] Within the next sixty years no less than three men testify to its worth: Berno of Reichenau, who cites chapter lxix (§ 1); [58] Bruno of Würzburg, who uses chapters xi (§§ 4–8) and xiii of the preface in his own *Expositio psalmorum;* [59] and Durand, bishop of Troarn, who quotes Cassiodorus on Psalm 109 in his own *Liber de corpore et sanguine Christi contra Berengarium et eius sectatores*.[60] Ekkehard, in his *Chronicon universale* (written *ca.* 1100), also speaks of the excellence of our author's work,[61] while Abelard, writing somewhat later, cites Cassiodorus' remarks on Psalm 50.[62] Further mention appears in the *Annales* of St. Rudbert in Salzburg [63] and in the *Auctarium Garstense* [64] (both of the twelfth century) and in the chronicle of Sicardus of Cremona [65] and in the annals of Admont [66] (both of the thirteenth century).

De anima   The *De anima* occurs in seven medieval catalogues: those at St. Emmeran's at Regensburg (tenth century), Liège (eleventh century), St. Bertin, Bec, Corbie, Michelsberg (near Bamberg), and St. Peter's at Salzburg (all of the twelfth century). It is used frequently by subsequent writers—in the ninth century, for example, by Rabanus Maurus

[51] Thiele, p. 411.
[52] *M.G., Ep.*, IV, 468.
[53] Thiele, p. 414.
[54] *M.G., Ep.*, V, 357.
[55] Manitius, I, 420.
[56] *Ibid.*, II, 158, 165.
[57] *Ibid.*, p. 698, note 3.
[58] *Ibid.*, pp. 62, 65.
[59] *Ibid.*, p. 73.
[60] *Ibid.*, p. 117.
[61] *M.G., SS.*, Vol. VI.
[62] Manitius, III, 112.
[63] *M.G., SS.*, Vol. IX.
[64] *Ibid.*
[65] *Ibid.*, p. 31.
[66] *Ibid.*, Vol. IX.

in his *De anima* [67] and by Hincmar in his *De diversa et multi-plici animae ratione.*[68]

Other theo-logical works   Cassiodorus' other theological works seem to have had little influence. His *Complexiones in epistulas et acta apostolorum et apocalypsin* and the *Expositio epistolae quae scribitur ad Romanos unde Pelagianae haereseos pravitates amovi* were not widely known. One other work, the *Liber titulorum quem de divina scriptura collectum memorialem volui nuncupari*, has been lost.

De orthographia   The *De orthographia* proved to be a useful work. Though it occurs in only two medieval catalogues—those of St. Vaast at Arras (eleventh century) and of Anchin (twelfth century)—it is the basis of much of the writing in this field by Isidore,[69] by Alcuin,[70] and, in the twelfth century, by William of Malmesbury.[71]

Variae   Cassiodorus' letters (*Variae*) are listed in a single medieval library catalogue—the tenth-century catalogue of Lorsch. Most of the extant manuscripts were written in the next five hundred years.[72] In the twelfth century the work is cited by Ralph Diceto in his *Abbreviationes chronicorum* [73] and by Giraldus Cambrensis in the parts of his remarkable *Topographia Hibernica* in which he discusses birds [74] and music.[75] At the end of the same century or the beginning of the thirteenth the work is cited twice by Alexander Neckam, once in connection with his account of birds.[76]

Chronicon   The *Chronicon* appears in two ninth-century catalogues—one of Reichenau and the other of Würzburg. Apparently unknown to Isidore, Bede, or Paulus Diaconus, it is first cited by Marianus Scottus in the eleventh century [77] and is used somewhat later as the basis for chronicles or annals by Hermannus Contractus (extensively) [78] and by Bernold, a monk of St. Blasien.[79] It is known in the twelfth century

[67] *M.G., Ep.*, V, 515.   [68] *Manitius*, I, 42.   [69] Thiele, p. 411.
[70] *De orthographia*, p. 307.   [71] Manitius, III, 469.   [72] *Ibid.*, I, 41.
[73] *Ibid.*, III, 638.   [74] *Ibid.*, p. 625, note 5.   [75] *Ibid.*, p. 626, note 3.
[76] *Ibid.*, p. 786 (birds). For the second citation, *ibid.*, p. 787.
[77] *Ibid.*, II, 392, 792. Cf. *M.G., SS.*, Vol. V.
[78] Manitius, II, 760, 761; *M.G., SS.*, Vol. V.
[79] Manitius, III, 405 (Manitius wrongly indexes this reference as "bei Helmold"); *M.G., SS.*, Vol. V.

to the writer of the *Historia pontificalis* [80] and to the author of the annals of Disibodenberg.[81]

History of the Goths   The earliest recorded use of any of Cassiodorus' works is the use of his *History of the Goths, ca.* 551, by Jordanes, whose work is a mere résumé of the original, which disappeared entirely in the eighth or the ninth century.[82]

The Historia tripartita   Two translations produced under Cassiodorus' direction—the so-called *Historia tripartita* and the Vivarian version of Josephus' *Antiquitates*—had a wide influence. The first is listed in fifteen medieval catalogues: three of the ninth century (those of Reichenau, St. Gall, and Würzburg), one of the tenth (that of Tegernsee), three of the eleventh (those of Toul, St. Vaast's at Arras, and Trier), and eight of the twelfth (those of St. Bertin, Bec, Corbie, Michelsberg, near Bamberg, Prüfening, St. Maur de Fossés, an unknown English cloister, and Constance). It is familiar to Isidore [83] and is mentioned by Paulinus of Aquileia in a letter written between 776 and 802.[84] Bishop Adalhard of Corbie had a manuscript copy made *ca.* 820.[85] The subsequent use of the work is extensive. Thus, in the remaining three-quarters of the ninth century it is employed by the authors of the acts of the Council of Paris (in 825),[86] by Almannus in his *Vita et translatio Helenae*,[87] by Frechulf in his universal chronicle,[88] by Walafrid Strabo in his *De exordiis et incrementis rerum ecclesiasticarum*,[89] by Sedulius Scottus in his *Liber de rectoribus christianis*,[90] by Anastasius Bibliothecarius,[91] and by Hincmar in his *De regis persona et regio ministerio*.[92] Chapters v and xlv are cited *ca.* 965 by the author of the *Miracula Sancti Gorgonii* in support of one of his his-

---

[80] *M.G., SS.,* Vol. XX.

[81] Manitius, II, 393. Thiele, p. 416, erroneously cites Manitius, II, 792, and assigns the work to the eleventh century.

[82] Manitius, I, 212 and 43.   [83] Thiele, p. 411.

[84] *M.G., Ep.,* IV, 526.   [85] Manitius, I, 407 and note 3.

[86] *M.G., Conc.,* Vol. II, Part 2, pp. 487 ff.

[87] A. Ebert, *Allgemeine Geschichte der Literatur des Mittelalters* (Leipzig, 1895), III, 203.

[88] *Ibid.,* II, 384.   [89] Thiele, p. 415.

[90] Edition of S. Hellmann, in *Quellen und Untersuchungen zur lateinische Philologie des Mittelalters* (Munich, 1920), I, 207.

[91] Manitius, I, 685, 686.   [92] Thiele, pp. 415–416.

torical incidents (chapter xxii).[93] In the eleventh century the work is employed by Marianus Scottus,[94] by Cardinal Humbert (in his work *Adversus simoniacos*),[95] by the author of the second revision of the *Vita III. Willibaldi*,[96] by Manegold of Lautenbach (in his *Liber ad Gebehardum*),[97] by Wido of Osnabrück,[98] and by the anonymous author of the *De unitate ecclesiae conservanda*.[99] In the twelfth it appears in the *Abbreviatio chronicorum* of Ralph Diceto,[100] in the *Chronica pontificum et imperatorum Tiburtina* [101] (which corrects the *Historia tripartita*), and in a notice by Wibaldus, abbot of Corvey.[102] Finally, in the thirteenth century, it is the basis of part of the three chronicles written respectively by Sicardus of Cremona,[103] Robert of Auxerre,[104] and Albertus Miliolus.[105]

Josephus' Antiquitates The translation of the *Antiquitates* is listed in at least fourteen medieval catalogues: four of the ninth century (those at Reichenau, St. Gall, Fontanelles, and St. Riquier), three of the tenth (those at Lorsch, at an unnamed "bibliotheca Francogallica," and at Freising), and seven of the twelfth (those at St. Amand, St. Bertin, Bec, Corbie, Michelsberg, near Bamberg, Durham, and at an unnamed English cloister). Alcuin cites this translation,[106] and Frechulf uses it in his universal chronicle.[107] Two centuries later Ekkehard IV shows knowledge of it in his *Casus Sancti Galli*,[108] while Lantbert of Deutz cites it in his *Vita Heriberti*.[109] The *Chronicon Ekkehardi*,[110] William of Malmesbury's *Gesta regum Anglorum*,[111] and the *Gesta abbatum* of Weingarten [112] all make use of it in the twelfth century. In the thirteenth century the chronicle of Sicardus of Cremona [113] and the *Chronica imperatorum* of Albertus Miliolus [114] both show knowledge of Josephus and of the

---

93 Manitius, II, 196.
94 *Ibid.*, p. 392. Cf. *M.G., SS.*, Vol. V.
95 Manitius, III, 24.
96 *M.G., SS.*, Vol. XV.
97 Manitius, III, 27.
98 *Ibid.*, p. 29.
99 *Ibid.*, p. 43. Two passages from the *Historia tripartita* are cited.
100 *M.G., SS.*, Vol. XXVII.
101 *Ibid.*, Vol. XXXI.
102 *Monumenta Corbeiensia*, § 167, cited by Thiele, p. 416, note 122.
103 *M.G., SS.*, Vol. XXXI.
104 *Ibid.*, Vol. XXVI.
105 *Ibid.*, Vol. XXXI.
106 *M.G., Ep.*, Vol. IV, No. 162.
107 Ebert, *op. cit.*, II, 384.
108 *M.G., SS.*, Vol. I.
109 Manitius, II, 365.
110 *M.G., SS.*, Vol. VI.
111 *Ibid.*, Vol. X.
112 *Ibid.*, Vol. XV.
113 Thiele, p. 417.
114 *M.G., SS.*, Vol. XXXI.

Antiquitates as well, while actual use of the Vivarian translation is made by Konrad (in his chronicle of Scheier),[115] by Alberic of Troisfontaines,[116] and by the author of the *Chronicon imperatorum et pontificum Bavaricum.*[117]

VI. THE MANUSCRIPTS OF "AN INTRODUCTION TO DIVINE AND HUMAN READINGS"

Manuscript tradition yet to be established
To obtain a detailed account of the important manuscripts of the *Institutiones* and appropriate *stemmata codicum* the reader should consult Mynors, pp. x–xlix and lii–lvi; the modifications (especially those concerning the relationship of manuscripts B and M) suggested in Rand; and the additional modifications suggested in van de Vyver, *Vivarium,* pp. 59–76, particularly those concerning the anterior date of *α* (the archetype, now lost, of the *first* edition, which is represented by the Φ and Δ families) and the posterior date of *β* (the *definitive* edition made by Cassiodorus, now represented by the Ω family), as well as those concerning the nature of the Φ and Δ families. Of these three somewhat divergent accounts van de Vyver, *Vivarium,* which adopts many of the views of Mynors and of Rand, *New Cassiodorus,* is the most recent and the most persuasive. It is the only one which presents a single stemma for both Book I and Book II. The discussion in van de Vyver, pp. 284–292, is largely outmoded.

List of Manuscripts
A list of the more important manuscripts is given below to indicate the wide dissemination of the *Institutiones.*[1]

---

[115] *Ibid.,* Vol. XVII.   [116] *Ibid.,* Vol. XXIII.   [117] *Ibid.,* Vol. XXIV.

[1] This list is based upon Mynors, pp. x–xlix. In addition to the *sigla* noted below the following designations of Mynors are occasionally used in the notes attached to my translation: for Book I, Θ (archetype of *θ* and FV), Ξ (archetype of CXG); for Book II, Ω (archetype of the authentic version, which is itself divided into groups BMUp, of which B is the archetype and SKLTO, of which Σ is the archetype); Σ₂ (KLTO); Φ (archetype of the first interpolated version, to which WAPm belong); and Δ (archetype of the second interpolated version, to which MSS *α–λ* and *πχ* belong).

Manuscripts containing Books *i* and *ii* [2]

BAMBERG HJ.iv.15 (Patr.61), written in a Beneventan hand of the second half of the eighth century (B).[3]

PARIS, Bibliothèque Mazarine 660, ff. 75–142, produced in the early tenth century by at least three Italian scribes, one of whom displays Beneventan characteristics [4] (M).

VATICAN Urbinas lat. 67, ff. 71–119, derived from B at some time in the twelfth century (U).

In addition to these three manuscripts there have been at least three others—one at Reichenau, written under Abbot Ruadhelm (A.D. 838–842), the second at Murbach in the ninth century, and the third at Cluny in the mid-twelfth century.

Manuscripts containing Book *i* only

ST. GALL 199, of the ninth–tenth century (*θ*).

FLORENCE Ashburnham 13 (57–14), of the ninth century, from the Chapter Library at Beauvais (F).

VALENCIENNES 353 (294 Molinier, 284 Mangeart), of the ninth century, from St. Amand (V).

CASSEL theol. fol. 29 (from Fulda), written in the mid-ninth century in several hands under more or less strong insular influence (C).

HEREFORD, Cathedral Library O.III.2, ff. 127ᵛ–162ᵛ, written in two good Carolingian hands of the later ninth century and descended from a MS in insular minuscule (H).

WÜRZBURG M.p.th.f. 29 (Dombibliothek No. 63), tenth century (X).

WOLFENBÜTTEL Weissenburg 79 (4163), of the early tenth century (G).

VATICAN Palatinus lat. 274, of the eleventh century, possibly from Augsburg (Q).

BERLIN cod. 162 (Phillipps 1737), ff. 38–43, containing a fragment of Book i in a hand of the ninth or tenth century (D).

---

[2] *St. Gall 199,* which represents the union of separate traditions, is treated below.

[3] The letter in this position is a conventional symbol used to designate the manuscript.

[4] Rand, *New Cassiodorus,* p. 445, suggests a connection with some such center as Vercelli.

Book I appears to have circulated widely in the twelfth century and later, often as part of a well-defined corpus of works dealing with earlier Christian literature. Among these later MSS are the following:

ARRAS, Bibl. municipale 732 (684), s. xi, from St. Vaast (a copy of V).

BAMBERG B.V.30 (Patr. 38), s. xv on paper, from Michelsberg.

BERNE 225, ff. 32–87, s. xi–xii (a).

BRUSSELS 8327–8342 (1031), ff. 133–end, s. xiv (b¹).

BRUSSELS 10615–10729, s. xii, the "medii aevi florilegium longe pretiosissimum" which belonged to Nicholas of Cusa; written at Liège (b²).

CAMBRIDGE, Corpus Christi College 68 (and King's College 9), written in 1432 for Walter Crome of Gonville Hall, Cambridge (c¹).

CAMBRIDGE, University Library Kk.IV.6, s. xii, a miscellany whose compilation is attributed to William of Malmesbury (c²).

DOUAI, Bibl. municipale 295, ff. 1–48, s. xii, from Anchin (from V or the Arras MS above).

ESCORIAL f.II.13, s. xvi on paper.

HUNTINGTON LIBRARY 627, s. xii, from Aulne in the diocese of Tournai; formerly Cheltenham, Phillipps MS 4621 (h).

LEYDEN Vossianus f°. 103, s. xiii (k).

LONDON, Royal 5.B.VIII, s. xii, perhaps from Westminster (l¹).

LONDON, Royal 10.B.XV, s. xiii (l²).

LONDON, Royal 13.A.XXI, ff. 151–192, s. xiii (l³).

LONDON, Cotton Vespasian B.XIII, s. xiii (l⁴).

LONDON, Lambeth Palace 76, volume I, s. xii *in.*, from Rochester, in a fine Canterbury hand (l⁵).

MILAN, Ambros. D 35 *supra, s.* xv, with numerous marginal notes in the hand of Archbishop Francesco Pizzolpasso (*ob.* 1443), who presented it to the Cathedral of Milan (m). Closely related to b² and probably copied from it. Pizzolpasso borrowed books from Nicholas of Cusa.

OXFORD, St. John's College 115, s. xii, with numerous notes

in the hand of Thomas Gascoigne, the Oxford scholar (1403–1458) (o¹).

OXFORD, The Queen's College 319, ff. 1–45, *s.* xii (o²).

OXFORD, Trinity College 34, *s.* xii (o³).

OXFORD, Bodley 391 (2222), *s.* xii *in.*, from Canterbury, in a Canterbury hand (o⁴).

OXFORD, e Museo 31 (3574), *s.* xii *ex.*, from Bury St. Edmunds (o⁵).

OXFORD, Rawlinson D 338 (13125), *s.* xii, from Durham (o⁶).

PARIS lat. 1791, ff. 1–74, *s.* xii, formerly Pithou's, then Colbert's (p¹).

PARIS lat. 1792, *s.* xii, from Abingdon, then "Cl. Puteani"; it has the same contents as o¹, with which it agrees very closely (p²).

PARIS lat. 1906, *s.* xii late; it has the same contents as o⁵ (p³).

PARIS lat. 12160, *s.* xii *ex.*, formerly "sancte Marie de Longoreto" and "sancti Cygiranni" (the latter in the diocese of Bourges) (p⁴).

PARIS lat. 17402, *s.* xii, from Vaux de Cernay, with the same contents as p³ and o⁵ (p⁵).

ROUEN 490, *s.* xii *ex.*, from Lyre and St. Ouen (r).

SALISBURY, Cathedral Library 88, *s.* xi *ex.*, a copy of H (s).

TROYES 56, *s.* xii (t¹).

TROYES 855, *s.* xii, from Clairvaux (t²).

VATICAN lat. 569, on paper; "Ioannes Franciscus Crescius Scriptor Bibliothecae Scribebat. Anno salutis 1558."

VATICAN Reginensis 551, *s.* xiii (v).

VIENNA cod. lat. 766 (Univ. 171), *s.* xii; this must be akin to C and X.⁵

YORK, Chapter Library XVI.I.8, *s.* xiii–xiv, from Rievaulx.

Mynors lists ⁶ copies of Book II in the twelfth- to fourteenth-century catalogues of nineteen monasteries in England: Reading, Meaux (Melsa), Durham, New Minster, Hexham, Ford, Exeter, Cirencester, Stoneleigh, Ipswich (Holy Trinity), Merton, Woburn, London (St. Paul's), Waltham, St. Alban's, Canterbury

---

⁵ The same is true of an Austrian thirteenth century copy owned by E. P. Goldschmidt of London. ⁶ Page xlv.

(Christ Church), Buildwas, Waverly, and Sherborne. He makes no attempt to list copies in the later monastic library catalogues of the continent of Europe.

Manuscripts containing Book II only (authentic form)

St. Gall 855, *s.* ix (S).

London Harley 2637, written late in *s.* ix, formerly in the Hospital of Nicolaus Cusanus at Cues (L).

Karlsruhe Augiensis 241, written late in *s.* ix (K).

Berlin 176, formerly at Fleury, then Phillipps MS 1780, *s.* x (T).

Chartres 130 (148), written early in *s.* x, from St. Père (O).

Paris lat. 8500, written in *s.* xiv in North Italy and formerly the property of Petrarch (p).

Manuscripts containing Book II only (first interpolated form)

Würzburg M.p.misc.f.5^A (Dombibliothek No. 58), in an insular hand of the late eighth century (W).

Karlsruhe Augiensis 171, *s.* ix *in.* (A).

Paris lat. 2200, ff. 1–85, *s.* ix; formerly the property of Pithou, de Thou, and Colbert (P).

Milan, Ambros. D.17 *infra,* written in 1642.

Manuscripts containing Book II only (second interpolated form)

Berne 212, ff. 1–110, *s.* ix (*a*).

Paris lat. 13048, ff. 59–82, *s.* ix, apparently from Corbie (*κ*).

Valenciennes 195 (172 Molinier, 164 Mangeart), *s.* ix, presumably from St. Amand (*ι*).

Cheltenham, Phillipps MS 16278 (Libri 229), second half of *s.* ix (*λ*).

Berne 234, *s.* ix/x; in two hands, the first insular, the second under insular influence (*β*).

St. Gall 199, pp. 115–374, probably early *s.* x (*θ*).

Paris lat. 12963 (Sangermanensis 782), first half of *s.* x, presumably from Corbie (*ζ*).

Chartres 90, *s.* x, from St. Père (*χ*).

CHARTRES 102, *s.* x, from the Chapter Library (γ).
KARLSRUHE Augiensis 106, *s.* x (ε).
RHEIMS 975, *s.* x, from the Chapter Library (η).
PARIS lat. 8679 *s.* x (π).
GLASGOW, Hunterian MS 281, *s.* x *ex.*/xi *in.* (δ).

VII. PRINTED EDITIONS OF "AN INTRODUCTION TO DIVINE AND HUMAN READINGS"

The reader is referred to Franz (pp. 129–137) for a reasonably complete list of the various printed editions and translations of all of Cassiodorus' works up to 1872.

First edition: No edition of any part of the *Institutiones* ap-
Book II peared until 1528, when Bebelius published
Johannes Sichardus' *Disciplinarum liberalium orbis, ex P. Consentio et Magno Aurelio Cassiodoro* at Basel. In this work, intended to be a textbook, Consentius supplies the grammatical portion and Cassiodorus (Book II) the compendia of the other six arts. The source was some manuscript of the △-type. Vascosanus published another edition at Paris in 1540.

First edition: Book I of the *Institutiones* was first published
Book I at Antwerp in 1566 by Christopher Plantin;
this edition, an early product of the distinguished editor Jacobus Pamelius, depended entirely upon a defective manuscript from St. Amand (now *Valenciennes 353* [*294*]). Pamelius deserves credit for making the first contribution to our knowledge of the library at Vivarium by appending a *Catalogus commentatorum veterum selectiorum in universa Biblia,* in which he marks with a star the authors and works mentioned by Cassiodorus.

First edition: Books I and II first appeared together in the
Books I & II folio edition of Gulielmus Fornerius, which
was published in Paris by Sebastian Nivellius in 1579 and reprinted in 1589. The editor employs *Paris lat. 2200* for Book II, filling up the lacunae in the sections on rhetoric and mathematics (the former from Sichardus) ; for Book I, however, he does not use the two manuscripts which he borrowed,[1] but instead the text

[1] Mynors, p. li.

of Pamelius, whose notes are repeated without acknowledgment and whose errors are preserved unaltered.

Garet

The Paris and Geneva editions published during the seventeenth century did nothing to improve the text. In 1679 Johannes Garetius brought out his *Opera omnia* at Rouen; this work was reprinted in Venice in 1729 and again in Migne's *Patrologia Latina* (Vol. LXX) in 1865. Garet's sources are listed below. For Book I: *Rouen 490,* an unidentified manuscript from the Cistercian house of la Noé (in the diocese of Évreux), and notes made from other manuscripts by Juretus; for Book II: *Paris lat. 12963,* the collection made by Simon Bougis of de Thou's manuscript (later *Paris lat. 2200*), and the collation made by Petrus Pelhester of *Paris lat. 8679.* Garet rejects spurious insertions of Fornerius and adds the "Praefatio" (from A. de Chesne's edition of Alcuin), but his work leaves much to be desired.

Mynors

The first critical edition of the *Institutiones* is the excellent work of R. A. B. Mynors, *Cassiodori Senatoris Institutiones,* published at Oxford in 1937. Though already challenged in part by Rand, *New Cassiodorus,* and subject to change in the light of further investigation, the text is really "edited from the manuscripts"; it lays the foundations for a new study of Cassiodorus. The work is equipped with much that will delight the reader—a full introduction, an appendix, an *index rerum,* an *index nominum,* and an *index auctorum.*

An Introduction to Divine and Human Readings

Book One
DIVINE LETTERS

PREFACE

1. Perceiving that the schools were swarming with students because of a great longing for secular letters (a great part of mankind believed that through these schools it attained worldly wisdom), I was, I confess, extremely sorry that the Divine Scriptures had no public teachers, since worldly authors were rich in instruction beyond doubt most distinguished. I strove with the most holy Agapetus, bishop of the city of Rome,[1] to collect subscriptions and to have Christian rather than secular schools receive professors in the city of Rome, just as the custom is said to have existed for a long time at Alexandria and is said even now to be zealously cultivated by the Hebrews in Nisibis,[2] a city of the Syrians, that thereby the soul might obtain eternal salvation and the tongue of the faithful might be adorned with a holy and completely faultless eloquence. But although my ardent desire could in no way have been fulfilled because of the struggles that seethed and raged excessively in the Italian realm, inasmuch as a peaceful affair has no place in anxious times, I was driven by divine charity to this device, namely, in the place of a teacher to prepare for you under the Lord's guidance these introductory books; through which, in my opinion, the unbroken line of the Divine Scriptures and the compendious knowledge of secular letters might with the Lord's beneficence be related—books not at all fluent, perhaps, since in them is found, not studied eloquence, but indispensable narration; to be sure, they are extremely useful, since through them one learns the indicated origin of both the salvation of the

[1] That is, pope; consecrated 535.
[2] The (Jewish) school at Nisibis is also mentioned by Junilius, bishop of Africa, in the letter prefixed to his work *De partibus divinae legis ad Primasium episcopum* (Migne, *Pat. Lat.*, LXVIII, 15, middle). See chap. x, note 5 below. On the school see Hermann and Nelz.

soul and secular knowledge. In them I commit to you, not my own learning, but the words of men of former times, which it is right to praise and glorious to proclaim for future generations, for whatever is said about men of former times by way of praise of the Lord is not considered hateful display. Add to this the fact that one is pleased with a venerable teacher if one consults him frequently; moreover, whenever one desires to have recourse to such teachers, one will find no harshness in them.

2. On this account, most beloved brothers, let us climb unhesitatingly to the Divine Scripture by means of the laudable expositions of the Fathers, as if by a certain ladder in Jacob's vision, in order that, borne aloft by their words, we may deserve to reach an effectual contemplation of the Lord. For this is perchance Jacob's ladder,[3] on which angels climb up and down; on which the Lord leans, extending a hand to the faint and supporting, through their contemplation of Him, the weary steps of the climbers. Therefore, if you please, we ought to preserve this kind of reading, that the novices of Christ, after they have learned the psalms,[4] may in the beginning study the divine authority with perpetual practice in faultless books, until under the Lord's guidance it becomes very well known to them, for fear lest the mistakes of scribes become fixed in unpolished minds; since that which is manifestly implanted and rooted in the recesses of the memory cannot easily be torn out. Happy indeed the soul which through the Lord's bounty has hidden in the recesses of the memory the secret of such a great gift; but much happier the man who through critical searching has learned the paths of knowledge and in consequence zealously drives human thoughts from himself and, to his salvation, is filled with divine communications. For we remember that we have seen that many men, mighty in strength of memory, when asked about very unintelligible points, have solved the questions brought forward merely by examples drawn from divine authority, inasmuch as that which is evidently said rather obscurely in one book is set down more clearly in another. A witness of this fact is the apostle Paul, who in great measure in the letter which is written to the Hebrews clarifies

---

[3] Genesis 28:12. (Subsequent references to the Bible follow this style of citing first the chapter and then the verse.)
[4] Cf. *Comm. Psalt.* pref. xvi. D.

the writings of the Old Testament by referring to their recent fulfillment.

3. On this account, dearest brothers, after the soldiers of Christ have filled themselves with divine reading and, strengthened by frequent meditation, have begun to know the properly designated passages of the books,[5] then someone, perhaps, will not vainly pass over the instructions of the present work, in whose two books are set forth in a manner most appropriate to each passage involved and in compact style the things which ought to be read; students will consequently learn by what Latin interpreters the separate items have been explained. But if in these writers one discovers something carelessly said, then let those to whom the tongue is known inquire which items have been wholesomely treated by Greek interpreters, that in the school of Christ the lukewarmness of carelessness may be removed and necessary knowledge sought by zealous minds.

4. And so it appears that the Divine Scriptures of the Old and the New Testament from the very beginning to the end have been expounded in the Greek language by Clement of Alexandria, surnamed Stromateus,[6] and Cyril, bishop of the same city, and John Chrysostom, Gregory, and Basil, and other studious men whom eloquent Greece celebrates. But with the Lord's aid we follow rather after Latin writers, that, since we are writing for Italians, we may most fitly seem to have pointed out Roman interpreters as well. For more gladly is that narration undertaken by every man which is told in the language of his fathers, whence it is possible for a task which cannot be completed through the use of new teachers to be completed through the use of old ones. On this account it will be enough to have pointed out to you the most learned writers, since to have sent one to such men is generally proved to be an appropriate completeness of instruction; for in your case as well it will be more efficacious not to sip at the cup of audacious novelty, but to drink deeply from the fount of the ancients. Hence it follows that I teach you in leisurely manner and instruct you without false assurance; and I believe that this kind of teaching will be profitable for us also—this training of others in such a way that we may seem most opportunely to

---

[5] That is, "assigned reading" for novices.
[6] = στρωματεύς, a writer of miscellanies (στρώματα).

have avoided the snares of those who represent us in a false light.

5. In the first book, therefore, present and ready you have masters of a bygone generation to teach you not so much by their tongues as by your eyes. Wisely, then, studious brothers, restrain your eager desires, learning in the proper order what should be read, imitating, of course, those who long to have bodily health. For those who want to be healed ask the doctors what to eat at their first repast and what to eat at their second, lest disorderly greediness overwhelm rather than reinvigorate the very delicate strength of their feeble limbs.

6. In the second book, which concerns the arts and disciplines of liberal letters, a few things ought, of course, to be culled; here, however, one would make a mistake with less danger if in making it he preserved his faith steadfast. Moreover, whatever will be found in the Divine Scriptures concerning such matters will generally be better understood because of previous knowledge. For it is agreed that in the origin of spiritual wisdom, as it were, evidences of these matters were sown abroad in the manner of seeds, which instructors in secular letters later most wisely transferred to their own rules; we have shown our approval of this action in a suitable place, perhaps in our expounding of the Psalter.[7]

7. Therefore, beseeching the Lord, from Whom comes every advantage, read, I pray, unremittingly; bring yourself to this task again and again with loving care; for the mother of understanding is constant and eager contemplation. Nor does it escape me that the most eloquent Cassian, in the fifth book of his *Collations*,[8] said that a certain simple old man had been asked about a very obscure passage of the Divine Scripture and that as a result of very frequent prayer he had recognized its meaning by means of a celestial light, so that suddenly, filled with a divine inspiration, he had expounded most difficult matters to his questioners—matters which he had not previously learned through human teachers. Of the same sort is that famous story of St. Augustine, which he tells in the books *On Christian Learning:*[9] a certain foreign servant, unskilled in letters, through frequent

---

[7] *Comm. Psalt.* pref. 15; cf. on Psalms 23: 11.
[8] *De institutis cenobiorum.* v. xxxiii.   [9] *Prologue,* §§ 4 ff.

prayer suddenly read a book which had been handed to him as
if he had been brought to perfection by long practice at school.
St. Augustine later says of this matter: though these were amazing miracles and though it be established that "all things are possible to them that believe," [10] we, however, ought not to long for
such things frequently, but we ought rather to abide by the common practice of teaching, lest when we boldly seek after those
things which are above us, we seem rather to risk the blame of
temptation contrary to the injunction of the Lord, who says, in
Deuteronomy, "Thou shalt not tempt the Lord thy God," [11] and
again, in the Gospel, "An evil and adulterous generation seeketh
after a sign," [12] and so forth. Let us, therefore, pray that those
things which are closed to us be opened, and let us in no manner
be cut off from the pursuit of reading; for even David, although
he was continually occupied with the law of the Lord, nevertheless cried out to the Lord, saying, "Give me understanding, that
I may learn thy commandments." [13] For so exceedingly sweet is
the gift which this thing offers, that the more it is received, the
more it is sought after.

8. But however much all Divine Scripture may shine with celestial light, and however much the excellence of the Holy Ghost
may manifestly illumine it, nevertheless, I have spent the greatest and most zealous toil upon the Psalter and the Prophets and
the Epistles of the Apostles, since they seemed to me to stir up
greater profundity of thought and, as it were, to encompass the
height of all Scripture and its most glorious depth. Insofar as my
age has allowed, I have gone over all nine codices of divine authority, reading them carefully, after a comparison of ancient
codices and previous reading on the part of friends; and in them
I admit that with the Lord's help I have worked hard not to lack
melodious eloquence and not to mutilate the holy books with rash
presumption.

9. We have believed that this too ought to be brought to
mind: St. Jerome, driven by consideration for the simple brothers, said in the preface to the Prophets [14] that because of those
who had not learned the marks of punctuation at the schools of

---

[10] Mark 9:22 (9:23). [11] Deuteronomy 6:16. [12] Matthew 12:39.
[13] Psalms 118:73 (119:73). [14] Preface to Isaiah.

instructors in secular letters he had indicated points of division
in his translation, just as it is read today, through the use of
cola and *commata*.[15] We too, impressed by the authority of this
very great man, have decided that this system ought to be followed although other works may be embellished by marks of
punctuation. By all means let those instructions which the above-
named man gave, just as has been stated above, for separation
by *cola* and *commata* suffice for the most simple reading, lest we
seem through blameworthy presumption to have gone beyond
the judgment of this great man. But I have left the remaining
codices, which are not marked by such punctuation, to be read
again [16] and corrected by scribes who are, however, particular
about taking pains; and although they will not be able to preserve entirely insignificant points of spelling, they will, nevertheless, in my opinion hasten in every way to accomplish the correction of ancient codices. For they have a knowledge of the
critical marks [17] used in their profession, which for the most part
have to do with expertness in correction and encourage it. But
that ingrown error may in some measure be taken from their
midst, we have set down a few remarks summarily and in accordance with their mental capacity in the book which follows
on the rules of spelling, that the unpolished presumption of hasty
correctors may not be handed down for posterity to revile. I have
also determined to find as many ancient orthographers as possible, through whose use the scribes may seem, if not made alto-

[15] An arrangement by which certain texts are divided into lines or short periods
to facilitate reading; in other words, into "sense-lines." In the preface cited (to
Isaiah) St. Jerome tells us that for convenience of reading he has followed the system of the MSS of Demosthenes and Cicero and arranged his translation in this new
style of writing. But actually he had found the same system already followed in the
Psalms, Proverbs, and other poetical books of the Old Testament—the very places in
which one would naturally expect to find the first experiment in casting the text into
sense lines.

[16] "Relegendos." "Relego" usually means simply "read" in C., but cf. chap. xv
below ("read and correct"). In Late Latin a compound verb frequently is used with
the force of the simple form.

[17] C. is clearly thinking here of spelling as well as punctuation; he therefore probably refers to the regular system of signs used in correcting and annotating a MS,
as the use of the asterisk (*) and obelus (—). On punctuation and the critical signs
used by scholars shortly after C.'s death see Isidore, *Etymologiae* I (De grammatica),
chap. xx (De positura), and chap. xxi (De notis sententiarum). Note also the various
items which C. calls *notae* in chap. xxvi below. (*Notae* clearly cannot mean shorthand
[Isidore's *notae vulgares*] here or in chap. xxvi.)

gether correct, nevertheless in large measure improved. If, indeed, among the Greeks spelling is for the most part clear and without ambiguity, among the Latin writers, however, it lies neglected because of its great difficulty, and hence even now it requires considerable zeal on the reader's part.

10. Since the arrangement of the work here undertaken has been proclaimed, it is now time for us to come to the most wholesome glory of religious teaching, the light of devoted souls, the heavenly gift and joy to abide without end. This joy, I believe, has been briefly intimated in the two books which follow.

Here ends the preface of Cassiodorus Senator. Here begins the first book of his Introduction, that on divine readings, and the order in which they ought to be read is clearly set forth.

Here through God's grace begins the table of contents for Book I

[18] From ἁγιόγραφα ("things written by inspiration"); among the Hebrews the portion of the O. T. not in the Law and the Prophets; here all the books of the O. T. not contained in the five chapters which precede.

[19] *Relegi* here means "to be read with pen in hand for the making of corrections" rather than "to be reread." *Relego* in C. sometimes means simply "to read" and once "to translate."

Here through God's grace ends the table of contents for Book I.

Here begins the work promised by our author.

I. ON THE OCTATEUCH

1. The first codex of the Divine Scriptures is the Octateuch, which with its historical narration, starting with Genesis, is the beginning of our inspiration. St. Basil has written a commentary in the Attic tongue [1] on selected passages from Genesis, and Eustathius, a most fluent speaker, has translated the work into Latin in such a way that the natural ability of this most learned man seems to have equaled the power of his eloquence. He has composed nine books, extending up to the creation of man, and in them he has set forth the nature of heaven and earth, and the condition of air and water and practically all living things, so that what was neglected in his source [2] for the sake of brevity may in his fuller treatment be learned in most minute and accurate fashion.

2. Father Augustine has expounded the text of Genesis so carefully in the two books of his dispute with the Manichaeans that almost nothing in it is left uncertain. And so it has come about that the heresy which he refuted, in view of his brave vic-

---

[1] *Homiliae in Hexaëmeron.* St. Basil was archbishop of Caesarea from A.D. 371 to A.D. 379.

[2] That is, the Sacred Scriptures.

tory, involuntarily gives us the means for the more careful instruction of the orthodox. In my mind our addition of these books to the volume of the Basil just mentioned has been, perhaps, proper, in order that the text of the aforementioned Genesis may be explained more clearly to readers.

3. Next, St. Ambrose, a clear and very delightful interpreter, in his eloquent fashion has written six books which he has called *Hexaëmeron.*[3]

4. On these same beginnings St. Augustine too, a fluent and extremely wary disputant, has written twelve books, which he has clothed in the glory of a learning practically complete. These books he has therefore called *On Genesis Considered Word for Word;* and although he has treated the very matter in which the blessed Basil and St. Ambrose have been abundantly praised for their conspicuous success, nevertheless, through the Lord's bounty he has extended his work to a far greater length, a feat usually difficult of accomplishment for one who comes after eloquent speakers. He has also written thirty-three books against Faustus the Manichaean, in which he has clearly demonstrated Faustus' exceedingly wretched depravity and has again disputed in remarkable wise concerning the book of Genesis. The same man has likewise composed two books, to which he has given the title *Against the Enemy of the Law and the Prophets,* in which in like manner he has united the knots of many questions of divine law; in opposing the men involved he has become so inflamed by the heat of his piety that he has spoken against them more earnestly and more vigorously than against believers in other heresies. In his *Confessions* as well, in the last three books, he has written on the interpretation of Genesis, admitting the profundity of the subject which he has treated so often with repeated explanations. Those questions too which were of such nature as to be hidden within the sacred volumes and consequently hard to answer he has made clear by a very necessary syllogistic demonstration in seven books, bending every effort, most excellent teacher and sagacious man that he is, to the end that a matter generally agreed to be important for the salvation of souls may in no way through deadly negligence be left with-

---

[3] That is, *The Six Days of the Creation of the World.*

out discussion. He has also written seven other remarkable books *On the Modes of Speech,* in which he has set forth both the figures of speech characteristic of secular letters and many other ways of speaking peculiar to the Divine Scripture—ways of speaking, that is, which do not belong to ordinary usage; he takes care lest the reader's mind on discovering the strangeness of the compositions be troubled by some aversion, and at the same time, outstanding master that he is, he takes care to show that, though the general modes of expression (that is, the figures of speech of the grammarians and the rhetoricians) have proceeded from the Scripture, the Scripture nevertheless retains something as its peculiar property—something which no secular teacher up to the present time has been able to imitate. It is said too that he has written seven sermons on the seven days of Genesis, for which we seek unremittingly and which we eagerly hope to find.

5. St. Ambrose, moreover, has published seven books on the Patriarchs and has agreeably clarified many points in the Old Testament on which questions have arisen.

6. St. Jerome too, in a single volume on the book of Genesis, has solved the Hebrew questions propounded, which go through the Divine Scriptures of both Testaments like a line drawn with equal grace by a single pen. These questions are necessarily read by the orthodox, since with the solution of such great questions the text is left quite intelligible and is set forth in full clarity. Moreover, in a single volume by means of his own translations into Latin, he has clarified for us the explanations of Hebrew names and places which have been set down in the text of ancient books to bring about a more complete understanding. He has also composed a companion book on the New Testament, in which the most careful teacher has freed from obscurity the questions pertaining to that law.

7. St. Prosper, too, ought to be read most carefully; he has narrated in one hundred fifty-three chapters three books of the entire Divine Authority—fish, as it were, which the evangelical nets have dragged from the troubled depths of this life.[4]

8. Further, Origen's sermons on the Octateuch in three books

---

[4] John 21:11.

are unusually eloquent; and St. Jerome, in most fluent language, has translated into Latin some short works of this man, whom the opinion of many Fathers brands as a heretic. Though the authority of so many Fathers has previously assailed him, nevertheless at the present time it is well known that he has been condemned again by Bishop Vigilius,[5] a most blessed man. Moreover, Theophilus, bishop of the church of Alexandria, by using the truth of orthodoxy, has proved that thirty-five conceptions of his are distorted by heretical irregularity; and Epiphanius the Cypriot, of the church of Salamis, persecutes him with great hatred, most sorrowfully using his authority as bishop to confute the sayings which are most dangerous because of their perverted cleverness. St. Jerome, however, has fitly pointed out in the letter [6] which he has written to Tranquillinus how he ought to be read, in order not to keep those who so desire from a needful reading of him and, on the other hand, in order not to hurl the unwary to destruction. Certain men have said, not without cause, that he ought to be compared to anise, for, though he [7] seasons the food of sacred letters, he himself is, nevertheless, thrown away when he has been boiled down and the juice extracted. Concerning this man it has been conclusively stated, "When he writes well, no one writes better; when he writes badly, no one writes worse"; [8] and therefore he must be read with caution and wisdom,[9] in order that we thus may drink most healthful medicine from him and at the same time not absorb the poison of his perfidy, which is inimical to our salvation. That remark may fitly be applied to him which Virgil made during his reading of Ennius, when he was asked by someone what he was doing—"I am seeking gold in a dung-pile." [10] Therefore, in the works of this same Origen, insofar as I have been able in my search to

[5] Bishop of Rome; *i.e.,* pope.

[6] *Epistula 62.*

[7] The *Thesaurus linguae latinae,* through a misunderstanding, makes "anise" the subject of "seasons" and the other verbs which follow and gives this as the only example in Latin in which *anethum* ("anise") is masculine.

[8] I am reminded of the nursery rhyme: "When she's good she's very very good and when she's bad she's horrid."

[9] Garet compares this to Sulpicius Severus *Dialogus* I. vi–vii; and to Bk. XVII of the *Commonitorium* of Vincent of Lérins.

[10] Cf. Jerome, *Epistula* 107, § 12; Aponius on *Song of Songs,* chap. ix, beginning (ed. Rom. p. 172) ; Donatus' life of Virgil, p. 31 (Brummer).

discover passages which have been spoken contrary to the rules of the Fathers, I have marked them with the sign of repudiation —"rejected"—[11] that he may not have power to deceive a man who ought to be warned of these irregular notions by such a sign. Later writers, however, say that he ought to be avoided completely, since he subtly deceives the innocent; but if, with the Lord's help, caution is employed, his poison can do no harm.

9. Besides, through the Lord's beneficence I have left you, if you desire to read them, the sermons of the above-mentioned Origen, that is, sixteen sermons on Genesis, twelve on Exodus, sixteen on Leviticus, twenty-nine on Numbers, four on Deuteronomy, in which there is an exceedingly minute and subtle exposition, twenty-six on Joshua, and nine on Judges. In the case of Ruth I have been unable in any way to discover the old interpretation; I have, however, persuaded a most devout man, the priest Bellator, to prepare a new one, and in two books he has had many laudatory things to say about this woman and other women who came after her; these books I have added, suitably perhaps, to the expositions of Origen, that the interpretation of the entire codex of the Octateuch may be complete to the very end.

10. But that the text of this Octateuch may be made available for us in somewhat abridged form, we have thought that the summaries for the entire text which are described in running order by our ancestors ought to be set down at the beginnings of the books in order that the reader, profitably warned, may be brought to a wholesome attention and that on seeking he may easily find everything which he perceives has been briefly pointed out to him.

II. ON KINGS [1]

1. In the second codex, that of Kings, since I have been unable to find an exposition of the complete text, I have clothed certain bits of the work of most skillful men in a single garment, as it

---

[11] "Achresimi." Not in *Thesaurus linguae latinae.* Cf. *chresimon* (χρήσιμον) below, ix. 3 (Mynors 33. 16) and Isidore, *Etymologiae* 1. xxi. 22; cf. also *achriston* (ἄχρηστον) below, ix. 3 (Mynors 33. 17).

[1] In the King James Version I Kings = I Samuel, II Kings = II Samuel, III Kings = I Kings, and IV Kings = II Kings. The Paralipomena (= I and II Chronicles) are also treated in the present chapter of Cassiodorus' work (sections 11 and 13).

were, that from the collection so assembled there may become known, limb by limb, what could in no way be found in a single body.

2. I have discovered four sermons of Origen on the first book.

3. Concerning this same book the blessed Augustine, writing to Simplicianus, bishop of Milan, has solved six questions, the first of which is about the passage in which he says "And an evil spirit from the Lord troubled Saul"; [2] the second question concerns the same book: in what manner "It repenteth me that I have set up Saul to be king" [3] was said; the third is whether the unclean spirit [4] which was in the witch could have caused Samuel to be seen by Saul in order that they might have speech with one another; the fourth has to do with the second book of Kings at the place in which it says "Then went King David in and sat before the Lord"; [5] the fifth concerns the speech of Elijah in the third book of Kings: "O Lord, I am a witness of the widow with whom I sojourn and thou hast brought evil upon her by slaying her son"; [6] the sixth [7] is in the same book and has to do with the lying spirit by whom King Ahab was deceived.

4. Concerning the second book we have also found a single sermon [8] by the same Augustine on Absalom, who in his passionate desire for the kingdom decided to destroy his father David.

5. I have also discovered three very illustrious questions of the blessed Augustine on the same codex, of which the most important is that about the first book of Kings at the place in which David fought with Goliath; [9] the second is about Elijah and the widow of Sarepta [10] in the third book of Kings; the third has to do with the fourth book of Kings at the point at which Elisha blessed the deadly waters.[11]

6. Moreover, the blessed Jerome, writing to Abundantius, has explained three other very unintelligible questions: first, why David, who went forth of his own accord with Achish, king of the Allophylians,[12] to conquer Saul, later killed the man who

---

[2] I Kings 16:14 (I Samuel 16:14).   [3] *Ibid.* 15:11 (I Samuel 15:11).
[4] *Ibid.* 28:7 ff. (I Samuel 28:7).   [5] II Kings 7:18 (II Samuel 7:18).
[6] III Kings 17:20 (I Kings 17:20).   [7] *Ibid.* 22:21 ff. (I Kings 22:21).
[8] *Sermo in II Regum*, 15.   [9] I Kings 17 (I Samuel 17).
[10] III Kings 17:10 ff. (I Kings 17:10). Sarepta is the town Zarephath.
[11] IV Kings 2:19 ff. (II Kings 2:19).
[12] *Allophylorum*: properly designating European or Asiatic peoples other than Indo-European or Semitic; here equals the Philistines.

announced the death of this same Saul;[13] second, why David on his deathbed admonished his son Solomon to kill Joab, the commander of his army;[14] the third question is about Shimei, who unjustly heaped intolerable curses on the fleeing David and cast stones at him.[15]

7. On the second book of the present codex I have not discovered a single homily by the Origen mentioned above.

8. On the third book of the above-mentioned codex St. Ambrose, bishop of Milan, has composed a sermon which has to do with the judgment of Solomon;[16] on this subject St. Jerome too has written with an interpretation, as usual, most delightful; and we have learned from him that St. Augustine published a most excellent sermon in order that such a miracle might be undisputed if told by worthy writers.

9. Concerning this book the St. Jerome mentioned above has also written to the bishop, Vitalis, on the manner in which Solomon and Ahaz are said to have begotten sons when they were both eleven years old, which was not at all a normal occurrence.

10. Moreover, while St. Augustine, a most eloquent disputant, is speaking, among other things, on the periods treated in Kings, he has properly clarified the prophecy of Anna [17] in chapter iv of the seventeenth book of his work *On the City of God*.

11. On the second book of Chronicles I have discovered only a single long homily by Origen.

12. I have gathered all these items within the framework of a single codex that with the Lord's guidance you may read by way of commentary the matters which pertain to these particular books. And to this codex I have also appended blank quires in order that what has thus far been discovered concerning the above-mentioned work [18] may be added to the interpretations already described.

13. In the case of the two books of Chronicles mentioned above, whose great usefulness is proclaimed by the Fathers— books which contain a knowledge of events in a form certainly

---

13 II Kings 1 (II Samuel 1).

14 III Kings 2:5 (I Kings 2:5).

15 II Kings 16:5 ff. (II Samuel 16:5).

16 III Kings 3:16 ff. (I Kings 3:16).

17 Luke 2:36 ff.

18 That is, I and II Samuel and I and II Kings as a whole.

brief, but most complete—since I have not discovered the ancient summaries, I have written down summaries in imitation of those which previously existed, in a manner suitable, I believe, to each section of the text, in order that the nature of our devotion may be recognized, however humble our style may be.

III. ON THE PROPHETS

1. St. Jerome, the first man to make annotations for novices and for the young on the entire fifth [1] codex, that of the Prophets, has explained their writings in a manner at once competent and brief; through the Lord's beneficence I have left you these comments in a codex recently annotated. The metaphor of grape clusters may perhaps be appositely applied to these very annotations in order that the vineyard of the Lord, filled with a heavenly fertility, may seem to bear very sweet fruit. For those, however, who are mature and already possess some power of meditation the man named above has produced other very full and very clear interpretations, through the bounty of our Lord Christ; in some cases by providing diverse translations and in others by resolving knotty points in allegories he has caused the abstruse and obscure words of the Prophets to be understood in such fashion, pious teacher that he is, as to reveal to earthly understanding the great mystery of the heavenly King.

2. Isaiah, who "ought to be called not so much a prophet as an evangelist" [2] because of his clear account of the mysteries of Christ and the church, has been gloriously expounded in eighteen books by the St. Jerome mentioned above.

3. In forty-five sermons in the Attic tongue Origen has interpreted Jeremiah, who "mourned the destruction of his city in quadruple alphabet"; [3] I have found fourteen of these sermons

---

[1] See below on chap. iv (*third* codex) and chap. v (*fourth* codex). The question of the order of the books in C.'s various Bibles is a thorny one; see for instance the discussion of Chapman, *Amiatinus*, 1926, pp. 147 ff. especially, and 1927. Cf. p. 34, notes 95, 97, and 98, above. The order Prophets *fifth,* Psalter *third,* and Solomon *fourth,* given at the beginning of chapters iii, iv, and v and in chapter xxvi, is taken from the *antiqua translatio,* or Septuagint (chap. xiv), and is used in C.'s nine-volume Bible. Just why C. takes up the three groups in their present order in the *Institutiones* is hard to discover.

[2] This description echoes that of Jerome in Migne, *Pat. Lat.,* XXIV, 18A.

[3] Jerome, *ibid.,* XXV, 17A.

translated and have left them to you. St. Jerome also wrote a commentary on Jeremiah in twenty books; we have been able to find only six of these, but with aid of the Lord we are still seeking the rest.

4. St. Jerome in fourteen books has explained Ezekiel, whose style in Hebrew is neither completely fluent nor completely halting; [4] and likewise, in three books, the same St. Jerome has explained Daniel, who, though he is by no means counted among the group of the prophets by the Hebrews, is, nevertheless, numbered among the writers of the Hagiographa.[5]

5. The remaining Prophets, who because of the brevity of their books are commonly [6] called Minor, have been interpreted in twenty books by the St. Jerome just mentioned, as follows: Hosea in three books, Obadiah in one book, Amos in three books, Joel in one book, Jonah in one book, Nahum in one book, Habakkuk in two books, Zephaniah in one book, Haggai in one book, Zechariah in three books, Micah in two books, and Malachi in one book. That nothing about them may be left ambiguous, he has also pointed out in most splendid fashion, with proper etymologies, the manner in which their names ought to be interpreted in Latin. Thus, through the Lord's bounty the field of the Lord, ploughed as it were by certain hired workers and sprinkled with heavenly moisture, has yielded us spiritual fruit.

6. It is said that St. Ambrose too has composed a commentary on the Prophets in his usual charming style; up to the present, however, I have not in any way been able to find it. I leave the zealous search to you, so that the augmented exposition made by skilled interpreters may bring you abundant knowledge and most joyous salvation of the soul.

IV. ON THE PSALTER

1. The third [1] codex, which contains the Book of Psalms, follows; it is the first work undertaken in my program of com-

---

[4] Cf. Jerome, *loc. cit.*

[5] The last of the three Jewish divisions of the O.T., or that portion not in the Law and the Prophets, which in Hebrew is called *Ketubim* (*Kethubhim*).

[6] Sermo vulgūs (gen. sing.) in MS.

[1] See above on chap. iii (*fifth* codex) and below on chap. iv (*third* codex).

mentating,[2] but it is fourth in order. The blessed Hilary and the blessed Ambrose and the blessed Jerome have treated certain psalms, but the blessed Augustine has treated them all at some length with zeal beyond measure; with the Lord's help I have already collected Augustine's commentary on twenty [3] of the psalms.

2. Borrowing light, in my usual fashion, from his light, I have written something about the Psalter, with the help of the Lord, in order that the famous saying of the Mantuan bard may be truly exemplified in my case:

> And I cackle as a goose among melodious swans; [4]

and in our discussion we have confused no topic by digressive narration, but by way of annotation we have briefly stated what the nature of the text itself required in every passage. If anyone possibly deigns to read my remarks after reading such men, he will perceive, as other Fathers have stated in no uncertain terms, that something has arisen from the Divine Scriptures which teachers of secular letters have subsequently transferred to their own studies. And as each passage has produced this something, with the Lord's aid we have indicated it, if I am not wrong, to the best of our ability.[5]

3. One should also read the little book entitled *On the Book of Psalms,* by Athanasius, bishop of the city of Alexandria, which the author composed and sent to Marcellinus as a most pleasant refreshment after an illness; with various admonitions he discloses the excellence of the Psalter by a well-documented discussion, bringing forward in charming manner the different misfortunes of mankind and their remedies. If I may suggest two metaphors, the Psalter is a heavenly sphere thick with twinkling stars and a very beautiful peacock adorned by eyes of many decorous colors; it is indeed the paradise of souls,[6] containing countless fruits to fatten the human spirit in charming manner.

4. We have decided that this entire collection of psalms [7]

---

[2] So Chapman, *Amiatinus,* 1926, pp. 147 ff. Another possible translation, though less likely, is: "it is the first work in the amount of labor required."

[3] *Duas decadas. Decas* sometimes means a work divided into ten books.

[4] Vergil, *Eclogues,* 9, line 36.   [5] Cf. *Comm. Psalt.* pref. xv.

[6] *Ibid.* (near the beginning).   [7] *Ibid.* (col. 9c).

ought to be written in three volumes of fifty psalms each, in order that the number of years before a jubilee [8] may thrice announce to you the long desired benefits of remission of sins which arise from the Holy Trinity, and in order that the brothers may receive hope of precious salvation through such a distribution of the psalms, since a single volume may be found heavy for some of them, and in order that through the guidance of the Lord many [9] may find advantage and salvation in reading the psalms in this way. May your library possess a copy of this work, may you have recourse to it if you have fallen into error, and may the parts of the work be distributed so that the curiosity of the brothers may be satisfied.

V. ON SOLOMON [1]

1. The fourth [2] codex contains Solomon, whose first book, entitled Proverbs, I have found to be divided into four parts; I have felt that certain admonitions ought to be made concerning these parts in the prologue of this same codex, in order that from a reading of this prologue the purpose of the book may quickly become clear.

2. As an expounder of this book,[3] we have discovered Didymus [4] in Greek, whose work with the aid of the Lord has been most carefully translated into Latin by our friend Epiphanius, a very well-spoken man. With justice and prophetic inspiration the blessed Anthony, father of monasticism, has spoken of this Didymus as possessing sight, though he was physically blind, for with a clear mind he perceived that which could not be seen by corporeal eyes. It is astonishing to relate the number of studies [5] and arts in which mere listening instructed a man who, on account of his blindness, was unable to examine even the forms of the letters. This, as I read it, would have seemed almost impossible to me, I admit, had not a certain man named Eusebius happened to

---

[8] Jubilee = the year of jubilee among the Jews, in which all slaves were set free and all lands reverted to their former possessors; it took place every fifty years.

[9] That is, three readers could thus consult the Psalms simultaneously, each using a separate volume.

[1] That is, Proverbs, Ecclesiastes, and the Song of Solomon.

[2] See above on chap. iii (*fifth* codex) and chap. iv (*third* codex).

[3] That is, Proverbs.   [4] Didymus Videus.   [5] "Disciplines."

come to us from the region of Asia and to tell us that, when he
was a child of five years he had been blinded so that his left eye
was hollowed out, as the extremely deep socket revealed; his
right eye, disordered and glassy in appearance, fruitlessly turned
without sight. He had stored away so many books in the library
of his memory that he gave readers most excellent advice concerning the part of the codex in which they might find what he
had previously mentioned. He held all studies [6] in his mind and
expounded them most clearly. He pointed out, moreover, that
the tabernacle and temple of the Lord was formed like a vault;
I have, as seems fitting, provided an accurate drawing of it with
a suitable design in the larger Latin pandect.[7] Moreover, on the
subject of priestly vestments he wove together many secrets of
the Lord, maintaining that nothing was useless, even if it did
not give a very excellent idea of a particular matter; he also de-
clared that Josephus, Origen, and Jerome had mentioned the
same principle in their works. Why should I say more? He made
me believe the stories about Didymus, whom he himself exemplified. And, admonished by his instruction, I have discovered many
ancient codices which were unknown to me. Though thus far he
has been held back by the delusion of the Novatian schism, we
think that with the help of the merciful Lord he ought to be
filled with the light of upright faith, so that the Lord, who caused
him to learn His Scriptures, may bid him to wax strong in the
integrity of the orthodox faith.

3. The second book of Solomon, which is called Ecclesiastes,[8]
has been effectually expounded by the blessed Jerome; he calls
the book "Contionator" [9] in Latin because it addresses the people and because its language is not directed toward one man in
particular, but toward all in general. Our "Ecclesiastes" is Christ
the Lord, who "hath made both one, and hath broken down the
middle wall of partition between us, having abolished in his flesh

---

[6] *Idem.*

[7] Apparently the pandect (a collection of all the books of the Bible) mentioned
again in *Inst.* I. xiv. 2 (Mynors 40. 6–7): "in codice grandiore littera clariore con-
scripto." This pandect is to be distinguished from the "pandectem . . . minutiore
manu . . . conscribendum" of chap. xii, § 3 (Mynors 37. 20–22). Both are to be distinguished from the "Graecum pandectum" of chap. xiv, § 4 (Mynors 41. 6) and
chap. xv, § 11 (Mynors 47. 24). Cf. *Comm. Psalt.*, 14, 1 and 86, 1.

[8] That is, "the Preacher."   [9] "Haranguer of the multitude."

the enmity." [10] He says that above all things the divine commandments should be followed, calling to mind that everything
of this world is "vanity of vanities." [11] Victorinus,[12] first orator
and then bishop, has also had something to say about this book.

4. In the case of the Song of Songs [13] the same St. Jerome,
illustrious propagator of the Latin tongue, has prepared the two
expository sermons of Origen for us in a translation of his usual
excellent quality. The most eloquent interpreter Rufinus [14] has
in three books explained the work in greater detail, with certain
passages added, as far as the precept which says: "Take us the
foxes, the little foxes, that spoil the vines." [15] And after these
men Epiphanius,[16] bishop of Cyprus, has briefly treated the entire work in Greek in one book. With the aid of the Lord we
have had this book, among others, translated into Latin by our
friend Epiphanius, a most fluent interpreter. I have consequently
included the most careful expounders of the Song of Songs in a
single codex, in order that all interpreters of a single work may
be presented to readers at the same time. St. Ambrose has also
made many profitable and excellent remarks on this work in the
third book of his treatise *On the Patriarchs,* in which he speaks
about the character of Isaac.

5. The oft-mentioned Father Jerome, moreover, maintains [17]
that the book of Wisdom [18] was not written by Solomon, as most
people hold, but rather by a certain very learned Jew named
Philo; he has designated the book as one bearing a false title,[19]
since it usurps a name other than that of the author. The priest
Bellator, as we know, has undertaken the exposition of this work
in eight books; we preserve this exposition along with other short
works by the same writer. Both Father Augustine and St. Ambrose have pronounced sermons on the name of this book,[20] a
name exceptionally pleasant and truly resplendent in its worthi-
ness.

---

[10] Ephesians 2:14.   [11] Ecclesiastes 1:2.
[12] Victorinus Petaviensis (end of third cent. A.D.); see Teuffel, § 385. 6.
[13] Also known as the Song of Solomon, or Canticles.
[14] *Ca.* A.D. 345–410.   [15] Song of Solomon 2:15.   [16] A.D. 298–403.
[17] Pref. to the books of Solomon (Proverbs, Ecclesiastes, Song of Solomon).
[18] Deuterocanonical among Roman Catholics; one of the Apocrypha among Protestants.
[19] That is, Wisdom of Solomon.   [20] Wisdom.

6. The St. Jerome just named recounts that the book Ecclesiasticus [21] is the work of Jesus, son of Sirach, and may be called "Congregator" [22] in Latin. The Fathers, however, made this distinction, that Ecclesiastes may refer to Christ the Lord alone, whereas Ecclesiasticus may without restriction refer to all just preachers who are wont to assemble the congregation of the Lord with most holy counsel. At any rate, it is clear that the present book has done this very thing, and because of the excellence of its qualities St. Jerome calls it "all-virtuous," [23] that is, able to hold all virtues; so great is its clarity and so pure its Latin style that the text is its own commentary; may the ease with which its excellence is imitated in actual deeds equal the speed with which it is comprehended by the mind.

7. We have, with the aid of the Lord, taken pains to mark the summaries of these books, in order that in such an essential text, as it is often said, the novice may not be left strangely confused.

VI. ON THE HAGIOGRAPHA

1. Next comes the sixth codex, which contains eight books of the Hagiographa, of which the first is Job, a remarkable and glorious specimen of patience. The Latin language has gained a very careful translation and exposition of this work, as it has of many other works, through the labors of the blessed Jerome. And by his interpretation Job is shown to have made all his complaints without blame, as the Lord himself deigned to bear witness.[1]

2. How many sweet, mysterious words that book contains, as the blessed Jerome says in the letter which he composes and directs to Paulinus:[2] "It begins in prose, continues in poetic form, ends in prose again, and it determines every point by the application of a major premise, a minor premise, a verification, and a conclusion in accordance with the law of logic." If this is true

---

[21] Not placed by the Hebrews or St. Jerome among the canonical Scriptures, but quoted as such, and even attributed to Solomon, by many Christian writers of the second century. Also called the Wisdom of Jesus, son of Sirach. Now deuterocanonical among Roman Catholics, and one of the Apocrypha among Protestants.

[22] That is, one who assembles the multitude; cf. Ecclesiastes ("the Preacher").

[23] panaretum ($= \pi\alpha\nu\acute{\alpha}\rho\epsilon\tau o\nu$). Jerome, preface to the books of Solomon.

[1] Job 42:7.   [2] *Epistula* 53, § 8.

—and it cannot be different from that which the authority of such a great man has proclaimed it to be—where are those who say that dialectics did not begin with the very Holy Scriptures? "Single words in it are full of enigmas, subjects for investigation, and sacred questions; and, not to mention other things, it prophesies the resurrection of the flesh in such a way that no one seems to have written anything more clearly and more carefully on this topic. For it says: "For I know that my redeemer liveth and that I shall stand at the latter day upon the earth. And I shall be clothed again in my skin, and in my flesh I shall see God; Whom I shall see for myself and mine eyes shall behold, and not another. This my earnest desire is preserved in my bosom." [3]

3. St. Augustine too, in annotating the same book, has treated it with his customary diligence. Moreover, a certain anonymous writer, who from his style we suspect is the blessed Hilary, has written a methodically arranged commentary on the book; if you read it attentively, it will instruct you carefully. Clearly Job is a great book and one written for the consolation and profit of mankind, since a holy man is shown to have borne so many great burdens that every sinner lightens for himself whatever burdens he sees he is bearing.

4. Moreover, Latin interpretations of Tobit in five books, of Esther in six books, of Judith in seven books, and of Maccabees in ten books have been written by the labors of the aforementioned priest Bellator insofar as he has had the power to do so.

5. I have, however, collected the summaries of these books in concise form, since pointing out in a few words matters which are very widely scattered is believed to be not the least advantage in instruction; instructed by these aids, the reader's mind courses eagerly through the very profitable sequence of the Scriptures. Though these books are historical and though they are expressed in a very simple narrative style, do you nevertheless realize on account of their most excellent moral character that they were written to impart to our minds in becoming fashion patience, hope, charity, fortitude, even in women, a life on God's account contemptuous of the present, and other kinds of virtue which under the guidance of the Lord flourished in them.

[3] Job 19: 25–27.

6. On each of the two books of Esdras I have found written in Greek a single sermon of Origen, which in each case has been translated through the efforts of the same devout Bellator. St. Ambrose, moreover, in the book *On the Patriarchs*,[4] at the point at which he speaks of Joseph, cites for the sake of example the second book of Maccabees, the greatest part of which he has laid open to view by the very sweet fluidity of his eloquence in order to describe tolerance. The books of Maccabees with the Lord's help have been provided with a careful commentary by our friend Bellator, mentioned above, in order that a text so great, which shows you so many examples of virtues, may not possibly be left unexplained.

VII. ON THE GOSPELS

1. The seventh codex of the Divine Scripture, which is the first of the New Testament and which has provided us with a beginning worthy of adoration and a necessary aid, shines with the celestial light of the four evangelists. St. Jerome has very diligently treated the peculiar characteristics of all of them; and I have collected his writings in a single volume in order that the reader's effort may not be hindered by writings distributed among several codices. The blessed Jerome again has written a commentary on Matthew in four books. St. Hilary has explained it in a single volume, and Victorinus,[1] first orator and then bishop, has also treated it. St. Ambrose has gloriously expounded Luke. The blessed Augustine has explained John in a full and excellent commentary and has also invested his four books *On the Harmony of the Evangelists* with an exceedingly subtle and necessary argument.

2. Eusebius of Caesarea, moreover, has collected the *Canons* of the Gospels in compendious form, in order to point out with the greatest possible discrimination the passages in which the Gospels agree and the passages in which they disagree; and in this collection the marvellous teachings of the different writers flourish in proportion to their fullness of faith.

---

[4] Actually in St. Ambrose's *De Iacob et Vita beata*, II. xi–xii, and not in his *De patriarchis*.

[1] Victorinus Petaviensis.

VIII. ON THE EPISTLES OF THE APOSTLES

1. The eighth codex contains the canonical epistles of the Apostles. In the thirteen [1] epistles of St. Paul, at the very beginning of my text, I have found annotations written which used to be considered so distinguished as to cause very learned men to say with zeal that they had been written by St. Gelasius, bishop of the city of Rome: [2] this is the practice of those who desire to defend faults by giving them the authority of a glorious name. After a careful reconsideration on my part in the light of the earlier texts, they are in my eyes clearly very subtle and very concise words, but the poison of the Pelagian heresy has been instilled into them; and, in order that the heretical delusion may be far from you, I have purged the first letter to the Romans [3] with all the care possible, and left the rest written in a papyrus codex to be emended by you. And this emending will easily be within your power, since one imitates more boldly because of the example which leads the way.

2. Nevertheless, seriously disturbed by these cares, I have discovered a certain anonymously annotated codex, conferred upon us by divine foresight, which treats the thirteen epistles of St. Paul in a commentary not without excellence. This codex, if carefully read, will provide you, through the bounty of the Lord, with a second and safe kind of commentary.

3. We have had Mutianus, a most skillful writer, translate into Latin the thirty-four homilies written in Greek by St. John, bishop of Constantinople, [4] on the epistle to the Hebrews, in order that the continuity of the epistles may not be broken by a sudden indecorous ending.

4. On the canonical epistles—specifically, on the first epistle of St. Peter, the first and second of St. John, and on the epistle of James—Clement of Alexandria, who is called "the writer of

---

[1] The Epistle to the Philippians is omitted altogether in the present chapter (though a quotation from it, 3:20, occurs below in Bk. II, chap. iii, § 5, the last line). If this epistle is included, the number of Pauline epistles becomes fourteen. This is the number mentioned in chaps. xii, xiii, and xiv, below (in the last two, Philippians is mentioned by name as well).

[2] That is, Pope. Consecrated 492.   [3] Cf. *De orthographia* (p. 144, l. 5).

[4] Chrysostom.

miscellanies," [5] has published certain writings; and in them he
has said many things subtly, but some things incautiously. We
have had his remarks translated into Latin in such a way that
his doctrine may be heard more safely after having been purified by the exclusion of causes of offense.

5. St. Augustine too has discussed the epistle of the apostle
James with his customary earnest diligence; I have left you his
discussion written in a parchment codex.

6. As considerable worry about the remaining canonical
epistles was tormenting us, suddenly through the Lord's bounty
the codex of Didymus written in Greek to explain seven canonical epistles was granted us; and with the Divinity's aid this codex
was translated by Epiphanius,[6] a very clear writer.

7. In ten sermons on the first epistle of the blessed John, St.
Augustine has said many things in wondrous fashion concerning
charity.

8. I have discovered a third codex [7] of the epistles of St.
Paul which is said by some to contain the blessed Jerome's very
concise annotations; this I have likewise left you through the
bounty of Christ.

9. In addition to these three similar commentaries which we
have mentioned, Peter, an abbot of the district of Tripolis, is
said to have written another on the epistles of St. Paul, by means
of illustrations taken from the shorter works of the blessed Augustine, in such a way as to announce the sacred secret in his
heart through another's mouth; he has adapted these illustrations
to the individual passages so becomingly that one feels that this
work has been completed rather through the efforts of the blessed
Augustine. It is indeed remarkable for one man to have written
an exposition drawn from another in such a way as to have fulfilled his heart's desire, apparently, without the addition of a
single word of his own. This codex, among others, ought through
God's grace to be sent you from Africa.

10. So the entire series for the canonical epistles, including
those of St. Paul as well as those of the other apostles, has been
made complete. The blessed Ambrose is also said to have writ-

---

[5] Stromatheus = στρωματεύς.   [6] Epiphanius Scholasticus.
[7] In addition to the two mentioned in sections 1 and 2, above.

ten and left a codex filled with a most delightful exposition of all the letters of St. Paul; up to the present, however, I have not been able to find it, but I am diligently searching for it.

11. This completes our account of the concise annotations of the epistles by the several expositors. Let us now state in order, just as we did in the case of the Prophets, the names of the writers who have preferred to expound the epistles at greater length, in order that the first type of exposition may seem to be given to novices and the second type reserved for those who have finished their training.

12. The first of all the epistles of St. Paul and the most wonderful is that intended for the Romans, and Origen has expounded it in the Greek tongue in twenty books; the Rufinus previously mentioned has reduced this exposition to ten books and has now for the first time translated it into Latin in its entirety. St. Augustine began a commentary on this very epistle; he states that he produced one book on the salutation alone, and, if I may use his own words,[8] "deterred by the magnitude of the work itself and by the labor involved," he was "turned away to other easier tasks." In a letter to Simplicianus, bishop of Milan, he has treated some lofty and excellent questions concerning the same epistle; we have decided to insert these questions in the codex just mentioned, in order that the reader's purpose may not be harmfully put off by searching for the scattered parts of an exposition.

13. The same St. Augustine, moreover, has written at greater length in explanation of the Epistle to the Galatians, and St. Jerome has written an extensive commentary on it in three books. The same Father Jerome has carefully explained the Epistle to the Ephesians in another three books. He has also set forth an exposition of the Epistle to Titus in a single book. He has, moreover, explained the Epistle to Philemon in one book.

14. St. Jerome is said to have been responsible for the interpretations of the remaining [9] epistles of St. Paul, that is, the two epistles to the Corinthians, the two to the Thessalonians, the

[8] *Retractationes* I. xxv (xxiv).
[9] The Epistle to the Philippians is omitted here. Cf. § 1, note 1, above.

one to the Colossians, and the two to Timothy; and from them much wisdom is granted, when the ignorant chance to learn that which they are seeking. Because of the compassion of the Lord we are sure that we shall receive them without delay from different places in which we have had them sought, and we ought zealously to preserve that which we know will be sent us; and so it comes about that if by chance some part of them happens to appear to any of you before the arrival of those which I am seeking, let him strive zealously to transcribe this part and to add it to the work of the expositors mentioned above, in order that the library of the monastery may derive profit through the Lord's aid and your toil, a combination through which very great accomplishments have been effected. But if before these things are done our old age perchance, at the Lord's bidding, reaches the end we desire, with our sins forgiven—and I beg you to pray that it will, the object for which we have hoped, as it is proper to believe, will some day come to you.

15. In the previously mentioned [10] eighth bookcase, where the Greek codices are assembled, I have left a commentary in Greek by John Chrysostom on the epistles already described in order that in the absence of more extensive Latin commentaries that which will furnish very full knowledge may from time to time be translated from it, to the end that through the Lord's bounty the commentaries of the ancients on the entire seventy-one canonical books [11] (this is the number of the holy father Augustine) may be offered for use at your banquets as though they were the spiritual fruit of Paradise.

16. If some doubtful passages are perchance left in the works which have just been mentioned and if in the fullness of their explanations they are unable to satisfy you, by no means do I forbid your use of modern interpreters, provided, however, you cautiously seek for orthodox writers, since with the passing of time the grace of the Godhead, which was perchance hidden from the ancient doctors, is newly imparted to many.

[10] Not previously mentioned, but mentioned below in chap. xiv, § 4, sentence 1: "in armario supradicto octavo."

[11] Cf. chap. xiii, below.

IX. ON THE ACTS OF THE APOSTLES AND
THE APOCALYPSE

1. The ninth codex contains the Acts of the Apostles and the Apocalypse, inasmuch as this Apocalypse, that is, Revelation, is also known to be the product of the apostle John. On the Acts of the Apostles we have found the commentary written in Greek by St. John, bishop of Constantinople, and our friends, with the Lord's aid, have translated it in two codices containing fifty-five sermons in all.

2. The Apocalypse, which effectively leads the minds of readers to heavenly contemplation and makes them see in their mind's eye that by actual sight of which the angels are blessed, is available to you in the interpretation of St. Jerome. The bishop Victorinus, often [1] mentioned above, has treated certain difficult passages of this book in concise form. Vigilius as well, bishop of Africa, has written in very full and careful style about the interpretation of the thousand years [2] which is contained in the previously mentioned Apocalypse and is to some a source of considerable confusion.

3. Ticonius the Donatist,[3] moreover, has made some remarks on the same volume which are not to be rejected, but he has also intermingled with them some of the dregs of his own poisonous heresy; in a manner which seems to me appropriate, whenever in my search I have been able to find good and bad in him, I have affixed the sign "approved" [4] to his good sayings and the sign "rejected" [5] to his bad ones. We urge you to do likewise when expositors are under suspicion, lest the reader's mind perchance be disturbed and confused by the intermingling of unspeakable dogma.

4. St. Augustine has also interpreted many points which concern the present volume in admirable and careful fashion in the various books of his work *On the City of God*. In our own times

---

[1] Only twice.   [2] Apocalypse 20: 2–7.
[3] A partisan of the heresy of Donatus.
[4] Chresimon (χρήσιμον). Cf. Isidore *Etymologiae* I. xxi. 22 and i. 8, second sentence from the end, above: *achresimi repudiatio.*
[5] Achriston (ἄχρηστον). But this word must have suggested the equally appropriate meaning "Unchristian."

as well, the Apocalypse mentioned above has been minutely and diligently expounded in five books through the zeal of the blessed Bishop Primasius, prelate of Africa. And to these five books there has been added another, with a very careful argument, on the subject "What makes a heretic?" May these books be offered as sacred gifts at the sacred altars in the temple of the Lord.

5. Inasmuch as we have mentioned all the ancient expositors whom we have been able to find and all whose works we have had translated from Greek and fashioned in a new tongue,[6] let us now say something about the six modes of understanding, in order that by frequent reference to the discussion we may avoid pernicious errors.

X. ON THE MODES OF UNDERSTANDING

1. The first thing for us to do after having been instructed by the present manual is to return solicitously to the writers of introductory works on the Sacred Scripture, writers whose works we have eventually [1] discovered: that is, Ticonius the Donatist,[2] St. Augustine *On Christian Learning*, Adrian,[3] Eucherius,[4] and Junilius; [5] I have collected their works with sedulous care in order that codices with the same purpose may be held united in a single collection; by their various explanations and examples these men make known matters which were previously unknown.

2. But if some things are perchance overlooked by the writers of the introductory works, let us then carefully seek the expositors of the books in question and matters which were previously unknown will begin to be made known.

3. Next, let us read the orthodox teachers most zealously, for they solve most obscure questions by the application of logical reasoning.

---

[6] That is, Latin.

[1] *Postea* ("afterwards").

[2] *Liber regularum.*

[3] *Isagoge in Scripturas.*

[4] *Formulae.*

[5] *De partibus divinae legis ad Primasium.* Also called *Instituta regularia divinae legis.* Junilius, an African, composed his work in 551 (?). It reproduces the views of Theodore of Mopsuestia with which Junilius had become familiar during a residence at Constantinople through the discourses of the Persian, Paul, who taught at the school of Nisibis. On Nisibis see pref. i, sentence 2, above.

4. In the fifth [6] place we ought to note with great diligence passages of special importance which are cited for the sake of illustration throughout individual books and letters of the different Fathers. The result of such a noting on our part is a thorough examination of various orthodox writers—an examination most proper, since they disclose their intentions in becoming manner and great knowledge comes to us from the questions which are treated in their works.

5. Finally, let frequent conversation be sought with elders of extraordinary accomplishments, for by conversing with them we suddenly notice what we did not imagine was existent, since they zealously relate to us what they have been able to learn in their long lives. It is indeed profitable to traverse these six modes of understanding with eager desire rather than to be sluggish because of impious stupidity.

XI. ON THE FOUR ACCEPTED SYNODS

1. Let us now tell how the universal and sacred councils have strengthened the wholesome sacraments of our faith, in order that we may avoid pernicious errors by perceiving in these councils the mystery of the true religion. The first synod to be approved by the holy Church and approved deservedly is said to have been convoked at Nicaea,[1] the second at Constantinople,[2] the third at Ephesus [3] (that is, the earlier synod of Ephesus), and the fourth at Chalcedon; [4] they have provided our faith with such great light that we ought not to fall with blinded hearts

---

[6] The first four modes of understanding perhaps include reading of the following: (1) the present work (§ 1), (2) the "introductory" books (§ 1), (3) the expositors (§ 2), and (4) the orthodox teachers (§ 3). But some scholars (C. H. Turner in particular) feel that there is a lacuna before § 4, and the two London Regius MSS of the twelfth and thirteenth centuries, respectively, bear the words "Note that two modes are lacking" ("Nota quod desunt duo modi") ; the repetition in the Latin text ("quae prius clausa manserunt") at the end of §§ 1 and 2 gives some ground for this suspicion.

[1] In Bithynia, on Lake Ascanius, formerly called Antigonia, the modern Isnik. The date is 325. This council condemned the Arian heresy and promulgated the Nicene creed.

[2] This council condemned the Macedonian and other heresies and reaffirmed the Nicene creed.

[3] 431. This council condemned the Nestorian heresy.

[4] 451. This council condemned the Eutychian heresy.

upon the rock of irreligion if we are guarded by the Lord, our protector. The most holy Fathers, moreover, not tolerating harm to upright faith, have preferred to establish ecclesiastical rules at these councils and have destroyed the stubborn contrivers of new heresies with the divine sword, decreeing that no one ought to trouble them with new questions, but that, content with the authority of the excellent men of old, they ought to obey the wholesome decrees without evasion and treachery. There are, indeed, some who think it a fine thing to know some fact which is at variance with the ancients and to find something new that they may thereby seem clever.

2. The Codex Encyclius [5] bears witness to the synod of Chalcedon and extols the synod's authority with such great praise as to deem it (with justice) worthy of being compared to the authority of the Sacred Scriptures. We have had this codex—that is, this collection of letters intended for the entire world—translated from Greek into Latin by the most skillful writer Epiphanius.[6]

3. But since with the Lord's help we have assembled sacred letters in nine codices and added to them, so far as has been within our power, introductory works and writings of practically all the Latin expositors, let us now see how the divine law has been divided in three different ways by different Fathers; the Church of all lands, however, in its acceptance of this law is reverent and of one mind.

XII. THE DIVISION OF THE SACRED SCRIPTURE ACCORDING TO ST. JEROME [1]

1. According to St. Jerome the divine authority is divided into the two Testaments as follows: [2]

[5] A collection of papal letters (encyclicals) addressed to the bishops of the world, or at times to the bishops of one country, on a matter of interest to the Church.

[6] Epiphanius Scholasticus.

[1] On chaps. xii–xiv cf. the Codex Amiatinus of the Bible, fols. vi, 8, and vii.

[2] Jerome's division, as presented below, is surprising in several particulars: (1) Judges and Ruth are separately listed, though they are usually coupled as a single book; (2) Kings, here omitted altogether, normally follows Samuel; (3) Ecclesiasticus replaces Ecclesiastes, which is omitted altogether; and (4) Daniel, normally found after the Song of Songs, is also omitted. The arrangement found in the text

The Old. The Law: Genesis, Exodus, Leviticus, Numbers, Deuteronomy. The Prophets: Joshua, Judges, Ruth, Samuel, Isaiah, Jeremiah, Ezekiel, the book of the twelve Prophets.[3] The Hagiographa: Job; David;[4] the books of Solomon—Proverbs, Ecclesiasticus,[5] the Song of Songs;[6] the Diaries[7] (that is, Chronicles), Esdras, Esther.

The New.[8] The Gospels: Matthew, Mark, Luke, John. The Epistles of the Apostles: 14 of Paul,[9] two of Peter, three of John, one of James, one of Jude. The Acts of the Apostles. Revelation[10] in one book.

is unsatisfactory, first, because it includes only twenty-one items (and in the second sentence of § 2, below, Jerome is said to have arranged the books to correspond to the twenty-two letters of the Hebrew alphabet), and second, because the arrangement differs from that presented by Jerome in his own works. In his *prologus galeatus*, e.g., (*Biblia Sacra vulgatae editionis Sixti V. & Clementi VIII Pont. Max. auctoritate recognita . . . editio nova notis chronologicis historicis et geographicis illustrata juxta editionem Parisiensem Antonii Vitré.* Antverpiae apud Joannem Baptistam Verdussen . . . 1740, p. vii) Jerome combines Judges and Ruth, adds Kings (= III and IV Kings) after Samuel (= I and II Kings), has Ecclesiastes after Proverbs, and does not include Ecclesiasticus among the canonical books, adds Daniel after the Song of Songs, and, finally, comments on the identification of the twenty-two books of the Old Testament with the letters of the Hebrew alphabet. In his *Epistola LIII ad Paulinum Presbyterum* (*Biblia Sacra iuxta Latinam Vulgatam versionem ad codicum fidem iussu Pii PP. XI cura et studio monachorum Sancti Benedicti commissionis pontificae a Pio PP. X institutae sodalium praeside Aidano Gasquet S. R. E. Cardinale edita. I. Liber Genesis . . .* D. H. Quentin. Rome, 1926), p. 24, line 4, Malichim (= III and IV Kings) follows Samuel; and, p. 30, line 1, Daniel follows Ezekiel. It is to be noted that in Jerome's computation of twenty-two books the twelve minor prophets count as one book, Ruth is coupled with Judges, Ezra and Nehemiah are coupled in the book Esdras (also known sometimes as I and II Esdras), Lamentations is considered a part of Jeremiah, and the following double books are thought of as single—I and II Samuel, I and II Kings (= Jerome's III and IV Kings), and I and II Chronicles.

[3] The minor prophets: Hosea, Joel, Amos, Obadiah, Jonah, Micah, Nahum, Habakkuk, Zephaniah, Haggai, Zechariah, Malachi.

[4] Psalms.

[5] Also called The Wisdom of Jesus the Son of Sirach and now generally considered deuterocanonical among Roman Catholics and apocryphal among Protestants. Perhaps the reading of the Θ and Ξ groups of MSS (= Ecclesiastes) is to be preferred here.

[6] The Song of Solomon.

[7] *Verba Dierum* or *Paralipomena* (= "things omitted," "supplement").

[8] Jerome gives a similar account in his *Epistola LIII ad Paulinum Presbyterum* (Dom Quentin's edition, cited above, pp. 32–33): eleven epistles are named for Paul, but since Corinthians, Thessalonians, and Timothy have two books each the total number of Pauline epistles becomes fourteen; a total of seven epistles is given for James, Peter, John, and Jude, collectively.

[9] Epistle to the Romans, I and II Corinthians, Galatians, Ephesians, Philippians, Colossians, I and II Thessalonians, I and II Timothy, Titus, Philemon, Hebrews.

[10] Often called The Apocalypse.

2. One should clearly understand that St. Jerome read and corrected the versions of different translators because he perceived that these versions by no means agreed with the Hebrew text. And in consequence of his experience he carefully translated all the books of the Old Testament from their Hebrew source into the Latin tongue and fittingly grouped them so that they accorded with the twenty-two letters of the Hebrew alphabet, by which all wisdom is learned and the record of words is preserved in written form for all time. To this translation the twenty-seven books of the New Testament were added; and the sum of the two amounts to forty-nine. Add to this the omnipotent and indivisible Trinity, by which these things were done and on whose account these things were said, and the result without doubt is the number fifty, since after the manner of the year of a jubilee it very compassionately forgives the transgressions and remits the sins of those who are absolutely penitent.

3. Because of the fullness of the text, we decided that this pandect [11] ought to be written in a rather small hand in fifty-three gatherings of six folios each in order that the compactness of the writing might shorten the inordinate length of the copious text.

4. We ought, moreover, to call to mind the fact that the aforesaid Jerome, according to his own testimony, arranged his entire translation of the divine authority by *cola* and *commata* [12] because of the simplicity of the brothers, in order that with the aid of this device those who were not at all able to understand the marks of punctuation employed in secular letters might pronounce the very sacred texts without blame.

XIII. THE DIVISION OF THE SACRED SCRIPTURE ACCORDING TO ST. AUGUSTINE

1. According to the blessed Augustine [1] the Sacred Scripture is divided into the two Testaments—the Old and the New—as follows:

[11] See chap. v, note 7, above.
[12] See Pref. 9, sentences 1 and 3, and note 15, above.
[1] *De doctrina Christiana* II. viii. 13.

The Old.[2] The History in 22 books, that is, five books of Moses,[3] one book of Joshua, one book of Judges, one book of Ruth, four books of Kings,[4] two books of Chronicles, one book of Job, one book of Tobit, one book of Esther, one book of Judith, two books of Esdras,[5] two books of Maccabees. The Prophets in 22 books: one book of the Psalter of David, three books of Solomon,[6] two books of Jesus the son of Sirach, four books of the Major Prophets (Isaiah, Jeremiah,[7] Daniel, Ezekiel), and 12 books of the Minor Prophets (Hosea, Joel, Amos, Obadiah, Jonah, Micah, Nahum, Habakkuk, Zephaniah, Zechariah, Haggai, Malachi).

The New. The four Gospels, that is, the Gospel according to Matthew, according to Mark, according to Luke, and according to John. The Epistles of the Apostles, that is, one Epistle of the Apostle Paul to the Romans, two to the Corinthians, one to the Galatians, one to the Ephesians, one to the Philippians, two to the Thessalonians, one to the Colossians, two to Timothy, one to Titus, one to Philemon, one to the Hebrews, two Epistles of Peter, three of John, one of Jude, one of James. The Acts of the Apostles in one book. Revelation in one book.

2. In the second book of his work *On Christian Learning* the blessed Augustine, in accordance with the afore-mentioned nine codices, which the Holy Church approves, describes the Sacred Scriptures as being contained in seventy-one books;[8] and if to this number you add the unity of the Holy Trinity, there will result a number appropriately and gloriously perfect in balance.[9]

---

[2] Tobit, Judith, I and II Maccabees, and I and II Jesus the son of Sirach (or The Wisdom of Jesus the Son of Sirach; also called Ecclesiasticus) are now considered deuterocanonical among Roman Catholics and apocryphal among Protestants.

[3] The Pentateuch: Genesis, Exodus, Leviticus, Numbers, and Deuteronomy.

[4] That is, I and II Samuel (called I and II Kings) and I and II Kings (called III and IV Kings).

[5] I Esdras = Ezra; II Esdras = Nehemiah.

[6] That is, Proverbs, Ecclesiastes, and Song of Solomon.

[7] Lamentations is considered a part of Jeremiah.

[8] Cf. viii. 15, above.

[9] Cassiodorus probably refers here to the Septuagint, the Greek translation of the Bible written by 72 scholars. The number was later reduced to a round 70 by the Church Fathers.

XIV. THE DIVISION OF THE SACRED SCRIPTURE
ACCORDING TO THE SEPTUAGINT

1. According to the ancient translation the Sacred Scripture is divided into the two Testaments as follows:

The Old.[1] Genesis, Exodus, Leviticus, Numbers, Deuteronomy, Joshua, Judges, Ruth, four books of Kings,[2] two books of Chronicles, five books of the Psalter,[3] five books of Solomon (that is, Proverbs, Wisdom, Ecclesiasticus, Ecclesiastes, and the Song of Songs),[4] the Prophets (that is, Isaiah, Jeremiah,[5] Ezekiel, Daniel, Hosea, Amos, Micah, Joel, Obadiah, Jonah, Nahum, Habakkuk, Zephaniah, Haggai, Zechariah, and Malachi, which is also known as The Messenger),[6] and Job, Tobit, Esther, Judith, two books of Esdras,[7] and two books of Maccabees.

The New. The four Gospels (that is, Matthew, Mark, Luke, and John), the Acts of the Apostles, the Epistles of Peter to the nations, the Epistles of James,[8] the Epistles of John to the Parthians,[9] the Epistles of Paul to the Romans in one book, to the Corinthians in two books, to the Galatians in one book, to the Philippians in one book, to the Colossians in one book, to the Ephesians [10] in one book, to the Thessalonians in two books,

---

[1] The following books are now considered deuterocanonical by Roman Catholics and apocryphal by Protestants: Wisdom (= The Wisdom of Solomon), Ecclesiasticus (= The Wisdom of Jesus Son of Sirach), Tobit, Judith, and Maccabees. II Esdras (also called III and IV Esdras) is considered apocryphal among both Roman Catholics and Protestants. The Septuagint is known to have included the following deuterocanonical books as well (apocryphal among Protestants): Esther (that is, the passages interpolated by the Alexandrian Jews and regarded as uncanonical by St. Jerome), the three additions to Daniel (The Song of the Three Children, The History of Susanna, and Bel and the Dragon).

[2] That is, I and II Samuel and I and II Kings.

[3] The Psalter, generally thought of as one book, may be divided into five books as follows: chaps. 1–41, 42–72, 73–89, 90–106, 107–150.

[4] That is, the Song of Solomon.

[5] Lamentations is considered a part of Jeremiah.

[6] That is, Malachi ("messenger" in Hebrew) means "the messenger of Jehovah."

[7] Esdras (also called I and II Esdras) = Ezra and Nehemiah.

[8] Jude, here omitted, precedes James in MS V[2]. To James the editors add "to the twelve tribes" ("ad xii tribus").

[9] John's first Epistle is directed to believers generally, but more particularly to Gentiles in Asia Minor, probably in the neighborhood of its chief city, Ephesus.

[10] The Epistle to the Hebrews is here omitted. Θ Ξ Q substitute "Hebreos" for "Ephesios," while H reads: "ad Eph. II ad Col. I ad Hebr. I ad Thess. II."

to Timothy in two books, to Titus in two books, to Philemon in one book, the Revelation of John.

2. The third division is to be found among the other divisions in the larger codex,[11] which is written in clearer script and has ninety-five quaternions containing the translation of the Old Testament by the seventy interpreters in forty-four books; and the twenty-six books of the New Testament are added; and taken together they become seventy books, auguring, perhaps, the number of palm trees which the Hebrew people found at their halting place at Elim.[12]

3. This text, altered by the translations of many scholars, as stated in the prologue of the Psalter, has been left in emended and perfected form by the zealous care of Father Jerome, and we have decided that all three types of division ought to be appended, in order that after a careful consideration and inspection they may seem not to conflict but rather to make one another mutually intelligible. Although many Fathers—that is, St. Hilary, bishop of the city of Poitiers, and Rufinus, priest of Aquileia, and Epiphanius, prelate of Cyprus—and the men assembled at the synod of Nicaea and at that of Chalcedon have made statements on this matter which are not contradictory but varying, all of them, however, through their divisions have adapted the sacred books to appropriate mysteries, just as is generally agreed to have been the case in the harmony of the Evangelists, in whom the faith in events is uniform and the manner of speaking divergent.

4. But inasmuch as the aforesaid Father Augustine gives the following instructions in the second book of his previously mentioned work, *On Christian Learning*,[13] saying: "In case of need, Latin codices (that is, codices of the Old and New Testament) should be corrected from the text of the Greeks, whence every translation subsequent to the Hebrew source has come to us"—on this account I have left you a Greek pandect composed of seventy-five books and containing . . . [14] quaternions in the afore-mentioned eighth bookcase,[15] in which I have of necessity

---

[11] This is apparently the "pandectes Latinus" of v. 2, sentence 7, above.
[12] Exodus 15:27.   [13] II. xv. 22.
[14] MS M shows a lacuna. MS Rotomagensis 490 (*saec.* xii *ex.*) reads "ninety quaternions" here.   [15] viii. 15, sentence 1, above.

assembled other Greek authors in various short works, lest something essential to your very holy instructions seem to be lacking. This number is consecrated to two miraculous events, for seventy-five souls came with the patriarch Jacob from the land of Canaan into the confines of Egypt [16] and Abraham was seventy-five years old when he joyfully received the promise of the Lord.[17]

5. It now remains for us to state at once the manner in which we ought to correct scribal errors in the Sacred Scriptures. For what profit is there in reading many texts and in not knowing what ought to be laudably corrected?

XV. THE CAUTION WHICH ONE SHOULD EMPLOY IN READING THE HEAVENLY AUTHORITY FOR THE PURPOSE OF CORRECTION

1. Do you, therefore, who have unusual knowledge of divine and secular letters and practical ability to discover what is inconsistent with ordinary usage, traverse the sacred texts in the following manner; for that which must be prepared for a simple and not very accomplished congregation ought to be done by a few learned men. On this account correct scribal errors only after a careful study, lest you be justly blamed for trying to emend others hastily; for this kind of correction is in my opinion surely the most excellent, and it is a glorious work for learned men.

2. In the first place, then, do not profane the customary idioms of the Scripture by any presumption, lest because of your desire to make the words intelligible to a lowly mind the purity of the heavenly words (perish the thought!) be destroyed. The idioms of the divine law are in fact called special modes of utterance, modes which ordinary usage is known not to possess, as for example:

"According to the cleanness of my hands," [1] and
"Let my sentence come forth from thy presence"—[2]
"Give ear unto my cry," [3] and
"Pour out your heart before him"— [4]

---

[16] Genesis 46:27.   [17] *Ibid.* 12:4. A reference to the Redemption.
[1] Psalms 17:21, 25 (18:20, 24); cf. 7:9 (7:8).
[2] *Ibid.* 16:2 (17:2).   [3] 38:13 (39:12).   [4] 61:9 (62:8).

"My soul followeth hard after thee"—[5]

"Thou hast greatly enriched it"—[6]

"There shall we rejoice in this thing," [7] and

"And he hath poured it out from this to that"—[8]

"He sent Moses his servant; and Aaron whom he had chosen"—[9]

"Mine eyes have failed for thy word"—[10]

"Let thine hand be with me to save me." [11]

Though ordinary usage is at variance with these expressions and a great many others like them, nevertheless, that authority which is beyond doubt sacred commends them, lest their destruction be permitted. But if you desire to know more about them, read St. Augustine's seven books *On the Modes of Expression,* which he wrote concerning the five books of Moses and the one book of Joshua and the one of Judges, and then you will be able to satisfy your desire in most bountiful fashion. You will, of course, have most abundant opportunity to find similar expressions in the Scriptural authority cited below.

3. Do not weaken certain Hebrew names of persons and places by any modification of form; let an integrity proper to their tongue be preserved in them. Let us change only those letters which can express the grammatical case [12] of the word, inasmuch as it is generally agreed that every one of these names— for example, Seth, Enoch, Lamech, Noah, Shem, Ham and Japheth, Aaron, David and the like— [13] has been applied, through an

---

[5] Psalms 62: 9 (63: 8).   [6] 64: 10 (65: 9).   [7] 65: 6 (66: 6).

[8] 74: 9 (75: 8).   [9] 104: 26 (105: 26).   [10] 118: 82 (119: 82).

[11] 118: 173 (119: 173).

[12] Hebrew words whose endings are analogous to those of Latin words are declined by Cassiodorus as if they were Latin: thus, "Saul," gen. "Saulis" (Mynors 17. 4) ; "Helias," abl. "Helia" (*ibid.* 16. 24) ; "Moyses," acc. "Moysen" (*ibid.* 89. 18) ; etc. Hebrew words whose endings are not analogous are left unchanged by him: thus, "David," nom. (*ibid.* 7. 20), acc. (*ibid.* 16. 19), and abl. (*ibid.* 148. 21) ; "Adam," abl. (*ibid.* 56. 27) ; "Chanaan," gen. (41. 12) ; and "Bethlehem," abl. (59. 20). Though the entire list quoted at 43. 7–15 belongs to the second group, none of the words except "David" can be used as evidence since none occurs in an oblique case in the *Inst.* Cassiodorus' "qualitatem" is of course not the technical word of Probus or Donatus (see Heinrich Keil, *Grammatici latini* [Leipzig, 1864], IV, 5, 373), which indicates either *nomina propria* (names of persons or gods) or *nomina appellativa* (names of animals or things).

[13] These names have the following meanings in Hebrew: "appointed," "dedicated," "destroyer," "rest" (or "wandering"), meaning uncertain, "warm," "extension," "light"(?), "beloved."

interpretation of the name itself, to some great mystery. Let us, moreover, with equal piety leave unchanged the names of such places as Zion, Horeb, Gihon, Hermon, and the like.[14]

4. In the third place, things which have a good and a bad meaning, as for example [15] "mount," "lion," "cedar," "lion's whelp," "shout," "man," "fruit," "cup," "calf," "shepherd," "treasure," "worm," "dog," and the like, are not to be profaned in any respect whatever. And those words which are used in place of other words are not to be changed; examples follow:

Satan, "he who departs from the upright path"—
"to wash one's hands," meaning "not to take part in"— [16]
"feet," used to indicate "the performance of an act"— [17]
"expectation," frequently used by the Scripture for "hope"— [18]
"once," in the sense of "unchangeable determination"— [19]
"to swear" by God, meaning "to affirm." [20]

Let us desire to have these things revealed to us by expounders; let us not mutilate any of them with impious inclination.

5. Nor should those words be altered [21] which are sometimes found to be opposed to the rules of ordinary grammar but are justified by the authority of many codices, since that which is known to have been said with the inspiration of the Lord cannot be corrupted, as for example: [22]

"We have not forgotten thee," [23] and that famous phrase,
"Bloody and deceitful men"— [24]
"The temple was built," [25] and

[14] The meanings are: "lifted up," "desert," "river," "lofty."
[15] Cf. *Comm. Psalt.* under the words which follow.
[16] Adrian, *Isagoge in Scripturas,* § 70; Psalms, 25:6 (26:6) and 72:13 (73:13); Matthew 27:24.
[17] *Isagoge,* § 74; cf. *Comm. Psalt.,* 37. 17.
[18] *Isagoge,* § 76; Psalms 38:8 (39:7), *et al.*
[19] *Isagoge,* § 56; cf. Augustine *De civitate Dei* v. 9. Psalms 61:12 (62:11) and 88:36 (89:35).
[20] *Isagoge,* § 79; Psalms 88:4 (89:3), *et al.*
[21] The word "altered" is almost equivalent to "inflected" here.
[22] The grammatical violations are of course not apparent in the English renderings given below.
[23] Psalms 43:18 (44:17); "obliti sumus" with acc.
[24] *Ibid.* 54:24 (55:23); "viri sanguinum," etc.
[25] Masculine adjective with neuter noun. Or "he built the temple." Zechariah 8:9.

"His head shall be shaved," [26] and

"She shall swell in her belly" for "her belly shall swell"— [27]

"If any man's wife shall have gone astray," [28] and

"They shall put upon the altar all the vessels thereof, where-with they minister about it"— [29]

"The land that they dwell in," [30] and

"The searchers brought up an evil report of the land which they had searched"— [31]

"My only one from the hand of the dog," [32] and

"The rivers shall clap their hands"— [33]

"Then shall all the trees of the woods rejoice." [34]

6. And inasmuch as the inflection and character of nouns and verbs cannot sometimes suit human rules, but the general wish of the Church favors their use, let the authority of two or three ancient and emended codices be sought (for it is written,[35] "In the mouth of two or three witnesses shall every word stand") and let no change be made in that which is supported by holy communication; [36] in the twenty-first Psalm,[37] for example, "To a people that shall be born, which the Lord hath made," and in those words of the Gospel [38] "Go ye therefore, and teach all the nations, baptizing them [39] in the name of the Father, and of the Son, and of the Holy Ghost," and similarly in the one hundred forty-third Psalm [40] "Happy is that people, whose God is their Lord," and the like.

---

[26] Numbers 6:9. This is a loose use of the reflexive *suum*.

[27] Numbers 5:27: "inflabitur ventrem" for "inflabitur ventre."

[28] *Ibid.* 5:12: "viri viri [*sic!*] si," etc.

[29] *Ibid.* 4:14: "in quibus" followed by "in ipsis" causes difficulty.

[30] *Ibid.* 13:19 (13:18): "terra in qua habitant in ea."

[31] *Ibid.* 13:33 (13:32): "terrae quam exploraverant eam."

[32] Psalms 21:21 (22:20): "hand" is the difficult word.

[33] *Ibid.* 97:8 (98:8): "manibus in se" is a troublesome phrase and the metaphor is unusual.

[34] *Ibid.* 95:12 (96:12): a bold metaphor.

[35] Deuteronomy 19:15, *et al.*

[36] That is, the Sacred Scriptures.

[37] Psalms 21:32 (22:31): or for "which . . . made" read "that the Lord hath done this."

[38] Matthew 28:19.

[39] "eos" = masculine whereas a feminine might be strictly expected here after *gentes* ("nations").

[40] Psalms 143:15 (144:15). The apparent difficulty here is the presence of "eorum" as well as "cuius."

7. Do not, therefore, wholly follow the rules of Latin style, that is, the *Quadriga* of Messius,[41] when you are convinced of the authority of ancient codices; for upon occasion it is advantageous to overlook the idioms of human speech and to observe instead the criterion of divine communication. Do not correct the prosaic beginning and ending of an heroic verse; do not venture to reject five long syllables and as many short ones; let a laudable neglect hide a triple trochee. Pay no attention at all to the mispronunciation of final *m* elided before a vowel and to the hiatus of vowels, since matters which teachers of the liberal arts are known to preserve regularly cannot have any place here. The avoidance of these faults is proper in human words; in divine communications, however, such stylistic arrangements are found by no means blameworthy. May a phrase which is known to have pleased God remain uncorrupted wherever it occurs, so that it may shine with its own splendor and not be subject to the enfeebling influence [42] of human desire. For it instructs the untutored pleasantly, and in becoming fashion it delights the learned in proportion to their reverence.

8. After the general treatment above, in which we have stated that the idioms of the divine law ought not to be altered and so forth, the subject prompts me to set down also, in the manner of our ancestors, the detailed treatment which follows, in order that we may arrive more clearly at the small points. For how could the most learned Aristotle have made his work *Perihermenias* clear if in his treatment of every subject he had not preserved the order of divisions, subdivisions, and subordinate subdivisions? Following his example, we shall now state the letters concerning which scribal errors ought to be corrected.

9. In the case of words which are the objects of prepositions that govern the accusative and the ablative, pay careful attention to rest and to motion, inasmuch as scribes without knowledge of grammar are acknowledged to make most of their mistakes on this point; for if you add or take away the letter *m* indiscrimi-

---

[41] Arusianus Messius (*ca.* A.D. 395). His work is so called (= "the four-horse team") because it contains examples of style taken from Terence, Vergil, Cicero, and Sallust.

[42] "Carpienda." For *carpio, -ire = carpo, -ere* see *Thesaurus linguae Latinae*, Vol. III.

nately, the whole expression is confused. Examine carefully the cases of nouns, except those which have but one case-ending, and the conjugations of verbs which are not defective, and all the parts of speech (where, however, the sacred authority does not impugn such action) and preserve that which fits each particular passage, lest with order of words confounded an unseemly confusion (perish the thought!) possess the whole. Do not allow *b* to remain for *v*, *v* for *b*, *o* for *u*, or *n* for *m* if the letters are corrupt and contrary to the rules of correct spelling; remove an aspiration if it is superfluous or add one if it is fitting. Where, however, you are permitted to do so, preserve carefully the cases of nouns and the tenses of verbs; for in the authority [43] you will frequently find things which disagree with established custom, and these you are not at liberty to alter. But in such instances let the reading of the emended codices be retained; recorrect other readings which have been erroneously changed, inasmuch as scribes offend rather than please when they do not know how to observe Latin usage methodically. Do not allow *a* [44] to stand at the end of an adverb; do not, on the other hand, remove *a* [45] from the genitive case. For the sake of euphony, moreover, we do well to change many letters because of those which follow, as for example in such words as *illuminatio, irrisio, immutabilis, impius, improbus*. Take away the superfluous *r* from *narratio;* [46] for a spelling of the noun with a single *r* comes from *gnarus*, that is "skillful" or "practiced." *Quod* should be written with *d*, not *t*, when it is a pronoun; with *t*, not *d*, when it is a numeral adverb. *Quicquam*—for the sake of euphony, which we are taught to observe, *c* ought to be placed in the first syllable rather than *d*. But why say more? Do you, however, take up the necessary corrections in due order in accordance with the rules laid down by writers on this art, [47] lest the glorious modulation of articulate speech become instead discordant and unseemly because of pollution by strange letters.

---

[43] The Sacred Scriptures.

[44] That is, in the combination *ae* (hence V² reads Æ).

[45] In *ae* (V² reads Æ again).

[46] The *r* is regularly retained, however. The information in this sentence and in the next two as well comes from Papirianus (*De orthographia*, pp. 159-160).

[47] That is, rhetoric or grammar.

10. Frequently reread the ancient orthographers. In chapter xxx below, where one reads about scribes, I have noted the need for making excerpts from these writers to provide useful information for copyists; moreover, to the separate book in which I have placed these excerpts I have given the title *On Orthography*. And so it happens that it is profitable for the student to read this book, for in it he perceives what he should not by any means profane in the Sacred Scriptures, and the places in which generally supposed faults are corrected necessarily become more widely known.

11. If, however, some words are found to be set down irrationally, one should either correct them intrepidly from the codices which the blessed Jerome emended in his edition of the Septuagint and translated from the Hebrew or, as the blessed Augustine says,[48] have recourse to the Greek pandect,[49] which is known to have collected all divine law; and let not those to whom it is possible refuse to consult the Hebrew Scripture and its teachers, for it is suitable for a seemly emendation to come from the same source from which an authoritative translation came to us. For rightly did our Fathers concern themselves particularly with this matter, namely, that the tunic of the Lord our Savior, which the cruel soldiers were not allowed to cut,[50] be not put in the power of unskilled emenders. May the Holy Spirit hear unblemished what It has bestowed; may It receive unadulterated what It has given; then will It perceive that we are faithful to It if we do not rend Its words with any presumption. For in what manner do we desire to be saved if (perish the thought!) we willfully destroy the means of salvation?

12. But in order to add apparent embellishment to all these things, place marks of punctuation in every section of the text, marks which the Greeks call *theses*,[51] that is, points very small and also round (except in the translation of St. Jerome, which is arranged in *cola* and *commata,* as already described in the preface) [52] because they make the composition plain and clear, since, as is pointed out below, they are distinctively suitable to

---

[48] Cf. xiv. 4, sentence 1, above. [49] *Ibid.*
[50] John 19:23–24. [51] θέσεις.
[52] Preface, § 9.

the individual passages. What an experience it is to pass with uninterrupted step through the most sacred thoughts, and to understand accurately the saving nature of the injunctions; to fix properly one's own limits for the measured voice, and to divide a whole composition into members in such a way that these members, viewed in the light of one's divisions, become beautiful! For if our body needs to be known through its members, why should a text be left with its parts apparently disordered? These marks or points of punctuation are, as it were, paths for thoughts and beacon lights for words, and render the readers as easily taught as they would be if they were being instructed by the most intelligible interpreters. The first is the half stop, the second the quarter stop,[53] and the third the full stop; it is generally agreed that they were invented by our ancestors in order that the voice, when tired from long speaking, might regain its strength by employing pauses at definite intervals. And if, O eager reader, you prefer to know them well, read Donatus, for he can instruct you briefly and carefully in this matter. We bear in mind that we have set down these marks of punctuation in the Psalter which serves as a pattern, and with the Lord's help we have in great measure brought light to its obscure passages by employing a remedy of this sort.

13. The number seven is so complete in a twofold sense [54] that it is quite clear in my opinion what matters we should refrain from correcting and what matters we should venture to correct in Holy Scriptures. But, however, if this need for correction can be satisfied in another way, may you desire to satisfy it, lest we seem after man's fashion to have left some necessary thing undone.

14. We must now speak about the manner in which we ought to emend texts other than the Holy Scriptures. Let every corrector read commentaries on the divine law, epistles, sermons, and books of the ancients in such a way as to associate their correction with the works of teachers of secular letters, and wherever errors are found in excellent writers, let the corrector in-

---

[53] That is, *subdistinctio,* weaker than the half-stop.

[54] It is perfect in its mystic significance and indeclinable in form. The number seven is here considered of sufficient importance to warrant its being introduced here as a separate topic.

trepidly set the mistakes right again, since the aforesaid writers should be thought of as having written their words in such manner as to have observed the grammatical rules which they had learned. Let the epistles of the Fathers too, the words and books of various writers, and the homilies and disputes of the faithful with heretics be read with great zeal, since they reveal the conflicting passages in the Sacred Scripture pleasantly and diligently, in order that with certain lamps properly lighted, as it were, in the Church of the Lord the whole may with His help shine clearly and brightly. If anything is discovered in them suitable for the expounding of the Sacred Scriptures, do not hesitate to associate it with the divine books, as we have done in the books of Kings. Many rather extensive remarks on the divine books are found to have been made by very excellent writers when opportunity offered in another work, and these remarks are of course properly accommodated to the sacred authority. Hence I beg you, when you have fully read not merely those codices which we leave you but also those which you will have the good fortune to discover, to finish more perfectly in Christ's name that which we have by no means been able to expound because of our scant reading.

15. I also beseech you who venture to make corrections to form the added letters so beautifully that they may be thought to be the product of scribes. It is surely inappropriate for anything unsightly to be found in this glorious work to offend the eyes of students hereafter. Consider, then, the nature of the cause entrusted to you, the serving of Christians, the guarding of the Church's treasure, the lighting of souls. And consequently take pains lest there be any residue of faultiness in its truth, of alteration in its purity, of erroneous letters in its correctness.

16. But inasmuch as we have first treated the nine codices of the divine law and with the Lord's help have described the writers of introductory works and also the expounders of the codices with all the diligence in our power, and have subsequently referred to the three divisions of all the divine law which were given us by our ancestors, and have added next the cautious manner in which the heavenly authority ought to be emended lest it be rent by audacious presumption or lest an unseemly confusion

be handed on to our descendants, we must now discuss fully the excellence of the Divine Scripture, in order that every passage may be filled with an appropriate sweetness.

XVI. ON THE EXCELLENCE OF THE DIVINE SCRIPTURE

1. Consider, most excellent companions, how wonderful, how agreeable are the ordered words which flow through the Divine Scriptures, the object of ever-increasing desire, the endless sufficiency, the glorious object for which the blessed hunger; an excessive desire to attain this object is not blamed, but extreme eagerness to do so is praised—and justly so, for from them comes the knowledge of things which pertain to eternal salvation and on their account everlasting life is offered to those who believe them and carry out their bidding. They describe the past without falsehood; they show the present as more than it seems; they report the future as if it had already been completed. Everywhere in them truth holds sway; everywhere the divine excellence beams forth; everywhere matters of use to mankind are related. And in view of the condition of earthly affairs, the heavenly truth is announced to us, in accordance with our intellectual capacity, by means of parables and dark sayings, as the truth itself bears witness in the seventy-seventh Psalm:[1] "I will open my mouth in parables, I will utter dark sayings from the beginning." They also hand down to us, in order that all burdens may be relieved, a knowledge of the Holy Trinity which is worthy of adoration, a knowledge which mankind has not known, because of his blind and lamentable devotion to idolatry for so many generations; they permit us to know that the Father, the Son, and the Holy Ghost, one God, the [2] creator and ruler of all living things, does "whatsoever he pleaseth in heaven and in earth."[3] If you seek his compassion, give ear to the compendious expression "A helper in due time in tribulation";[4] if you seek his power, hear "And who shall resist thy power?";[5] if you seek his justice, read "And he shall judge the world in equity."[6]

---

[1] Psalms 77:2 (78:2).   [2] The more recent MSS add "powerful."
[3] Psalms 134:6 (135:6).   [4] Psalms 9:10 (9:9).
[5] Psalms 75:8 (76:7); Wisdom 11:12.   [6] Psalms 9:9 (9:8) and 95:13 (96:13).

God in His entirety is most clearly shown to be omnipresent in the words of the psalm-writer: "Whither shall I go from thy spirit? and whither shall I flee from thy presence? If I ascend up into heaven, thou art there: if I descend into hell, thou art present," [7] and the remaining words contained in the sacred books concerning His majesty.

2. Human reason did not discover these books, but heavenly virtue communicated them to holy men; and they can be well understood only when a devout mind believes that they state what is true and useful. What utility and agreeableness will you not find in these books, if you approach them with undefiled clearness of mind? The entire text is full of excellence, a communication not idly uttered,[8] and it does not delay the performance of its promises, bringing eternal salvation to the obedient and decreeing everlasting punishment for the proud. We are therefore admonished not merely to listen to it but also to fulfill its bidding with holy works. At one moment it points out God's fraternal charity; at another it recommends contempt of present affairs, which are about to pass away; at still another it tells you to be mindful of that heavenly home in which you will abide forever. It counsels patience; it gives hope; it praises the benefits of humility; it always reproaches baneful pride; it prompts the frequent giving of pious alms. And then, in the most indulgent of all compassionate acts, the Judge himself bears witness that he has accepted repentance, since he forgives the words with which the most merciful Redeemer is questioned; he causes dread in order to set men right; he threatens in order to spare; and he enjoins us to live in such a manner as to deserve to be the companions of the pious angels and to cause that which is agreeable beyond measure and everlasting to be accomplished for us, namely, "that God may be all in all"; [9] and finally he enjoins us to live in such a way that "we may know him as he is" [10] and may be filled so full of his glory as not to be wearied by any spiritual barrenness arising out of further need. Who, then, would not seek to obey such injunctions except the man who is hastening in every way to eternal doom? To neglect the pre-

---

[7] Psalms 138:7–8 (139:7–8).   [8] Cf. III Kings 8:56 (I Kings 8:56).
[9] I Corinthians 15:28.   [10] I John 3:2.

cepts of one's Redeemer and to fulfill the desires of the most
unmerciful adversary [11] is to surpass all folly. There are as many
rewards as words; as many punishments as sentences! No instruction is useless providing the tongue is not silent concerning
mighty works. Would that their praises might never cease! Surely
the occasion for sin would be taken away if the restless mind of
mortals had no idle time.

3. In addition to these benefits, which are given for great
piety, we also have the adorable and venerable knowledge of the
Holy Trinity—a kind of life completely unknown to heathens,
who are unaware of sin. It now remains for us to name the men
who have had something reverent to say about the Holy Trinity
in their books. To strengthen our faith and to guard against the
snares of heretics you should read the thirteen books which the
blessed Hilary has written on the Holy Trinity in a profound
and very fluent treatise. You should also reflect carefully upon
the very clear and charming books which St. Ambrose wrote on
the same subject and sent to the emperor Gratian as well as the
fifteen remarkably profound books which St. Augustine wrote
on the Trinity. If, however, anyone chooses to get some knowledge concerning the Father, the Son, and the Holy Ghost briefly
and prefers not to tire himself with long reading, let him read
the book which the bishop Nicetas has written *On Faith,*[12] and,
filled with the perspicuity of heavenly teaching, he will be brought
expeditiously to the contemplation of God; this book is joined
to those which St. Ambrose composed and sent to the emperor
Gratian. O the incalculable kindness and excellence of the Creator! "The heavens were opened";[13] the Holy Trinity, disclosed to the hearts of the faithful, shone brightly; and pagan-
ism, which had seized an honor not its own, was confuted and
departed from the true Lord.

4. Also useful for the imparting of ecclesiastical instruction
are the three mellifluous books of the aforesaid St. Ambrose *On
Duties* and also the one book of the blessed Augustine *On the*

[11] The devil.

[12] Nicetas (*floruit ca.* 414), bishop of Remesiana in Dacia, wrote six books "conpe-
tentibus ad baptismum instructionis," of which Book III (*De fide unicae maiestatis*)
is the one mentioned here.

[13] Matthew 3:16.

True Religion and his four books *On Christian Learning;* and likewise the one book which he composed *On the Christian Struggle,* particularly necessary for you who strive in the Christian contest in this despised life. And in like manner you should very zealously read his book on moral philosophy, as it were, which he composed for the teaching and correcting of morals by drawing upon the divine authority and named *The Mirror.* Let us read with tireless zeal the twenty-two books which St. Augustine has written *On the City of God,* books in which disordered Babylon, the city of the devil, and glorious Jerusalem, the city of Christ the Lord, are pointed out as existing with suitable differences in man's way of life. He has also written five questions on the New Testament and sent them to the priest Honoratus and has written eighty-three others after extraordinary deliberation. Moreover, if after careful examination anyone desires to correct his own words and not to leave them rashly, let him read assiduously the two books of St. Augustine's *Retractations,*[14] in order that he embellish his own work through imitation of the other's, and he will perceive what an abundance of wisdom the divine favor has conferred upon the most blessed Father, in order that he whom no one, perhaps, could blame may after careful reconsideration correct himself. It is a long task to mention all the separate works of this man, since there exists a codex by no means small containing an index of his short works [15] and, although it gives a concise account of what he has said,[16] it nevertheless occupies numerous pages of text.

XVII. ON CHRISTIAN HISTORIANS

1. In addition to the various writers of treatises Christian studies also possess narrators of history, who, calm in their ecclesiastical gravity, recount the shifting movements of events and the unstable history of kingdoms with eloquent but very cautious splendor. Because they narrate ecclesiastical matters and describe

[14] That is, new treatments, with corrections, of subjects treated in his previous works.

[15] Perhaps the *Indiculus librorum Sancti Augustini* written *ca.* 432 (together with a *Vita*) by Possidius, bishop of Calama, the pupil and friend of St. Augustine.

[16] That is, the titles of his works.

changes which occur at various times, they must always of necessity instruct the minds of readers in heavenly affairs, since they
strive to assign nothing to chance, nothing to the weak power of
gods, as pagans have done, but to assign all things truly to the
will of the Creator. Such is Josephus,[1] almost a second Livy, who
is very diffuse in his *Jewish Antiquities,* a prolix work which, in
a letter to Lucinus Betticus,[2] Father Jerome says he himself
could not translate because of its great size. We, however, have
had it laboriously translated into Latin in twenty-two books [3] by
our friends, since it is exceedingly subtle and extensive. Josephus
has also written with remarkable grace seven other books entitled *The Jewish Captivity,* the translation of which is ascribed
by some to Jerome, by others to Ambrose, and by still others to
Rufinus; and since the translation is ascribed to men of this sort,
its extraordinary merits are explicitly shown. The next work to
be read is the history [4] written by Eusebius in Greek in ten books,
but translated and completed in eleven books by Rufinus, who
has added subsequent events. Among the Greek writers Socrates,[5]
Sozomenus,[6] and Theodoretus [7] have written on events subsequent to Eusebius' history; with God's help we have had the
work of these men translated and placed in a single codex in
twelve books by the very fluent Epiphanius, lest eloquent Greece
boast that it has something essential which it judges you do not
possess. Orosius,[8] who compares Christian times with pagan, is
also at hand, if you desire to read him. Marcellinus [9] too has
traversed his journey's path in laudable fashion, completing four
books on the nature of events and the location of places with
most decorous propriety; I have likewise left his work for you.

2. Eusebius has written chronicles,[10] which are the mere shad-
ows of history and very brief reminders of the times, in Greek;
and Jerome has translated this work into Latin and extended it

---

[1] A.D. 37–*ca.* 100.   [2] *Epistula* 71, § 5.
[3] That is, twenty books on the *Jewish Antiquities* plus two *Contra Apionem.*
[4] *Historiarum ecclesiasticarum libri X* (up to A.D. 325).
[5] *Historiarum ecclesiasticarum libri VII* (up to A.D. 439).
[6] *Historiarum ecclesiasticarum libri IX* (the same period as that covered by Socrates).
[7] *Historiarum ecclesiasticarum libri V* (written in 448/9).
[8] *Historiarum adversum paganos libri VII* (the events from Adam to A.D. 417).
[9] Marcellinus comes, *floruit ca.* 534.   [10] From the earliest times to A.D. 324.

to his own time in excellent manner.[11] Eusebius has been followed
in turn by the aforesaid Marcellinus the Illyrian, who is said to
have acted first as secretary of the patrician [12] Justinian, but
who later, with the Lord's help, upon the improvement of his
employer's civil status,[13] faithfully guided his work [14] from the
time of the emperor Theodosius to the beginning of the trium-
phant rule of the emperor Justinian,[15] in order that he who had
first been grateful in the service of his employer might later appear to be most devoted during his imperial rule. St. Prosper has
also written chronicles which extend from Adam to the time of
Genseric and the plundering of the City.[16] Perhaps you will find
other later writers, inasmuch as there is no dearth of chroniclers
despite the continual succession of one age after another. But
when, O diligent reader, you are filled with these works and your
mind gleams with divine light, read St. Jerome's book *On Famous Men,*[17] a work whose brief discussion has honored the various Fathers and their works; then read a second book, by Gennadius [18] of Marseilles, who has very faithfully treated and
carefully examined the writers on divine law. I have left you
these two books joined in a single volume, lest delay in learning
the matter be caused by the need of using various codices.

3. The authors of many venerable texts follow. These most
learned authors either compose books with divine inspiration, or
comfort each other with the easy elegance of letters, or describe
the people in a very charming sermon, or strive in an exceedingly
lively contest with heretics in such a way that certain ones of
their number enter controversies with unusual zeal and contend
in the midst of judges with glorious disputation. Thus, with the
Lord's help the faithful are strengthened by the destruction of
the faithless. You will, then, be able to choose for yourself amid
this most holy and most eloquent multitude of Fathers the one

[11] *Chronicon* (produced in 380/1; events up to 378 are described).

[12] A nontransferable title of person high in office at court from the time of Con-
stantine; usually awarded to one who had held the consulate.

[13] That is, his accession to the imperial throne.   [14] *Chronicon.*

[15] 379–534. The extant work also has a continuation as far as 548. (Theodosius
was emperor 379–395 and Justinian 527–565.)

[16] In 455, with which the later form of his work closes.

[17] An index of Christian writers.

[18] He continues Jerome's *On Famous Men* to 496.

with whom you converse most pleasantly. It is, moreover, difficult to state how frequently they effectually reveal the Sacred Scriptures at most suitable points, so that, as you read along, you unexpectedly become acquainted with that which you realize you have carelessly neglected. These most learned authors are extraordinary witnesses because of their various merits, and the ecclesiastical sky shines with them as if with glittering stars.

XVIII. ON ST. HILARY

1. Among their number St. Hilary, bishop of Poitiers, a profoundly subtle and cautious disputant, walks majestically and, reverently bringing the deep mysteries of the Sacred Scriptures before us, with God's help causes the things which were previously veiled in dark parables to be seen clearly.

XIX. ON ST. CYPRIAN

1. It is impossible to explain completely how useful, among other writers, the very blessed Cyprian is (except in the matter of repetition of baptism, which the practice and theory of the Church have rejected); a remarkably skillful declaimer and a wonderful teacher, he is like the ointment that runs down to make all things pleasant.[1] How many doubters he has saved from apostasy! How many apostates he has restored to spiritual health with his very powerful preaching! How many martyrs he has led all the way to martyrdom! And, lest he fail to attain the ideal described in his preaching, he too, with the Lord's aid, was adorned with the crown of martyrdom. Among the other famous monuments of his erudition which he has left us is a little book written with rhetorical charm to explain the Lord's Prayer, which is ever set as an invincible shield against the deceitful vices.

XX. ON ST. AMBROSE

1. St. Ambrose, too, utterer of eloquent speech, impassioned, but dignified, very agreeable in his calm [1] persuasion, a man

---

[1] Cf. Psalms 132:2 (133:2).
[1] Inviolenta: cf. the technical use of *violentus* and *violatio* for the form of argu-

whose teaching was like his own life, since the divine grace indicated its approval of him by no small miracles . . .

XXI. ON ST. JEROME

1. The blessed Jerome, distinguished propagator of the Latin tongue—who in his translation of the Divine Scripture has given us such a perfect rendering that it is practically unnecessary for us to consult the Hebrew sources, since he has filled us with the great richness of his eloquence—has blessed us, for whom with the Lord's help he has deigned to write, with numerous books and copious letters. Graceful, learned, charming, he turns his talents in every possible direction with ready fullness of style. At one moment he speaks softly and pleasantly to the meek, and at another he completely humbles the proud, now retaliating against his detractors with the necessary biting severity, now praising virginity, now defending chaste marriages, now extolling highly the glorious struggles of the virtues, now blaming wrongdoing on the part of priests and monks. But nonetheless, whenever opportunity is offered, he intermingles illustrations drawn from pagan peoples by way of agreeable variety, explaining the whole, embellishing the whole, and ever gliding along eloquently and evenly through various kinds of argument. Though he extends some books to a great length, nevertheless, one is always sad at reaching the end because of the charm of his words. I believe that he lived in Bethlehem and had leisure to write for no other reason than that his eloquence might shine for us like the sun rising in the east in that land of miracles.

2. He has written and sent an extraordinary letter [1] to Paulinus, who was first a senator and then a priest, teaching the cautious manner in which he should read the Sacred Scriptures, and in it he has pointed out the excellence of every book of the Old and the New Testament briefly but wonderfully. If I had read his letter earlier, I should perhaps have been satisfied to yield to his eloquence and to say nothing on this subject. But since our remarks in the work just completed with the Lord's help are

---

mentation which destroys a point made by an adversary and shows it to be favorable to our cause rather than to his.

[1] *Epistula* liii.

different from his, I believe that the diligent reader will not be employed unprofitably in the present work. He wrote for a reader untutored in divine law but nevertheless accomplished in secular literature, in order that he might compose a book on the emperor Theodosius wisely and elegantly; at that time apparently he did not have [2] a large number of authors of his own country whom he might recommend for reading one after the other, inasmuch as the soldiers of Christ had up to that time been laboring with the sweat that brings salvation in the training school of the divine law; and he himself later wrote many things in their midst. Our case has been different, first because we have written for the instruction of simple and unpolished brothers, in order that they may be filled with an abundance of Heavenly Scriptures by reading many authors who have been explained even in our own time; in order that they may be laudably imbued, not so much with us, who are poor in this matter, as with the copious and ancient Fathers. But lest those who have not attended worldly schools lack something, we have felt that they ought to be reminded, in the second book, of the arts as well as the sciences of secular letters, in order that skill in worldly letters, which except for the additions of certain learned men is known to have arisen from the Sacred Scriptures, may serve simple men as their slave. Consequently we are not blamed for our unusual presumption, and moments of thankfulness may perhaps arise for our relative lack of humility.

XXII. ON ST. AUGUSTINE

1. The distinguished teacher, the most blessed Augustine, subduer of heretics, defender of the faithful, and victor in famous contests, though exceptionally difficult and abstruse in some books, is so unusually clear in others that he is understood even by children. His clear words are charming; his abstruse words are richly packed with usefulness. If anyone should desire to know the liveliness of his intellect, let him read the books of his *Confessions*,[1] in which he reports that he has learned all the

[2] In his monastery at Bethlehem.
[1] *Confessions* IV. xvi.

mathematical sciences without a teacher, though others may scarcely reach that goal even with the help of learned expositors. With a full explanation he discloses our symbol,[2] the surety of our faith, the evidence of an upright heart, the undissoluble mystery of that which is promised us,[3] in order that through deeper knowledge of those things which we profess to believe we may most carefully keep our vows. One should also read the book in which he succinctly treats the various heresies subsequent to the bishop Epiphanius, since it is unnatural for a sane mind to find pleasure in moving upon those rocks upon which it [4] knows another man's ship has been wrecked. The opinions of those whom the provident Church has condemned should be completely avoided, and, if anyone dares to hold an heretical opinion in the future, shun it with unusual care.

XXIII. ON THE ABBOT EUGIPPIUS AND THE ABBOT DIONYSIUS

1. It is also proper for you to read the necessary works of the priest Eugippius, whom we ourselves have seen, a man to be sure not so accomplished in secular letters, but very well read in the Divine Scriptures. Selecting very profound questions and ideas and various other matters from the works of St. Augustine at the house of our relative Proba, a holy virgin,[1] he assembled them in accordance with the disposition required and arranged them in three hundred thirty-eight sections. This codex will be read with profit in my opinion, for the diligence of a learned man has been hidden in a single work, and this work can scarcely be found even in a great library.

2. Even today the Catholic Church produces illustrious men who are conspicuous for the elegance of their laudable learning. In our time there was a monk Dionysius, Scythian in race but altogether Roman in customs, a man exceedingly learned in both tongues,[2] imitating in his own deeds the righteousness about

---

[2] This and the next three expressions describe the Creed.
[3] That is, the promise of salvation.   [4] I translate *cognoverit* (*U Q et al.*).
[1] That is, a nun. She belonged to the family of the Anicii, whose library furnished Eugippius with the materials for his study. She wrote (in the fourth century) a *cento* on the creation of the world and on the Gospels.
[2] Greek and Latin.

which he had read in the books of the Lord. He had discussed the Divine Scriptures with such a great desire to know them and had comprehended them so well that whenever he was questioned he always had a suitable reply ready without any delay. He read philosophy with me and, through the Lord's beneficence, lived a long life in the manner of a glorious teacher. I am ashamed to state the presence of qualities in my colleague which I cannot discover in myself. He had great simplicity coupled with wisdom, humility coupled with learning, conciseness in speech coupled with eloquence, so that he set himself up as superior to no man, not even the lowliest servants, though without doubt he was worthy of conversations with kings. May he who used to pray with us pray for us, in order that we may now be helped by the kindness of him whose prayer is our support on this earth. At the request of Stephanus, bishop of Salona, as an expression of his own practices, he wrote *The Ecclesiastical Canons* [3] from Greek models with great and splendid eloquence, for he was a clear and fluent writer, and the Roman Church honors these canons today with constant use. You should read them too with unremitting zeal, lest you seem culpably to be without knowledge of such authoritative ecclesiastical rules. He also translated many other works which can be adapted to the service of the Church from Greek into Latin; he was wont to exhibit such great skill in his use of Latin and Greek as to translate into Latin without hesitancy whatever Greek books he took in his hands and, in turn, to translate Latin books into Greek in such fashion that one would believe that the words which streamed from his mouth with uninterrupted speed were actually written down.

3. It is a long task to narrate everything which concerns this man. Among other excellent qualities he had this unusual virtue, namely, not to despise taking part in conversations with the laity, though he had devoted himself wholly to God. He was very chaste, though he saw other men's wives daily; gentle, though he was struck by the furious whirlwind of raging men. Moved by the sting of conscience, he used to pour forth tears when he heard the prattling words of hilarity; he used to abstain from food without being censured by those who dined; and so gladly

[3] Canons which concern the government and discipline of the Church.

did he attend banquets that upon invitation he always displayed
his spiritual riches amid the corporeal feasts. If he occasionally
ate, however, he ate sparingly, and he took nothing but food
of a common sort. On this account I consider it the highest type
of patience to be present amid human allurements and to preserve the capacity for abstinence. But, if we may recount the
good qualities of his mind, he was completely orthodox, completely and perseveringly attached to the rules of his forefathers,
and, as all admitted, possessed of a remarkable knowledge of
whatever information readers may seek to find in various writers. Base men strive artfully to foist certain works upon his
glorious name, in order that they may thereby excuse their own
mistakes to some extent. But having already left the perversity
of the present life and having been admitted with the Lord's aid
to the peace which the Church brings, he must now be considered
a companion of the servants [4] of God.

4. Perhaps, moreover, I should narrate the remaining details
of this holy man's life, for they have been disclosed to us with
completely proved truth. In their stead, however, we must carry
out our plan, lest, while we are bound to fulfill one promise, we
seem to prolong our account of something else with unsuitable
loquacity. And in order that no deception concerning the rules
of our faith may harm you, read the materials which you have
at hand—the records of the council of Ephesus and those of the
council of Chalcedon, and also the *Encyclicals,*[5] that is, the letters of confirmation which have to do with the latter council;
and if you read them diligently, on no occasion will the cunning
of wicked men prevail over you.

XXIV. GENERAL RECAPITULATION: THE ZEAL
WITH WHICH THE HOLY SCRIPTURES
OUGHT TO BE READ

1. Let us therefore take pains, and after the introductory
books let us read the authority [1] and its expositors assiduously,
and let us follow with pious zeal the paths of knowledge discov-

---

[4] That is, the saints.
[5] On the *Codex Encyclius* of the Council of Chalcedon cf. xi. 2, above.
[1] The Scriptures.

ered by the labor of the Fathers, and let us not aim with a greedy superfluity at exceedingly empty questions. Let us consider as divine beyond doubt that which is found to be said rationally in the most excellent commentators; if anything happens to be found out of harmony and inconsistent with the rules of the Fathers, let us decide that it should be avoided. Indeed the source of the gravest heresy is the liking of the whole in the case of authors who excite suspicion and the injudicious desire to defend what one finds; for it is written "Prove all things; hold fast that which is good." [2]

2. But to sum up the things which should be mentioned, everything which ancient expositors have said well should be punctiliously retained; lest we tire ourselves with fruitless labor, the things which have remained uninvestigated by them should be examined thoroughly, first, to see what good qualities they possess or to what practices they will lead us, and, second, to see what we shall accomplish by reading them. For even though a text may seem unusually simple and even though it be clear in its historical narration, nevertheless, it either urges justice at one time or confutes impiety at another; it either commends tolerance or blames the faults of inconstancy; it either condemns pride or exalts the blessings of humility; it either checks the quarrelsome or consoles those who abound in charity or says something of the type which spurs one on to good conduct and leads one away from wicked thoughts and gives one a regard for piety. If God promised rewards [3] to the good alone, his mercy would grow cool from neglect; if he continually threatened the evil with destruction, despair of salvation would drive them headlong into vice. And therefore the pious Redeemer has guided both groups with our salvation in mind, to frighten sinners with a threat of punishment and at the same time to promise worthy rewards to the upright.

3. In general, therefore, let the mind always be aware of the purposes of books, and let us fix our minds upon that attentive consideration which not only addresses itself to the ears but is also clear to the inner eyes. Even if the narration seems simple, there is nothing empty and nothing idle in divine literature, but

[2] I Thessalonians 5:21.   [3] Salvation.

what is said is always said for some useful purpose in order that this purpose may be received in its proper meaning and may bring salvation. When, therefore, good deeds are related, let us be instantly aroused to imitation; when bad deeds which deserve punishment are set forth, let us dread to be engaged in the like. And so it happens that we always gain some advantage if we observe why statements are made.

XXV. COSMOGRAPHERS TO BE READ BY THE MONKS

1. Not without reason do we recommend that you ought to acquire some notion of cosmography, in order that you may clearly know in what part of the world the individual places about which you read in the sacred books are located. This knowledge will certainly come to you if you hasten to read carefully the short work of Julius Orator,[1] which I have left you; he has treated the seas, the islands, the famous mountains, the provinces, the cities, the rivers, the peoples, with a fourfold division [2] in such a way that his book lacks practically nothing which pertains to a knowledge of cosmography. Marcellinus too, concerning whom I have already spoken,[3] should be read with equal care; he has described the city of Constantinople and the city of Jerusalem in four short books in considerable detail.

2. Next read the brief *Picture of the World* of Dionysius [4] in order that you may contemplate almost as an eyewitness the things which you perceived with your ears in the above-mentioned book. Then, if a noble concern for knowledge has set you on fire, you have the work of Ptolemy,[5] who has described all places so clearly that you judge him to have been practically a resident in all regions, and as a result you, who are located in one spot, as is seemly for monks, traverse in your minds that which the travel of others has assembled with very great labor.

---

[1] Julius Honorius, a rhetorician, whose description of the earth is to be dated not later than the fifth century A.D.

[2] With four oceans (east, west, north, and south).

[3] Chap. xvii, § 1, end, and § 2, beginning, above.

[4] Dionysius Exiguus' *Penax* (= *Pinax mundi*).

[5] Claudius Ptolemaeus, who lived in the time of Marcus Aurelius (A.D. 161–180). His Γεωγραφικὴ ὑφήγησις (or *Cosmographia*) in eight books is our most important handbook of ancient geography.

XXVI. ON THE ADDING OF CRITICAL MARKS

1. We have also caused the following to be pointed out, in order that our toil may instruct you and furnish the pursuit of your salvation with a little gift, however humble it may be; with the Lord's help, insofar as either old age or the weariness caused by my long sojourn on this earth have allowed me to read and comment, in certain codices of the Fathers I have set down pertinent critical marks [1] as indices for the codices in red ink in a manner which seems to me appropriate for all the individual passages. To explanations of the Octateuch [2] we have given the sign $\overline{\text{OCT}}$; to explanations of Kings a second sign, $\overline{\text{REG}}$; to explanations of the Psalter a third sign, $\overline{\text{PSL}}$; to explanations of Solomon a fourth sign, $\overline{\text{SAL}}$; to explanations of the Prophets a fifth sign, $\overline{\text{PROP}}$; to explanations of the Hagiographa a sixth sign, $\overline{\text{AGI}}$; to explanations of the Gospels a seventh sign, $\overline{\text{EV}}$; to explanations of the epistles of the Apostles an eighth sign, $\overline{\text{AP}}$; to explanations of the Acts of the Apostles and of the Apocalypse a ninth sign, $\overline{\text{AAA}}$. I have always written these signs at the beginning of the codices which I have been able to study carefully, in order that you may recognize them in the text without ambiguity if you read the individual pages studiously.

2. Then, if it be found pleasing, you who venture to do so in consequence of your extensive reading will easily be able to imitate the best commentators. [3] And as a result there will arise thence another most intelligent and most excellent sort of interpretation, and that which our forefathers did not, perhaps, elucidate in their commentaries will be found thereby to have been in some degree explained.

We have also marked idioms of the sacred law, that is, expressions peculiar to it, with a character of this sort $\overset{\wedge}{\text{PP}}$, in order that these words, wherever found, may be profaned by no presumption.

---

[1] Cf. the critical marks mentioned in the preface, § 9, middle, above.

[2] Consult chaps. xii–xiv, above, and the notes for these chapters for an indication of the books of the Bible intended by the terms here used (Kings, Solomon, etc.).

[3] This sentence and the next do not follow naturally after what precedes. Have they been inserted later, or has something dropped out before and after them? The last sentence of this section resumes the thought of section 1, above.

XXVII. ON FIGURES OF SPEECH AND THE LIBERAL ARTS [1]

1. We have decided that you ought to be cautioned about this matter too: since we can understand much in sacred literature as well as in the most learned interpreters through figures of speech, much through definitions, much through the art of grammar,[2] much through the art of rhetoric, much through dialectics,[3] much through the science of arithmetic,[4] much through music, much through the science of geometry, much through astronomy, it is not unprofitable in the book which follows to touch briefly upon the elements of instruction laid down by secular teachers, that is, upon the arts and the sciences, together with their divisions, in order that those who have acquired knowledge of this sort may have a brief review and those who perhaps have been unable to read widely may learn something from the compendious discussion. Beyond any doubt knowledge of these matters, as it seemed to our Fathers, is useful and not to be avoided, since one finds this knowledge diffused everywhere in sacred literature, as it were in the origin of universal and perfect wisdom. When these matters have been restored to sacred literature and taught in connection with it, our capacity for understanding will be helped in every way.

2. May the task of the ancients be our task, in order that we may unfold very briefly in our second book, as has already been stated, what they set forth at great length in many codices; and may we with laudable devotion recall to the service of truth what they diverted for the practice of subtlety, in order that the learning which was thereby secretly removed may be honorably restored to the service of upright understanding. Surely in my opinion it is a necessary task, but in view of the difficulty an exceed-

---

[1] The word *disciplinae* (here translated "the liberal arts" = the archaic "disciplines") is obviously used loosely. The word *art* too is often used loosely. For strict meanings of both words see II. iii. 20, 22; and ii. 17. See Mynors' *index rerum* also. When the words are used strictly, C.'s distinction is very much like our present distinction between art and science.

[2] That is, literature; skill in the art of cultivated speaking and writing of prose and verse (II. i. 1).

[3] Generally called an art, but called either an art or a discipline in II. ii. 17.

[4] C.'s "disciplina" here and below in connection with geometry is rendered "science." Music and astronomy, though not so labeled here, are also "disciplinae" or "sciences."

ingly arduous one, to try to describe the very copious sources of divine and human letters in two books; and I must quote those well-known lines [5] of Sedulius on this subject:

> I ask great gifts, but thou know'st how to give them;
> The less one hopes to get, the more thou'rt grieved.

XXVIII. WHAT IS READ BY THOSE WHO CANNOT ENTER UPON PHILOSOPHICAL WRITINGS

1. But if certain simple-minded brothers cannot understand the excerpts which have been gathered in the following book, since practically all conciseness brings obscurity, let it be enough for them to examine briefly the divisions, usefulness, and excellence of these studies, in order that they may be seized with an eager striving of their minds to acquire a knowledge of the divine law. Through the various holy Fathers they will discover the source from which they can satisfy their ardent longing to the fullest extent. Let there be merely a genuine inclination to read and a sober wish to understand, and then may a suitable assiduity bring learning to those who were frightened at the start by the profundity of the text.

2. We know, however, that intelligence is not placed in letters [1] alone, but that God gives perfect wisdom "to everyone according as he will." [2] For if knowledge of good things were present in letters alone, surely unlettered men would not possess suitable wisdom. Since, however, many illiterate persons attain true understanding and feel an upright faith instilled from heaven, there is no doubt that God grants to pure and devout feelings that which He considers is advantageous to them. For it is written, "Blessed is the man whom thou shalt instruct, O Lord: and shalt teach him out of thy law." [3] With good deeds, therefore, and with constant prayer we must seek to attain in the company of the Lord the true faith and the very holy works in which our everlasting life lies. For one reads: "Except the Lord build the house, they labour in vain that build it." [4]

---

[5] *Carmen Paschale* I. 349–350. Sedulius *floruit* A.D. 470.
[1] "Letters" here = reading as part of a formal education.
[2] I Corinthians 12:11.   [3] Psalms 93:12 (94:12).   [4] *Ibid.* 126:1 (127:1).

3. Nevertheless, the very holy Fathers have not decreed that the study of secular letters should be scorned, for these letters are not the least important means of instructing our minds in the understanding of the Sacred Scriptures; they have decreed, on the other hand, that, if knowledge of these matters is sought soberly and reasonably with the support of the divine grace, we should not hope to be advanced spiritually by reading them, but in the course of our reading we should desire to have profitable and advantageous wisdom granted us by "the Father of lights." [5] How many philosophers through eager reading of secular letters alone have failed to arrive at the fount of wisdom and, deprived of the true light, have been plunged into the blindness of ignorance! For, as someone has expressed it, that can never be fully discovered which is not sought in the proper manner.

4. Again, many of our Fathers, trained in letters of this sort and living by the law of the Lord, have attained true wisdom, as the blessed Augustine relates in his work, *On Christian Learning,* saying: [6] "We see, do we not, with how much gold and silver and clothing Cyprian, a most agreeable teacher and a most blessed martyr, was enriched when he went out from Egypt? With how much Lactantius, and Victorinus, and Optatus, and Hilary were enriched?" We add Ambrose, and the aforesaid Augustine, and Jerome, and the many others included in the words "countless Greeks." Likewise enriched "was that most faithful servant of God, Moses himself, concerning whom it is written [7] that he 'was learned in all the wisdom of the Egyptians.'" And imitating them carefully, but unhesitatingly, let us hasten to read both bodies of doctrine,[8] if we can (for who would venture to doubt after the many examples of men of this sort?), with clear knowledge, as it has often been said before now, that the Lord can grant true and genuine wisdom, as the Book of Wisdom [9] says: "Wisdom is from the Lord God, and hath been always with him, and abideth for all time."

5. On this account, with every effort, with every exertion, with every desire let us seek to deserve through the Lord's bounty to

---

[5] James 1:17.   [6] II. xl. 61.   [7] Acts 7:22.

[8] That is, the Old and the New Testaments.

[9] Ecclesiasticus (= The Wisdom of Jesus Son of Sirach) 1:1. This book is not to be confused with The Wisdom of Solomon.

attain a gift of such quality and importance. For it is advantageous to us, beneficial, glorious, everlasting—a gift of such sort that death, change, and forgetfulness cannot take it away, but in that sweet fatherland it will make us rejoice in the Lord with eternal exultation. But if in the case of some brother, as Vergil puts it,

> The chill blood about the heart stand in the way,[10]

so that he cannot be perfectly trained in either human or divine letters, though he have a moderate endowment of learning, let him by all means choose what follows:

> Let my delight be the country and the running streams amid the dells,[11]

since it is not unsuitable for monks to cultivate gardens, to work fields, and to rejoice in the fertility of fruit trees. For one reads in Psalm CXXVII:[12] "For thou shalt eat the labours of thy hands: blessed art thou, and it shall be well with thee."

6. But if authors should be sought for this study, Gargilius Martial has written most excellently on gardens and has carefully explained the raising of vegetables and the virtues of the latter, so that by a reading of his treatise under the Lord's guidance everyone may be filled and restored to health; and among other codices I have left you this treatise. In like manner Columella and Emilianus among others are commendable authors on the tilling of the fields and on the keeping of bees, doves, and also fish. But Columella in sixteen books glides eloquently and fluently through the different types of agriculture, suited as he is to those skilled in careful speech rather than to the unskilled, so that those who study his work are filled not merely with ordinary food but also with most pleasant banquets. Emilianus, moreover, a most fluent author, has written with exceptional clearness on gardens, and cattle, and other matters, in twelve books; and, among other works, through the Lord's beneficence I have left his work to you to be read.

7. But when these things are prepared for strangers and sick people they become heavenly, however earthly they may seem to be. What a deed it is to refresh the sick with sweet fruits or to

---

[10] *Georgics* II. 484.   [11] *Ibid.*, I. 485.   [12] Psalms 127 : 2 (128 : 2).

feed them with young doves or to nourish them with fish or to
soothe them with sweet honey! Since, indeed, the Lord directs
that "in <His> name" even "a cup of cold water" be offered a
poor man,[13] how much more deserving of thanks will it be to give
especially sweet food to the different ones who are destitute in
order that in return on Judgment Day you may receive your reward with interest! One should not fail to employ every available means of helping a man in laudable fashion.

XXIX. ON THE SITUATION OF THE MONASTERY OF VIVARIUM AND THAT OF CASTELLUM

1. The site of the monastery of Vivarium invites you to prepare many things for strangers and those in need, since you have
well-irrigated gardens and, close beside them, the waters of the
River Pellena, which abounds in fish—a river which should not
be considered dangerous because of the greatness of its waves
or contemptible because of their smallness. It flows into your
grounds, skillfully directed wherever it is considered necessary,
adequate for your gardens and your mills alike. It is indeed present when it is wanted, and when it has satisfied your wishes it
goes far away; thus, being dedicated to a definite service, neither
is it dangerously rough nor can it be lacking when it is sought.
Seas too are so near you that they are accessible for various
kinds of fishing, and, when it pleases you, a fish once caught may
be shut up in the fish ponds. For there, with the help of the
Lord, we have made pleasant ponds, where a multitude of fish
may drift beneath the faithful monastery; the situation so much
resembles the caves in mountains that the fish in no way realizes
that it is a captive, and it is free to acquire food and to hide itself in the solitary caverns. We have also ordered baths to be
built of a sort suitable for sick bodies in a place where fitly flows
limpid water, which is most pleasant for drinking and for bath-
ing. Consequently, in all justice your monastery is sought by other
people rather than other places by you. But these matters, as you
see, are delights in present affairs, not a future hope of the faithful. The former are transitory; the latter will abide without end.

[13] Matthew 10:42; Mark 9:40 (9:41).

But, situated in the monastery as we are, let us be conveyed rather to the desires which make us reign with Christ.

2. Carefully read and willingly hear the priest Cassian, who has written about the instruction of faithful monks; he states in the very beginning of his holy argument that eight cardinal sins are to be avoided.[1] He penetrates so competently into the harmful disturbances of minds that he makes men practically see their excesses in physical form and avoid them, though through confused and dull perception they had no previous knowledge of them. In the matter of free will, however, he has been rightly blamed by the blessed Prosper, and we therefore admonish you that you ought to exercise caution in reading a man who oversteps the mark in topics of this sort. Victor Mattaritanus, bishop of Africa, has with the Lord's help corrected what Cassian has said and added what was lacking with such skill as to be justly awarded the palm in these matters; and we believe that we ought promptly to make this same Cassian, among others, conform to orthodox beliefs about the beginnings of monasticism in Africa. He violently arraigns other kinds of monks. But, dearest brothers, with God's aid choose those parts which Victor Mattaritanus has soundly praised.

3. But if through God's grace the monastic life should suitably instruct you at the monastery of Vivarium, as is proper to believe, and if purified souls should happen to desire something higher, you have the solitary sweetness of Castellum's hill, where, through the Lord's beneficence, you may happily live as anchorites. For there you will find places secluded and like a desert, since they are shut in and encompassed by ancient walls. It will therefore be appropriate for those of you who have already been trained and tested to choose this habitation, if the ascent has previously been made ready in your heart. For through reading you perceive one of two things—either what you can desire or what you can endure. It is a wonderful thing for an upright man who cannot teach others by precept to teach them by the piety of his conduct.

---

[1] *De institutis coenobiorum et de octo principalium vitiorum remediis libri XII.*

XXX. ON SCRIBES AND THE REMEMBERING OF CORRECT SPELLING

1. I admit that among those of your tasks which require physical effort that of the scribe, if he writes correctly, appeals most to me; and it appeals, perhaps not without reason, for by reading the Divine Scriptures he wholesomely instructs his own mind and by copying the precepts of the Lord he spreads them far and wide. Happy his design, praiseworthy his zeal, to preach to men with the hand alone, to unleash tongues with the fingers, to give salvation silently to mortals, and to fight against the illicit temptations of the devil with pen and ink. Every word of the Lord written by the scribe is a wound inflicted on Satan.[1] And so, though seated in one spot, with the dissemination of his work he travels through different provinces. The product of his toil is read in holy places; people hear the means by which they may turn themselves away from base desire and serve the Lord with heart undefiled. Though absent, he labors at his task. I cannot deny that he may receive a renovation of life from these many blessings, if only he accomplishes things of this sort, not with a vain show of ambition, but with upright zeal. Man multiplies the heavenly words, and in a certain metaphorical [2] sense, if one may so express himself, that which the virtue of the Holy Trinity utters is written by a trinity of fingers. O sight glorious to those who contemplate it carefully! With gliding pen the heavenly words are copied so that the devil's craft, by means of which he caused the head of the Lord to be struck during His passion, may be destroyed. They deserve praise too for seeming in some way to imitate the action of the Lord, who, though it was expressed figuratively, wrote His law with the use of His all-powerful finger.[3] Much indeed is there to be said about such a distinguished art, but it is enough to mention the fact that those men are called scribes (*librarii*) [4] who serve zealously the just scales (*libra*) of the Lord.

[1] Cf. Cato in Iulius Rufinus (C. Halm, *Rhetores latini minores*, Leipzig, 1863, p. 40, 8).

[2] *Contropabili:* not cited in Latin lexica.   [3] Exodus 31: 18, etc.

[4] C.'s etymology is defective; *librarii* comes from *liber* ("book," with short *i*), not from *lĭbra* ("scales").

2. But lest in performing this great service copyists introduce faulty words with letters changed or lest an untutored corrector fail to know how to correct mistakes, let them read the works of ancient authors on orthography, that is, Velius Longus, Curtius Valerianus, Papirianus, Adamantius Martyrius [5] on V and B, on first, middle, and last syllables, and on the letter B in three positions in the noun and adjective,[6] and Eutyches on the rough breathing, and Phocas on the differentiation of genders and moods; [7] I have collected as many of these works as possible with eager curiosity. And lest the obscurity left in the codices just mentioned disturb someone, since codices are for the most part brought into disorder by the confusion of ancient inflections, I have taken great pains to have selected rules reach you in a work separately compiled, which is entitled *On Orthography,* and to have the mind, with doubt removed, proceed more freely along the path of emendation. We have also found out that Diomedes and Theoctistus have written something on this art; if copies of their works are subsequently discovered, do you also make selections from them. Perhaps you may find other authors by whom your knowledge may be made greater. If, however, those who have been named above are read with unremitting zeal, they will completely free you from the fog of ignorance, so that what was previously unknown may become for the most part very well known.

3. In addition to these things we have provided workers skilled in bookbinding, in order that a handsome external form may clothe the beauty of sacred letters; in some measure, perhaps, we imitate the example in the parable of the Lord,[8] who amid the glory of the heavenly banquet has clothed in wedding garments those whom He judges worthy of being invited to the table. And for the binders, in fitting manner, unless I err, we have represented various styles of binding in a single codex, that he who so desires may choose for himself the type of cover he prefers.

4. We have also prepared cleverly constructed lamps which

---

[5] Manitius, I, 49; Schanz, Vol. IV, Part 2, pp. 219–221: of the first half of the sixth century.

[6] "Nomen" = noun and adjective in the Latin grammarians.

[7] See below II. i. 1, middle.   [8] Matthew 22:11.

preserve their illuminating flames and feed their own fire and without human attendance abundantly maintain a very full clearness of most copious light; and the fat oil in them does not fail, although it is burned continually with a bright flame.

5. Nor have we by any means allowed you to be unacquainted with the hour meters which have been discovered to be very useful to the human race. I have provided a sundial for you for bright days and a water clock which points out the hour continually both day and night, since on some days the bright sun is frequently absent, and rain water passes in marvellous fashion into the ground, because the fiery force of the sun, regulated from above, fails. And so the art of man has brought into harmony elements which are naturally separated; the hour meters are so reliable that you consider an act of either as having been arranged by messengers. These instruments, then, have been provided in order that the soldiers of Christ, warned by most definite signs, may be summoned to the carrying out of their divine task as if by sounding trumpets.

XXXI. ON DOCTORS

1. I salute you, distinguished brothers, who with sedulous care look after the health of the human body and perform the functions of blessed piety for those who flee to the shrines of holy men—you who are sad at the sufferings of others, sorrowful for those who are in danger, grieved at the pain of those who are received, and always distressed with personal sorrow at the misfortunes of others, so that, as experience of your art teaches, you help the sick with genuine zeal; you will receive your reward from him by whom eternal rewards may be paid for temporal acts. Learn, therefore, the properties of herbs and perform the compounding of drugs punctiliously; but do not place your hope in herbs and do not trust health to human counsels. For although the art of medicine be found to be established by the Lord, he who without doubt grants life to men makes them sound.[1] For it is written: "And whatsoever ye do in word or deed, do all in the name of the Lord Jesus, giving thanks to God and the Father by him."[2]

[1] Ecclesiasticus 38: 1 and ff.   [2] Colossians 3: 17.

2. But if the eloquence of Greek letters is unknown to you, you have first of all the *Herb Book* of Dioscorides, who has treated and portrayed the herbs of the fields with remarkable accuracy. After this read the Latin translations of Hippocrates and Galen (that is, the *Therapeutics* of Galen, addressed to the philosopher Glauco) and a certain anonymous work, which has been compiled from various authors. Finally, read Caelius Aurelius'[3] *On Medicine,* and Hippocrates' *On Herbs and Cures,*[4] and various other works written on the art of medicine; with God's help, I have left you these books, stored away in the recesses of our library.

XXXII. AN ADMONITION FOR THE ABBOT AND THE COMMUNITY OF MONKS

1. Do all of you, therefore, whom the walls of the monastery enclose observe the rules of the Fathers, as well as the biddings of your own superior,[1] and do you carry out willingly the orders which are given you for your salvation, because men are well rewarded for obeying without a single rebellious murmur commands which pertain to their salvation. And I beg you, most holy men, abbots Calchedonius and Gerontius, to arrange all matters in such a way as to lead the flock entrusted to you to the gifts of beatitude,[2] with the help of the Lord. Before all things, therefore, receive the stranger, give alms, clothe the naked, break "thy bread for the hungry,"[3] since that man is truly to be called comforted who comforts the wretched.

2. Do you, moreover, instruct the peasants who belong to your monastery in good morals; and do not burden them with the weight of increased taxes. For it is written, "My yoke is sweet and my burden is light."[4] May they be ignorant of sly dealings and may they be completely without knowledge of the worshiping of sacred groves—both matters which are generally acknowledged to be familiar to peasants, and may they live in

---

[3] Also called Caelius Aurelianus and Aurelius Caelius. Cf. Manitius, I, 45, 63. Called "methodicus Siccensis" in MSS: see Teuffel, Vol. III (1913), § 463. 1 ff.
[4] This second mention of Hippocrates' work is undoubtedly an interpolation.
[1] That is, a superior of monks.   [2] Salvation.
[3] Isaiah 58: 7.   [4] Matthew 11: 30.

innocence and happy simplicity. Let a subordinate manner of life
of the purest sort be imposed upon them; may they come frequently to the holy monasteries in order that they may be
ashamed to be called yours without being recognized by the
members of your institution. May they also perceive that God
in his kindness will impart fertility to their fields if they have
been wont to call upon him faithfully.

3. You have therefore been given a city of your own, O pious
citizens, and if with the help of the Lord you spend your time
concordantly and spiritually, you already enjoy a prefiguration of
the heavenly home. Do not delight in slothfulness, which you
know is hateful to the Lord. The authentic documents of the
Sacred Scriptures together with their interpreters attend you,
and they are truly the flowery fields, the sweet fruits of the heavenly paradise, with which faithful souls are imbued to their salvation and by which your tongues are instructed in a diction not
destined to die but to bear fruit. Therefore enter ardently upon
the mysteries of the Lord, in order that you may be able to point
out the way to those who follow, since it is a great shame to have
books to read and to be unable to teach their meaning through
ignorance.

4. And therefore, mindful of future blessedness, do you constantly read the lives of the Fathers, the confessions of the faithful,[5] the accounts of the sufferings of martyrs, which beyond
doubt you will find, among other things, in the letter of St. Jerome intended for Chromatius and Heliodora and which have become highly esteemed throughout the entire world, in order that
holy imitation may arouse you and lead you to the heavenly kingdom; knowing that crowns [6] are given not alone for martyrdom
or for virginity, but that all who overcome the failings of their
own bodies with God's help and believe rightly receive the palm
of holy recompense.[7] But in order that you may the more easily
conquer the deadly delights and the noxious allurements of this
world with the Lord's aid, as it has been said, and in order that
you may be pilgrims [8] in this life, as it is said of the blessed saints,

---

[5] Confessions of faith by martyrs before pagan judges.
[6] That is, rewards of a good life.   [7] Salvation.
[8] Cf. Hebrews 11:13.

do you at all times hasten to the satisfactory remedy of the first Psalm [9] in order to meditate on the law of the Lord day and night. The shameless fiend [10] will find no place when Christ has wholly occupied the mind. Father Jerome has expressed the idea excellently in the following words: [11] "Take pleasure in a knowledge of the Scriptures, and you will not take pleasure in the errors of the flesh."

5. Tell me, most prudent men, what is more fortunate than to keep Him well-disposed whose anger we cannot escape? If the voice of the herald should announce the prefect, if we should know that his car was passing by with its rumbling wheels, we should all cast aside the pleasures of the mind, should we not, since we fear his presence and authority? God thunders through the vault of heaven, he reveals his lightning in the clouds, he frequently shakes the very foundations of the world and (sorrowful to relate!) his presence is not feared, though he is acknowledged to be omnipresent and omnipotent. Let us not, therefore, believe that our Judge is absent, and we shall avoid coming as culprits to his judgment seat.[12] Let him who has sinned little give thanks, inasmuch as he has not been abandoned by the Lord's mercy so as to fall headlong into error; let him who has sinned much pray unceasingly. Let no one be turned to dishonest excuses and deceitful promises. Let those of us who have sinned willfully confess our guilt. Nothing is more stupid than to desire to impose upon him who can in no way be mocked. For mercy is ready if it is sought with heart absolutely pure. Before the pious judge no excuse is too poor except a petitioner's neglect of his own salvation.

6. Let us therefore pray, dearest brothers, that He who conferred such great blessings upon man as to deign to bring the lost sheep back on his shoulders [13] and break the chains of sinners through the incarnation,

may disclose the secrets of faith to those who are ignorant and estranged, vouchsafe us baptism, allow us martyrdom, urge the giving of alms,

and also cleanse us by the holy institution of prayer, and bid us

---

[9] Psalms 1:2.   [10] The devil.   [11] *Epistula* 125, § 11.
[12] There is a reference here to the Last Judgment.
[13] Cf. the Rule of St. Benedict, 27.

forgive the debts of our brothers in order that he in like manner may forgive our debts too; [14]

that we may turn the sinner to repentance in order that the bonds of our error may be loosed;

that we ourselves may most zealously seek penance;

that we may have abounding charity toward God and toward our fellow men.

7. And, in addition, the most merciful Redeemer has granted us the communion of His body and blood, in order that thereby the compassion of the Creator may be understood in the highest degree, since by this great gift He has brought about our forgiveness, if only we seek Him with pure heart. And now may He also increase his gifts; may He light up our minds; may He purify our hearts; in order that we may deserve to understand the Sacred Scriptures with mind most pure and, supported by His grace, may fulfill His commands.

XXXIII. PRAYER

1. Grant, O Lord, spiritual progress to those who read thy law, remission of all sins to those who seek thy law, in order that we who desire with great longing to attain the light of thy Scriptures may be blinded by no dark sins. Draw us toward thee with the strength of thy omnipotence; do not suffer those "whom thou didst redeem with thy precious blood" [1] to wander about of their own accord; do not allow thy image to be covered with darkness in our minds, for if it is guarded by thee it is always surpassing. Permit neither the devil nor us to subvert thy gifts, since whatever strives to withstand thee is wholly perishable. Hear us, O merciful King, despite our sins, and take them from us before thou dost justly condemn us on their account in thy examining. [2]

2. Why does our iniquity lie in wait for us? Why do trespasses which have no corporeal stability fight against us; why do they seek to destroy thy creature? Let the devil speak the real reason for his pursuing us with insatiable animosity. Did we advise him to become proud before thee, our Lord, and to fall from the beatitude which had been granted him when he pos-

[14] Matthew 6: 12.   [1] *Te Deum*, verse 20.
[2] This refers to the Last Judgment.

sessed honors of such great worth through thy agency? Let him be satisfied with having cast us down in the person of Adam; [3] why does the impious trickster press upon us with daily deceptions, and why does he seek to keep us from thy grace just as he has been kept from it by his own guilty fall?

3. Vouchsafe, O Lord, the merciful help of thy defense against a most unmerciful adversary, in order that he who does not cease to assail our weakness may depart confounded by thy strength. O good King, do not suffer a most violent foe to fulfill his vows concerning us. Why does he who has chosen to offend thee grievously "go about as a roaring lion"? [4] Why does he strive to devour us? Once for all we renounced him at the holy baptism; once for all we professed our faith in thee, O Lord. Grant that by thy defense we be kept as good, most august Creator, as thou didst warrant we should be by using the water of regeneration. [5] May we who have begun to be thine know no other lord. By thy grace we have been redeemed; with thy help may we carry out thy precepts. If Thou dost abandon us, that renegade will attack us; unexhausted and shameless, he is always at hand, counting human downfall as his gain. He entices only to deceive; he arouses only to destroy. [6] He deceives souls by means of our bodies particularly and, slipping into human desires, is diffused through them in such a way that almost no foresight, and certainly no stratagem, reveals his presence. It would be tedious to recount every detail. Who could withstand such an adversary, unless, O Lord, you had determined to thwart him? What indeed could he not do to us—he who dared tempt thee with crafty tricks when thou wert in human form? [7] Hear us, O Protector of mankind! Because of thy indulgence may thou now free us from him who labors to drag us off to hell. May our destiny carry us not to him, but rather to thee, O Lord. Deliver thy creature [8] from his destroyer. May he who has condemned himself not cause the condemnation of others, but instead may he who hastens to destroy all things perish with his kind.

4. Up then, dearest brothers! Hasten to profit from the

---

[3] This refers to the original sin. [4] I Peter 5:8.
[5] That is, baptism.
[6] See Cyprian, *Epistula* 43, § 6 at the end.
[7] This refers to the incarnation. [8] Man.

Sacred Scriptures, since you know that I have assembled by the Lord's grace these many excellent works to instruct you fully. And now, as you read, do for me what I have done for you: deign to supplicate the Lord continually in my behalf, inasmuch as it is written: "Pray one for another, that ye may be saved." [9] O the inestimable mercy and excellence of the Creator, since he promises that it will be for the common good if we supplicate the gracious Lord in behalf of one another!

[9] James 5: 16.

Book Two
SECULAR LETTERS

—————◆◆◆—————

PREFACE

1. The preceding book, completed with the aid of the Lord, contains, as you have seen, the principles of instruction for divine readings. It is comprised of thirty-three chapters, a number acknowledged to correspond with the age of the Lord when he offered eternal life [1] to a world laid low by sin and granted rewards without end [2] to those who believed. It is now the time for us to present in seven additional chapters the text of the second book, on secular readings; this number, continuously repeated throughout the weeks as they succeed one another, is ever being extended to the very end of the world.

2. One surely ought to know that the Sacred Scripture frequently expresses by means of this number whatever it desires to be understood as continuous and perpetual, as David, for example, says, "Seven times a day I have given praise to thee," [3] though he elsewhere vows, "I will bless the Lord at all times; his praise shall be always in my mouth," [4] and Solomon says, "Wisdom hath built herself a house, she hath hewn her out seven pillars." [5] In Exodus as well the Lord said to Moses, "Thou shalt make seven lamps, and shalt set them to give light over against it." [6] Revelation constantly mentions this number in various applications. [7] And this number leads us to that eternity which can have no end; with justice, then, is it always used whenever perpetuity is indicated.

3. Thus, the science of arithmetic is endowed with great praise, since God the Creator has arranged his dispensations by

[1] By his resurrection.
[2] Salvation.
[3] Psalm 118:164 (119:164).
[4] *Ibid.* 33:2 (34:1); cf. Augustine *De civitate Dei* XI. xxxi.
[5] Proverbs 9:1.
[6] Exodus 25:37.
[7] Revelation 1:4, 12, 16, etc.

the use of number, weight, and measure; as Solomon says, "Thou hast ordered all things in measure, and number, and weight." [8] Thus God's creation is known to have been ordered in number, since our Lord says in the Gospel, "But the very hairs of your head are all numbered." [9] And likewise God's creation has been ordered in measure, as our Lord bears witness in the Gospel: "And which of you by taking thought, can add to his stature one cubit?" [10] And likewise the prophet Isaiah says, "Who doth measure heaven with the span, and hold the earth confined in his hand." [11] Again, God's creation is acknowledged to have been ordered in weight, as it is written in the Proverbs of Solomon, "And he poised the fountains of waters," [12] and a little farther on, "When he balanced the foundations of the earth, I was with him." [13] For this reason God's extraordinary and magnificent works are necessarily confined to definite limits, so that just as we know that he has created all things we may in some measure learn to know the manner of their creation. And hence it is to be understood that the evil works of the devil are not ordered by weight or measure or number, since, whatever iniquity [14] does, it is always opposed to justice, as the thirteenth Psalm declares, saying, "Contrition and unhappiness in their ways: and the way of peace they have not known." [15] Isaiah also says, "They have abandoned the Lord of hosts and have walked along crooked paths." [16] God is really wonderful and extremely wise in having distinguished every one of his creatures by a unique dispensation lest unseemly confusion take hold of some of them; Father Augustine has discussed this topic in most minute manner in the fourth book of his work *On Genesis Considered Word for Word*.

4. Let us now enter upon the beginning of the second volume, and let us attend with some care, for it is crowded with etymologies and full of a discussion of definitions. In this book we must speak first of the art of grammar, which is manifestly the source and foundation of liberal studies.[17] The word "book" (*liber*)

---

[8] Wisdom 11:21.   [9] Matthew 10:30.   [10] *Ibid.* 6:27.

[11] Isaiah 40:12.   [12] Proverbs 8:28.   [13] *Ibid.* 8:29–30.

[14] The devil.

[15] Psalms 13:3 (not included in the Authorized Version).

[16] Isaiah 59:8; cf. 5:24.   [17] Literally "liberal letters."

comes from the word "free" (*liber*) ;[18] a book, in other words, is the bark of a tree, removed and freed—the bark on which the ancients used to write oracular responses before the invention of papyrus.[19] In view of this, therefore, we are permitted to make short books or extended ones, since we are allowed to limit the size of books in accordance with their nature, just as the bark encloses both tiny shoots and vast trees. We ought, moreover, as Varro says,[20] to understand that the elements of all arts came into existence because of some usefulness. "Art" is so called because it limits (*artet*) and binds us with its rules; according to others this word is taken over from the Greek expression *apo tes aretes*,[21] which means "from excellence," the term applied by well-spoken men to skill in every matter.[22] Second, we must speak of the art of rhetoric, which is deemed very necessary and honorable because of the splendor and fullness of its eloquence, especially in civil questions.[23] Third, we must speak of logic, which is called dialectic; according to the statements of secular teachers this study separates the true from the false by means of very subtle and concise reasoning.[24] Fourth, we must speak of mathematics, which embraces four sciences,[25] to wit, arithmetic, geometry, music, and astronomy. In Latin we may call mathematics the theoretical study; though we might apply this term to all studies which teach one to speculate on abstract principles, nevertheless, by reason of its excellence this study has claimed the common word strictly for itself, just as when "the Poet" is mentioned, Homer is understood in Greek writers [26] and Vergil in Latin writers, and when one refers to "the Orator," Demosthenes is indicated in Greek writers and Cicero in Latin writers, al-

[18] (Isid. I. v. 1; Rabanus III. 18.) This etymology, like many of the others which follow in this book, is incorrect. Here and elsewhere on the following pages references to authors who borrow from Cassiodorus are enclosed in parentheses.

[19] (Cf. Isid. VI. xiii. 3.)

[20] Fragment 117 G–S (233 *Fun.*), from *Disciplinarum libri IX;* see Servius *Commentarium in Donatum* (Heinrich Keil, ed. *Grammatici latini*, Vol. IV [Leipzig, 1864], p. 405, § 2), etc.

[21] ἀπὸ τῆς ἀρετῆς.

[22] (*Isid.* I. i. 2; v. 2.)

[23] Those within the range of common understanding which concern what is fair and good. Cf. below, ii. 1, at end.

[24] On this sentence and the one which precedes cf. Isid. I. ii. 1.

[25] Cf. I. xxvii, title, and note 1 on *disciplinae* (here translated "sciences").

[26] Cf. Seneca, *Epistles* lviii. 17; Justinian, *Institutes* I. ii. 2.

though many poets and orators are shown to have used both languages. Mathematics is the science which considers abstract quantity; abstract quantity is that which we separate from matter or from other accidents by our intellect and treat by reasoning alone.[27]

5. By stating the contents of the entire book in advance I have, as it were, given bail to secure the performance of my promise. Let us now, with the Lord's aid, give an account of the individual topics, as they have been promised, by means of their divisions and definitions, since learning is in a certain sense twofold in character, inasmuch as a clear description first carefully permeates the sense of sight and then, after having prepared the ears, penetrates the hearing.[28] And, moreover, we shall not fail to reveal the authors, both Greek and Latin, whose explanations of the matters which we discuss have become famous, in order that those who desire to read zealously may more lucidly understand the words of the ancients after having first been introduced to them in abridged form.

Here ends the preface to Book II. Here begins the table of contents for the same book.

Here ends the table of contents for the secular letters of Book II. Here begins our author's second book.

I. ON GRAMMAR

1. Grammar gets its name from the letters of the alphabet, as the derived character of the word itself shows.[1] Sixteen of these letters are said to have been invented by Cadmus,[2] who

---

[27] On this sentence cf. iii. 6, third and fourth sentences; iii. 21, first sentence.

[28] That is, C.'s preface permeates the sight and the book proper penetrates the hearing (= understanding).

[1] ἡ γραμματική is, as it were, the art of knowing one's letters (γράμματα). (Rabanus III. xviii; cf. Isid. I. v. 1.)

[2] Pliny VII. 192, etc.; cf. Varro VIII. xii. 4.

handed them down to the studious Greeks, who in turn supplied the rest by their liveliness of mind. On the positions and worth of the letters Helenus [3] has written a subtle treatise in Greek and Priscian [4] another in Latin. Grammar is skill in the art of cultivated speech—skill acquired from famous writers of poetry and of prose; its function is the creation of faultless prose and verse; its end is to please through skill in finished speech and blameless writing. But although such authors of earlier times as Palaemon,[5] Phocas,[6] Probus,[7] and Censorinus [8] have written on the art of grammar with variety of method and have been highly esteemed in their own day, nevertheless, for the good of all we intend to quote from Donatus,[9] who is considered to be especially appropriate for boys and suitable for novices; we have left you his twofold treatise in order that a twofold explanation may make even clearer him who is already clear. We have also discovered that St. Augustine has written a short course of instruction on the same topic for the simple brothers; and we have left you this work to read, lest anything seem to be lacking to the inexperienced who are being made ready for high achievement in this great study.

2. In the second part of his work [10] Donatus discusses the following topics: the spoken word, the letter, the syllable, feet, accentuation, punctuation and proper phrasing, the eight parts of speech (for the second time), figures of speech, etymologies, and orthography. A *spoken word* is a vibration of the air perceptible

[3] Cf. Varro VIII. xii. 5.

[4] His great work on grammar was completed at Constantinople by one of his pupils, the calligrapher Theodorus, in A.D. 526–527.

[5] Published his *Ars grammatica*, probably at Rome between A.D. 67 and 77.

[6] Published his *Ars de nomine et verbo* at Rome in the fifth century A.D. Cf. I. xxx. 3, above.

[7] The foremost grammarian of the first century A.D. (*floruit* 56–88, at Rome).

[8] A grammarian of the third century A.D., who wrote a work entitled *De accentibus*, now lost; cf. below, v. 10, end.

[9] Grammarian and rhetorician at Rome in the middle of the fourth century; he also wrote important commentaries on Terence and Virgil, the latter frequently cited by Servius. His *Artes* (1. *Ars minor* or *prima*, for boys and novices, and 2. *Ars maior* or *secunda*, for more advanced students) became the standard grammatical textbooks of the Middle Ages and the name of Donatus became practically synonymous with grammar.

[10] That is, in the *Ars maior*. (The *Ars minor* discusses the eight parts of speech.) Except for the definitions of accent and punctuation, all of this section of Cassiodorus through the *interjection* is derived from Donatus.

to the hearing in proportion to the power of the vibration.[11] A *letter* is the smallest part of a spoken word.[12] A *syllable* is a group of letters, or a single vowel, which can be measured as a unit.[13] A *foot* is a definite reckoning of syllables and of quantity.[14] *Accentuation* is the artistic pronunciation of a word without mistake. *Punctuation* or *proper phrasing* is a clear pausing in well-regulated pronunciation. The parts of speech, moreover, are eight in number: noun, pronoun, verb, adverb, participle, conjunction, preposition, and interjection.[15] A *noun* is a part of speech with case ending, signifying a person or thing as an individual or as a class: "Rome" and "Tiber" are examples of individuals; "city" and "river," of classes.[16] A *pronoun* is a part of speech which is used instead of a noun without causing any perceptible change in meaning and which sometimes admits person.[17] A *verb* is a part of speech which has time and person, but no case.[18] An *adverb* is a part of speech added to a verb to clarify and complete its meaning, as in such an expression as "I shall now make" or "I shall not make." [19] A *participle* is a part of speech so called because it partakes of the functions of a noun and of a verb; it receives gender and case from the noun, tense and meaning from the verb, number and form from both.[20] A *conjunction* is a part of speech which binds a sentence together and sets it in order.[21] A *preposition* is a part of speech placed before other parts of speech to change, complete, or curtail their meaning.[22] An *interjection* is a part of speech, without grammatical connection, which signifies a disposition of mind.[23] *Figures of speech* are transformations of words or thoughts, used for the sake of adornment; they are represented as being ninety-eight in number in the collection made by the grammatical writer Sacerdos; [24] this number therefore includes those which are considered faults by Donatus. Like Sacerdos, I too feel that it is unfortunate to label as faults those figures which are supported by the example of authors and particularly by the authority of the

---

[11] Donat., p. 367, l. 5.   [12] *Ibid.*, p. 367, l. 9.   [13] *Ibid.*, p. 368, l. 18.
[14] *Ibid.*, p. 369, l. 17.   [15] *Ibid.*, p. 372, l. 25.   [16] *Ibid.*, p. 373, l. 2.
[17] *Ibid.*, p. 379, l. 23.   [18] *Ibid.*, p. 381, l. 14.   [19] *Ibid.*, p. 385, l. 11.
[20] *Ibid.*, p. 387, l. 18.   [21] *Ibid.*, p. 388, l. 28.   [22] *Ibid.*, p. 389, l. 19.
[23] *Ibid.*, p. 366, l. 13.
[24] Marius Plotius Sacerdos (third cent. A.D.) wrote an *Artes grammaticae* in three books.

divine law. Figures of speech are common to professors of literature and to orators, and they are recognized as being well suited to both. I must also add something on etymologies and orthography, concerning which I am sure several men have written. *Etymology* is the true or probable demonstration of the origin of a word. *Orthography* is the art of composing correctly and without error; it applies alike to writing and to speaking.

3. Let these words, which concern brief definitions alone, suffice. But let him who desires wider and fuller knowledge of these matters read both preface and body of the codex which [25] I have had written on the art of grammar, in order that the careful reader may find the facts which he knows are considered to belong to this subject. Let us now come to the divisions and definitions of the art of rhetoric; as its extensiveness and richness deserve, it has been amply treated by many illustrious writers.

II. ON RHETORIC

1. Rhetoric is said to be derived *apo tou rhetoreuein*,[1] that is, from skill in making a set speech. The art of rhetoric, moreover, according to the teaching of professors of secular letters, is expertness in discourse on civil questions.[2] The orator, then, is a good man skilled, as has just been said, in discoursing on civil

---

[25] Instead of "which . . . subject" Φ Δ (and M²) read: "which we have formed because of our desire for knowledge, to wit, the *Art* of Donatus, into which we have introduced a second treatise, *On Orthography,* and a third, *On Etymology,* and to which we have added a fourth treatise as well, Sacerdos' *On Figures of Speech,* in order that the diligent reader may be able to find the facts which he knows are considered to belong to the art of grammar. (Cf. *De orthographia*—Heinrich Keil, *Grammatici Latini,* Vol. VII [Leipzig, 1880], p. 144, l. 7.) But, since the matter belongs properly to the art of grammar, we on our part have taken pains to append some remarks concerning the rules for noun and verb, rules which Aristotle (*Perihermenias, at the beginning?*) has quite rightly explained (as belonging in each case to a part of speech, *sic* Φ, *om.* Δ)." *Excerpts from Martianus Capella's treatise (produced c. 410–427) on the seven liberal arts follows in* Φ. Δ *omits these excerpts and adds:* Let him who desires the rest seek in another volume, for I, the describer, in my haste to get to more important matters, have forgotten the rest or have, perhaps, neglected it. (Δ *then supplies a list of the "parts of speech"* [the noun, whose "parts" are gender, number, case, etc.; the pronoun, etc.; the verb, etc.] *and a series of excerpts from Quintilian,* II–VII; cf. Mynors, Introduction, pp. xxvii and xxxvi–xxxvii.)

[1] ἀπὸ τοῦ ῥητορεύειν ("from speaking in public").

[2] Cf. II. pref. 4, middle, on the art of rhetoric, and note 23. (On this sentence and that which precedes cf. Isid. II. i. 1). On this sentence alone cf. (Rabanus III. xix) Quint. II. xv. 38.

questions.³ The function of an orator is speaking suitably in order to persuade; his purpose ⁴ is to persuade, by speaking on civil questions, to the extent permitted by the nature of things and persons. Let us now, therefore, take up a few matters briefly in order that we may understand the main points of almost the entire art and the excellence of the art from a description of several of its parts. According to Fortunatianus,⁵ a modern writer on rhetoric, civil questions are questions "which can fall within the range of common understanding, that is, questions which everyone can comprehend, since they concern what is fair and good." ⁶

2. Rhetoric ⁷ has five parts: invention, arrangement, proper expression, memorization, delivery. *Invention* is the devising of arguments which are true or which resemble true arguments to make a case appear credible. *Arrangement* is the excellent distribution in regular order of the arguments devised. *Proper expression* is the adaptation of suitable words to the arguments. *Memorization* is a lasting comprehension. by the mind of the arguments and the language. *Delivery* is the harmonious adjustment of voice and gesture in keeping with the dignity of the arguments and the language.

3. The three principal kinds of rhetorical case are these: ⁸

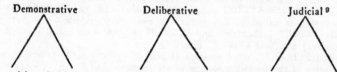

Demonstrative	Deliberative	Judicial ⁹
In praising In blaming	In persuading and dissuading	In accusing In accepting ⟨and defending⟩ and refusing a penalty

³ On this sentence and the preceding cf. Fortun. I. i. (On this sentence alone cf. Isid. II. iii. I.)

⁴ Cf. Quint. II. xv. 5; cf. Cicero, *De inventione* i. 6, and Fortun. *ibid.*

⁵ Claudius Chirius Fortunatianus (last half of the fourth century, A.D.). His *Artis rhetoricae libri III* (in the form of a catechism) is founded on Quintilian, with illustrations from Cicero.

⁶ Fortun., *ibid.* At this point Δ adds (from Cicero *De inventione* i. 8): "A case is a matter containing a subject for dispute into which definite persons are introduced; a question, on the other hand, is a matter containing a subject for dispute into which definite persons are not introduced."

⁷ All of § 2 = essentially Cicero *De inventione* i. 9.

⁸ All of § 3 = essentially Fortun. I. i.—At this point Δ adds: "Every function of speaking ⟨is⟩ either one or another of the three. . . . Aristotle uses *contionalis*

The *demonstrative* kind is that which points out a particular matter and contains praise or blame.[10] The *deliberative* kind is that which contains persuasion and dissuasion.[11] The *judicial* kind is that which contains accusation and defense, or the seeking and refusing of a penalty.

4.[12] The place in which a case rests is called its position;[13] the position arises out of the complaint and the answer.[14] The positions of cases are either rational[15] or legal.[16] There are four rational positions which are general:

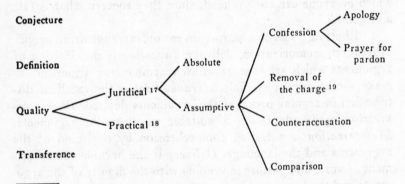

Conjecture

Definition

Quality ──┬── Juridical[17] ──┬── Absolute
          │   │
          └── Practical[18]   └── Assumptive ──┬── Removal of the charge[19]
                                               ├── Counteraccusation
                                               └── Comparison

Confession ──┬── Apology
             └── Prayer for pardon

Transference

['suitable for delivery before an assembly of the people'] instead of *deliberative*. [from Quint. III. iv. 1] ... The *deliberative* kind is that which takes counsel; the *judicial* kind is that which makes a judgment concerning cases."

9 Δ adds: "ΕΠΙΔΕΙΚΤΙΚΟΝ suitable for display" and "ΕΓΚΟΝΙΔΟΤΙΚΟ (*sc.* ἐγκωμιαστικόν) is called laudatory for the most part" (Quint. III. iv. 12) and "ΠΑΝΗΓΥΡΙΚΟΝ (panegyric) and "ΣΥΜΒΟΥΛΕΥΤΙΚΟΝ is called counselling" (deliberative) and "ΔΙΚΑΝΙΚΟΝ" (judicial).

10 Δ adds: "It occurs when someone is pointed out and made known through a description of the following sort, as in the twenty-eighth Psalm, in many other Psalms, and elsewhere: 'O Lord, thy mercy is in heaven, and thy truth reacheth even to the clouds. Thy justice is as the mountains of God,' and so on" [Psalm 35:6–7 (36:5–6)].

11 Δ adds: "that is, what to seek, what to shun, what to teach, what to prohibit."

12 (§§ 4–7 = Isid. II. v–vi.)

13 Fortun. I. xi and ii.—On the validity of the word "position" as a translation of *status* and also of *constitutio* in §§ 4–6, below, consult Howell, pp. 38–39.

14 Δ adds: "or the issue (*constitutio*). Some call the position the issue (*constitutio*); others call it the question; still others call it that which arises from the questioning," (from Quint. III. vi. 2).

15 That is, having to do with general reason and common law.

16 That is, having to do with statute law and texts.

17 To this item and the next Δ adds: "ΔΙΚΟΛΟΓΙΚΗ" and "ΠΡΑΓΜΑΤΙΚΗ."

18 *Negotialis.*

19 To this item and the next two Δ adds: "ΜΕΤΑСΤΑСΙС, ΑΝΤΕΓΚΛΗΜΑ" (*corrupt*), and "ΑΝΤΙСΤΑСΙС" (from Quint. VII. iv. 8–14).

But, as Cicero relates in his work *On the Orator* [20] in correction of his own statements, transference ought to be classed among the legal positions, for Fortunatianus says,[21] We "accept transference as merely legal. Why? Because no transference, that is, no demurrer, can exist without law." There are five legal positions: [22] letter and spirit, contradictory laws, ambiguity, reasoning or deduction, and legal definition.

5. The *conjectural* [23] position is that in which the fact charged by one side is vigorously denied by the other. The *definitive* [24] position is that in which we hold that the fact is not as charged, but in which we demonstrate its nature by the use of definitions. *Quality* [25] is the position in which the character of an act is sought; and, since the controversy concerns the import and essential nature of the act, it is called the general position. When a case depends either upon the fact that the proper man does not seem to be bringing the action or the fact that the action is not being brought against the proper man, or in the proper court, or at the proper time, or under the proper law, or with the proper charge, or with the proper penalty, the position in which the case rests is called *translative,* because the action seems to require transference and change.[26] The *juridical* [27] position is that in which the nature of the justice and right involved and the reasonableness of the fine or punishment are sought. The *practical* [28] position is that in which one considers what is right in accordance with civil custom and equity. The *absolute* position is that which contains the question of justice and injury in itself. The *assumptive* position is that which has no strength of defense in itself but assumes some defense from without. The *confession* is the position in which the accused does not defend that which has been done but begs to be pardoned; we have pointed

---

[20] Actually the *Rhetorica ad Herennium* I. ii.

[21] Fortun. I. xi.

[22] *Ibid.* I. xxii.—Δ adds: "ΡΗΤΟΝ Κ. ΔΙΑΝΟΙΝ (*sic*), ΑΝΤΙΝΟΜΙΑ, ΑΜΦΙΒΟΛΙΑ, ϹΥΛΛΟΓΙϹΜΟΝ" (from Quint. III. vi. 46).

[23] Fortun. I. xi.   [24] *Ibid.* I. xiii.

[25] For this sentence and the next see Cicero *De inventione* i. 10.

[26] This position, a transference of an indictment, is merely a technical question of procedure.

[27] For the text from this point to the end of § 5 see Cicero *De inventione* i. 14–15.

[28] On the exact meaning of C.'s term "practical" (*negotialis*), used also by Cicero, consult Howell, p. 162.

out that this has to do with penitents.[29] *Removal of the charge* [30] is the position in which the accused attempts by force of argument or influence to transfer the charge from himself to another. A *counteraccusation* is the position in which an act is said to have been lawfully done because the doer was previously provoked unjustly. *Comparison* is the position in which it is contended that as a result of the commission of the act charged some other worthy and useful deed has been done by one of the two parties to the dispute. *Apology* is the position in which the act is admitted but the blame set aside; it has three parts: ignorance, chance, necessity. A *prayer for pardon* is the position in which the defendant admits that he has been guilty and deliberately guilty and yet begs that he be pardoned; this type of plea will happen very rarely.

6. *Letter and spirit* [31] is the position in which the actual language of a written document seems to be at variance with the writer's intention. The position of a *contradictory law* is that in which two or more laws are recognized as disagreeing. *Ambiguity* is the position in which a written document seems to have two or more meanings. *Reasoning,* also called *deduction,* is the position in which something that is not written in the law is ascertained from that which is written therein. *Legal definition* is the position in which the force of a word on which the definition depends is sought, just as in the definitive position. According to some men, therefore, the total number of both rational and legal positions is quite surely eighteen.[32] According to Tully's [33] *Rhetorical Books,*[34] on the other hand, the number is found to be nineteen, because the author has, for the most part, assigned transference to the rational positions; in correction of his own classification, however, as has been stated above,[35] he has later joined transference to the legal positions.

7. Every subject for dispute, as Cicero says,[36] is either simple

---

[29] *Comm. Psalt.* chap. 31.   [30] Or "evasion."

[31] For the first five sentences of this section see Cicero *De inventione* 1. 17.

[32] That is, not counting *transference* at all, since it apparently may be applied to all five of the legal positions and thus does not necessarily constitute a separate category.

[33] That is, Cicero's.   [34] *De inventione.*

[35] § 4, middle, and note 20.

[36] On § 7 see *De inventione,* i. 17.

or complex; and if it is complex, one must consider whether it is made so because of the joining of several points or because of some comparison. A *simple* subject is that which contains a single complete point, as in the following question: "Shall we declare war against Corinth or not?" A *complex subject arising from the joining of several points* is that in which an inquiry is made concerning several matters, for example, whether Carthage should be destroyed, or whether it should be given back to the Carthaginians, or whether a colony should be transplanted there. A *complex subject arising from a comparison* is that in which an inquiry is made concerning the relative desirability of two or more acts; for example, whether an army should be sent into Macedonia against Philip to help our allies or whether it should be held in Italy to provide us with as many men as possible against Hannibal.

8. There are five kinds of legal cases: [37] honorable, paradoxical, insignificant, uncertain, obscure. An *honorable* case is one toward which the mind of the hearer is favorably disposed at once without utterance from the person involved. A *paradoxical* case is one by which the minds of those who are about to hear are made hostile. An *insignificant* case is one which is neglected by the hearer and seems unworthy of very much attention. An *uncertain* case is one in which either the judgment is doubtful or the cause partly honorable and partly discreditable so that it begets both good will and displeasure. An *obscure* case is one in which either the hearers are dull or the cause is apparently entangled in affairs which are somewhat hard to understand.

9. A rhetorical composition has six parts: exordium, narration, partition, direct argument, refutation, conclusion.[38] The *exordium* is an utterance which suitably prepares the hearer's mind for the rest of the discourse.[39] The *narration* is an exposition of the acts done or supposed to have been done.[40] The *partition* is that which, if properly made, renders the whole speech clear and intelligible.[41] The *direct argument* is that by means of whose proofs the speech induces belief and adds strength and support to our cause.[42] The *refutation* is that by means of whose

[37] On § 8 see *ibid.* § 20. (§ 8 = Isid. II. viii.)
[38] Cicero, *De inventione*, i. 19.   [39] Chap. i, § 20.
[40] Chap. i, § 27.   [41] Chap. i, § 31.   [42] Chap. i, § 34.

proofs the direct argument of adversaries is destroyed or weak-ened.[43] The *conclusion* is the termination and end of the entire speech, and in it there is sometimes employed a recapitulation of the chief points, calculated to bring forth tears.[44]

10. Although Cicero, the distinguished light of Latin elo-quence, has set these matters forth abundantly and carefully in his various works and seems to have included them in the two books of his *Art of Rhetoric*,[45] on which I have left you, in my library, a commentary composed by Marius Victorinus,[46] never-theless, Quintilian, a surpassing instructor, who after the streams of Tully's learning was still able to enrich his teachings, has taken at an early age a man morally good and skilled in speaking and has pointed out that this man ought to be trained in all the arts and disciplines of noble letters [47] in order that the prayers of the entire state may justly seek him out as a champion. We have concluded that the two books of Cicero's work, *On the Art of Rhetoric*,[48] and the twelve books of Quintilian's *Manual* ought to be joined, not in order that the size of the codex may be increased, but in order that both works may be at hand when they are needed. Suitably and conveniently perhaps, we have compressed Fortunatianus, a recent teacher, who has discussed this subject subtly and minutely in three books, into a small com-pass, in order that he may put an end to the reader's aversion and may fittingly cause him to arrive at the essentials. Let the lover of brevity read this author, for, though he has not ex-tended his work to many books, he has nevertheless discussed a large number of topics with an exceedingly acute reasoning. You will discover that these treatises, together with a special preface, have been assembled in a single codex.

11. Rhetorical argumentation [49] is treated as follows: [50]

---

[43] Chap. i, § 78.   [44] Chap. i, § 98.   [45] *De inventione.*

[46] Of African origin about the middle of the fourth century A.D.; author of several philosophical and rhetorical works and of a treatise on meter. He received the unusual literary distinction of a statue in the forum of Trajan.

[47] That is, the liberal arts.   [48] *De inventione.*

[49] (§§ 11–15 = Isid. II. ix.)   [50] Cicero, *De inventione*, i. 51.

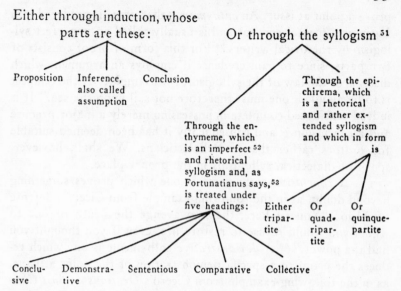

Either through induction, whose parts are these:

Proposition　　Inference, also called assumption　　Conclusion

Or through the syllogism [51]

Through the enthymeme, which is an imperfect [52] and rhetorical syllogism and, as Fortunatianus says, [53] is treated under five headings:

Through the epichirema, which is a rhetorical and rather extended syllogism and which in form is

Either tripartite　　Or quadripartite　　Or quinquepartite

Conclusive　　Demonstrative　　Sentencious　　Comparative　　Collective

Argumentation [54] is the term used, as it were, for the verbal expression of a clear mind; it is a statement by means of which we maintain that a proof which has been discovered is probable.[55] An *induction* is a statement which by the use of clearly known particulars seeks to gain approval for the generalization with which the induction was begun, whether among philosophers or rhetoricians or conversationalists.[56] A *proposition* is the part of an induction which of necessity introduces one or more points similar to the point to be admitted. An *inference,* also called an "assumption," is the part of an induction that introduces the point which is at issue and on account of which the similarities have been used.[57] A *conclusion* is the part of an induction which establishes the admission made in the *inference* or points out what is established from the admission.

12. A *syllogism* is a form of statement by means of which we

[51] That is, deduction.　　　　　[52] Unrhetorical: Isid.
[53] Fortun. II. xxix.
[54] The suggested etymology is partially correct. Before the word *argumentation* Δ inserts: "Propositions are single and double, or multiple if several charges are joined together."
[55] Fortun. II. xxviii.
[56] *De inventione* i. 51; Fortun. II. xxviii.
[57] On this definition and the next cf. *De inventione* i. 54.

prove a point at issue. An *enthymeme,* therefore, is rendered into Latin as a mental concept and is usually called an imperfect syllogism by rhetorical writers.[58] For this form of proof consists of two parts, since to gain credence it employs an argument which disregards the law of the syllogism; for example: "If the tempest is to be avoided, one must therefore not sail upon the sea." It is indeed considered complete in possessing merely a major premise and a conclusion,[59] and consequently it has been deemed suitable for orators rather than for dialecticians. We shall, however, speak of dialectical syllogisms in the proper place.

13. A *conclusive* enthymeme is one which proves something beyond doubt, as in the following example from Cicero's defense of Milo: "You sit here, then, to avenge the death of one to whom you would refuse to restore life, even if you thought you had the power." [60] A *demonstrative* enthymeme is one which reduces the proof to a specific demonstration of the point at issue, as in the following example from Cicero's *Orations against Catiline:* "And yet this man lives. He lives? Why he even comes into the Senate." [61] A *sententious* enthymeme is one whose authority is increased by the use of a maxim, as in the following example from Terence: "Complaisance makes friends, and truthfulness is the mother of unpopularity." [62] A *comparative* enthymeme is one which by a comparison to something used as a pattern portends a similar conclusion, as in the following illustration from Cicero's *Philippics:* "I wonder that you, Antonius, while you copy their deeds, do not shudder at their end." [63] A *collective* enthymeme is one in which all the proofs are collected into a single statement, as in the following example from Cicero's defense of Milo: "Did he then desire, when some people were sure to protest, to do what he refused to do when all would have been delighted? He did not venture to slay Clodius when he might have done so lawfully, advantageously, opportunely; and did he have no hesi-

---

[58] ([Boethius'] *Demonstratio artis geometriae,* p. 395, Lachmann.)

[59] The example in the preceding sentence appears again below, in the second sentence of § 14, as an enthymeme which consists of a major premise alone. For this reason Ω and many MSS of Isidore omit "and a conclusion" here.

[60] *Pro Milone* xxix. 79; Quint. v. xiv. 2.

[61] *In Catilinam,* oration I, chap. i, l. 2.

[62] *Andria,* l. 68.

[63] *Philippics,* oration II, chap. i, l. 1.

tation in slaying him unlawfully, inopportunely, and at the risk of his own life?" [64]

14. According to Victorinus, moreover, there is another definition of the enthymeme. It consists of a major premise alone, as has already been stated; for example: "If the tempest is to be avoided, one must not sail upon the sea"; or of a minor premise alone; for example: "There are those who say that the world moves without divine direction"; or of a conclusion alone; for example: "A divine judgment is therefore true"; or of a major and minor premise; for example: "If he is unfriendly, he will perish,[65] and he is unfriendly," and because a conclusion is lacking in the last case, the argument is called an enthymeme.

15. The epichirema follows. An *epichirema,* as we have said above, is a rather extended treatment of the rhetorical syllogism, proceeding from deduction and differing from the dialectical syllogism in amplitude and length of language, on account of which it is assigned to rhetoricians. A *tripartite* epichirematic syllogism is one which consists of three parts: major premise, minor premise, and conclusion. A *quadripartite* epichirematic syllogism is one which consists of four parts: major premise, minor premise, additional proof joined to either, and conclusion. In like manner a *quinquepartite* syllogism is one which consists of five parts: major premise and additional proof, minor premise and additional proof, and conclusion. This is the type of syllogism used in the following quotation from Cicero's *Art of Rhetoric:* [66] "If deliberative and demonstrative oratory [67] are types of speech, they cannot rightly be considered as subdivisions of a type, for the same object may be called a type by some people and a subdivision by others, but it cannot be called both a type and a subdivision by the same person"; more follows which falls within the limits of this syllogism. But I shall see to what extent the reader can exercise his ingenuity concerning the parts which I have omitted.

16. In his third book [68] the aforesaid Fortunatianus has made mention of the orator's memorization and of his delivery and manner of speaking; the monk will derive a certain advantage

---

[64] *Pro Milone* xv. 41; Quint. v. xiv. 3.   [65] Or "he will kill."
[66] *De inventione* i. 12.   [67] Cf. § 3, above.   [68] III. xiii ff.

from this book, since it seems not improper for him to adapt to his own uses that which orators have profitably applied to disputation. Duly cautious, he will pay heed to memorization, as applied to divine reading, when he has learned its force and nature from the afore-mentioned book; he will foster the art of delivery in reading the divine law aloud; and he will, moreover, preserve a careful manner of speaking in chanting the psalms. Thus, though he be somewhat occupied by secular books, he will be restored to holy work upon the completion of his instruction.

17. Let us now in due order come to logic, which is also called dialectic. Some have preferred to name it a science,[69] and some an art, saying that when it uses demonstrative arguments, that is, true arguments, in discussing a subject, it ought to be called a science and when it treats something probable and conjectural it is called an art.[70] Each of these terms is properly used because of the nature of proof in each case. For Father Augustine, impressed, I believe, by this consideration, has followed Varro in naming grammar and rhetoric sciences;[71] and, in addition, Felix Capella [72] has given the title *On the Seven Sciences* to his own work. A science is so named because it is a subject completely known,[73] and the name is justly applied, since the immutable rule of truth always follows in its track.

III. ON DIALECTIC

1. To be sure, the first philosophers had dialectic in their teachings, but they did not possess the skill to reduce it to an art. After their time, however, Aristotle, diligent expounder of all knowledge that he was, imposed rules upon the argumentation employed in this subject, which had previously had no definite principles.[1] By writing books of surpassing quality, he has brought great and glorious praise to Greek learning, and our countrymen, no longer permitting him to remain a stranger, have transferred him to the Latin language by means of translation and exposition.

---

[69] *Disciplina.*   [70] (Isid. I. xiii.)
[71] Cf. *De ordine* II. xii. 37; *Retractationes* I. v (6).
[72] = Martianus [Minneus Felix] Capella. His work is a treatise on the seven liberal arts: Cf. i. 3, note 25, above.
[73] (Isid. I. i. 1.)   [1] (Isid. II. xxii. 2.)

2. In his nine books of *Disciplines* [2] Varro distinguishes dialectic and rhetoric by using the following comparison: [3] "Dialectic and rhetoric are like man's closed fist and open palm," [4] one compressing its arguments into a narrow compass, the other running about the fields of eloquence with copious speech; one contracting its language, the other expanding it. If indeed dialectic is more subtle for the discussion of questions, rhetoric is more eloquent for the teaching of its objectives. One sometimes comes to the schools; the other constantly proceeds to the forum. One seeks a few studious men; the other the great mass.

3. But before we speak about syllogisms, in which the usefulness and worth of dialectic as a whole are manifested, we must say a few words about its elements, about certain underlying principles, as it were, in order that our arrangement of material may be designed in accordance with that established by our ancestors. In like manner, it is the custom among teachers of philosophy, before they come to the exposition of the *Isagoge,* to describe briefly the divisions of philosophy; [5] and in observance of this custom we too, not unjustly, believe that the divisions ought to be announced now.

4. Philosophy is divided into [6]

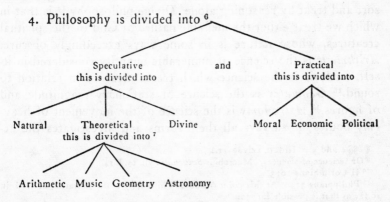

Speculative
this is divided into

and

Practical
this is divided into

Natural Theoretical Divine   Moral Economic Political
this is divided into [7]

Arithmetic Music Geometry Astronomy

[2] Now lost; the work treated the seven liberal arts and also medicine and architecture.

[3] (§ 2 here = Isid. II. xxiii. 1–2.)   [4] Cf. Quint. II. xx. 7, etc.

[5] (Cf. Isid. II. xxiii. 3.) *Isagoge:* an "introduction" to a subject; specifically, Porphyry's *Isagoge* (see below § 8, sentences 1, 2, 8).

[6] Δ reads: "Philosophy is divided as follows according to Aristotle, but not according to Plato: ΘΕΟΡΗΤΙΚΗ—ΠΡΑΚΤΙΚΗ."

[7] The divisions which follow in Δ (including a number of Greek terms) are very much confused; see Mynors 110.14, critical note.

5. Philosophy [8] is the probable knowledge of divine and human things insofar as it may be attained by man. According to another definition, philosophy is the art of arts and discipline of disciplines.[9] Again, philosophy is a meditation on death; this is better adapted to Christians, who, spurning the vanity of this world, lead a disciplined life in imitation of the life which they will lead in their future home; as the apostle says: [10] "For though we walk in the flesh, we do not war according to the flesh," and in another place: "Our conversation is in heaven." [11]

6. *Speculative* philosophy [12] is that by means of which we surmount visible things and in some degree contemplate things divine and heavenly, surveying them with the mind alone, inasmuch as they rise above corporeal eyes. *Natural* philosophy is that in which the nature of every material thing is discussed, for nothing is produced against the will of nature, but everything is allotted to the uses decreed by the Creator, unless perchance with God's consent some miracle is shown to appear. *Theoretical* philosophy is that which considers abstract quantity.[13] Abstract quantity is that which we separate in the intellect from matter or other accidents such as being even or odd or other things of this sort and treat by reasoning alone. *Divine* philosophy [14] is that in which we treat either the ineffable nature of God or the spiritual creatures, whose nature is in some ways exceedingly obscure. *Arithmetic* is the science of numerable quantity considered in itself.[15] *Music* is the science which treats measure in relation to sound.[16] *Geometry* is the science of stationary magnitude and of figures.[17] *Astronomy* is the science of the movement of heavenly bodies; it surveys all their forms and investigates the ac-

---

[8] (§§ 4 and 5 = Isid. II. xxiv. 9–11.)

[9] Or "science of sciences." Macrobius *Saturnalia* VII. 15. l. 14.

[10] II Corinthians 10:3.

[11] Philippians 3:20. At this point Δ adds: "Philosophy is the imitation of God, in so far as that is possible for man."

[12] (§§ 6–7 = Isid. II. xxiv. 11–16.)

[13] On this sentence and that which follows cf. above, II. pref. 4, last sentence; and below, II. iii. 21, first sentence.

[14] That is, theology.

[15] This sentence and the next three are repeated below in § 21, sentences 4–6.

[16] This sentence is repeated below in v. 4, sentence 2.

[17] This sentence is repeated below in vi. 2, sentence 1.

customed state of the stars in relation to themselves and to the earth.[18]

7. *Practical* philosophy is that which seeks to explain advantageous things [19] by a demonstration of the manner of their operations. *Moral* philosophy is that by means of which a proper manner of life is sought and habits are prepared which tend toward virtue. *Economic* philosophy is a wisely ordered management of domestic affairs. *Political* philosophy is that by means of which the entire state is advantageously administered.

8. After this treatment [20] of the all-embracing divisions and definitions of philosophy let us now take up the book by Porphyry which is entitled *Isagoge*.[21] Porphyry's *Isagoge* treats the five predicables: genus, species, difference, property, accident. *Genus* is the common attribute pertaining to species which is predicated of objects differing in species: animal, for example, is a genus, for through the individual species, that is, through man, ox, horse, and so forth, the genus animal is predicated and pointed out. *Species* is the common attribute which is predicated of several objects differing in kind; for man is predicated in the case of Socrates, Plato, and Cicero. *Difference* is the quality which is predicated of several objects differing in species, as rational and mortal are qualities predicated of man.[22] *Property* is the nonessential quality which is peculiar to every species and individual and which distinguishes them from others of the same class; for example, the property of laughing in man, and of neighing in a horse. *Accident* is the quality which is added and removed without detriment to the subject,[23] or it is the quality which is added in such a way as not to be completely removed.[24] Let him who desires to know these matters more fully read the

---

[18] This sentence is repeated in essentially the same form below in vii. 2, sentence 1.

[19] *Res praepositas* (προηγμένα), a Stoic term applied to wealth, beauty, etc., which are not to be called absolutely good.

[20] § 8 is drawn chiefly from Boethius' translation of the *Isagoge*.

[21] An "introduction" in Greek to the *Categories* of Aristotle which, in the translation of Boethius, had an important influence on the thought of the Middle Ages, Porphyry (A.D. 233–ca. 301–5) wrote many works, chiefly philosophical, philological, and historical.

[22] In other words, *difference* is that determinant distinguishing a species from other species of the same genus.

[23] A separable accident, presumably.   [24] An inseparable accident, presumably.

Introduction of Porphyry, who, though he says he is writing to make the work of another writer [25] useful, seems, nevertheless, not undeserving of praise himself for having fashioned such excellent words.

9. Next come [26] Aristotle's categories, or predicaments, by which in marvellous manner all discourse is encompassed through the use of various significations; their organs or instruments are three in number. The three organs or instruments of the categories, or predicaments, are: equivocal words, univocal words, and denominative words.[27] *Equivocal* words are those which have a common name but designate a different kind of substance in accordance with the name; for example, animals such as a real man and one in a painting. *Univocal* words are those which have a common name and designate the same kind of substance in accordance with the name; for example, animals such as man and ox. *Denominative,* that is, derivative, words are all those which have an appellation derived from a name and in accordance with it but with a different termination; for example, grammarian from grammar, and brave from bravery.[28]

10. Aristotle's categories, or predicaments, are ten in number: substance, quantity, relation, quality, action, passivity, place, time, position, possession.[29] *Substance* [30] is that which is indicated by the proper and primary and most definite sense of the word, that which is neither predicated of a subject nor present in a subject; for example, a particular man or a particular horse.[31] Second substances,[32] however, are species within which the above-mentioned primary substances are contained and included, as man, for example, is the species within which Cicero is contained. *Quantity* is either separate and has parts which are separated from one another and do not possess a common boundary, for example, number and speech, or it is continuous and has

---

[25] That is, Aristotle's *Categories.*

[26] §§ 9–10 are from Aristotle's *Categories.*

[27] Δ adds: ΟΜΩΝΥΜΑ ϹΥΝΟΝΥΜΑ ΠΑΡΩΝΥΜΑ.

[28] (Isid. II. xxvi. 4.) Δ adds: ΑΝΔΡΙΑϹ ΑΝΔΡΙΟϹ.

[29] Δ adds with various distortions: ΟΥϹΙΑ, ΠΟϹΟΤΗϹ, ΠΡΟϹ ΤΙ, ΠΟΙΟΤΗϹ, ΠΟΙΕΙΝ, ΠΑϹΧΕΙΝ, ΚΕΙϹΘΑΙ, ΠΟΤΕ, ΠΟΥ, ΕΧΕΙΝ.

[30] Equals "individual reality" here.

[31] (Isid. II. xxvi. 6.)

[32] "The universal substantial nature abstracted from first substances."

parts which are joined together at a common boundary, for example, line, surface, body, place, motion, time. One thing bears a *relation* to another if the very nature of the first is said to depend upon the second; for example, something greater, something double, condition, arrangement, knowledge, sensation, position. *Quality* is that by virtue of which certain of our species are said to be such as they are; for example, good, bad. Cutting and burning—in other words, doing something—are examples of *action*. Being cut and being burned are examples of *passivity*. Standing, sitting, and lying are examples of *place*. Yesterday and tomorrow are examples of *time*. In Asia, in Europe, and in Libya are examples of *position*. To have shoes and to have weapons are examples of *possession*. This work of Aristotle's should be read intently, since, as stated above, whatever man says is inevitably discovered to be present among these ten predicaments.[33] It is, moreover, of service in the understanding of books, whether they are connected with rhetoricians or dialecticians.

11. Next comes the book *Perihermenias*,[34] an exceedingly subtle and careful work with its various forms and repetitions, concerning which it has been said: "When Aristotle was in the process of writing *Perihermenias*, he used to dip the pen in his mind." [35] In the *Perihermenias* (which means *On Interpretation*) the afore-mentioned philosopher treats the following subjects: [36] noun, verb, clause, declaration, affirmation, negation, contradiction. A *noun* is an utterance which does not refer to time and is significant by convention but of which no part is significant when separated from the rest; for example, Socrates.[37] A *verb* is that which signifies time in addition to its proper meaning, that of which a part has no significance by itself, and which is always a sign of something said of something else; for example, "thinks," "disputes." A *clause* is a significant utterance of which any of

---

[33] (This sentence and the next occur in Isid. II. xxvi. 15.)

[34] περὶ ἑρμηνείας.

[35] (This sentence occurs in Isid. II. xxvii. 1.) The quotation is to be found in Suidas' *Lexicon* (written A.D. 950–976, from Greek sources), 3930 under the word Ἀριστοτέλης.

[36] (The remainder of this sentence and the rest of this section occur in Isid. II. xxvii. 4–7.)

[37] This sentence and the next five are from Boethius' translation of Aristotle's *Perihermenias*, chaps. ii–vi.

the parts when separated from the others is significant in itself; for example, "Socrates disputes." A *declarative* clause is a significant utterance concerning that which is or is not something; for example, "Socrates exists, Socrates does not exist." An *affirmation* is a declaration of something about something; for example, "Socrates is." A *negation* is a denial of something about something; for example, "Socrates is not." A *contradiction* is the opposing of affirmation and negation; for example, "Socrates disputes, Socrates does not dispute." All these matters are treated in very minute divisions and subdivisions in the work mentioned above. Let it suffice that we have briefly stated their definitions, since an appropriate explanation will be found in the work itself and particularly since the work has been expounded in a commentary in six books by Boethius, a man of distinction,[38] and the commentary left you among other codices.

12. Let us now come [39] to syllogistic figures and forms, with which the intellect of noble philosophers is continually occupied.

[38] "Vir magnificus." This appellative is used regularly of Boethius by C. (and once of Albinus, a writer on music; cf. chap. v, § 10, sentence 2, below). It does not occur in *Notitia,* the official register of all the offices, except municipal, which existed in the Roman Empire, or in any of the commentaries on this work (*e.g.,* Thomas Hodgkin, *Italy and Her Invaders: the Visigothic Invasion,* I, 200–233, J. B. Bury, *Later Roman Empire,* Vol. I, chap. iv, Gibbon's *Rome* (ed. by J. B. Bury), II, 549 f.), or in any of the epigraphical sources consulted (Dessau, Cagnat, etc.). Boethius was made consul at the age of thirty in A.D. 510, and even before that he had been dignified with the patriciate (cf. the title "patricius" in § 18, sentence 4, and at the end of note 104, below). On Sept. 1, 522, he was elevated to the highly important post of Master of the Offices, an office which he held at the time of his fall.

    The title "magnificus vir" would seem to have been one just below the older and higher dignity of "vir inluster." Both of these titles passed into the Gothic and Frankish kingdoms, in which also many other titles appeared, some of which were more indicative of social gradations than of political distinctions (see Samuel Dill, *Roman Society in Gaul in the Merovingian Age,* pp. 226–228; "viri magnifici" was applied even to assessors in the courts, who were probably landowners in the district, and also to a sprinkling of minor officials). "Magnificus vir" occurs several times in Frankish sources, both Merovingian and Carolingian, and lasts as late as 786 and 798 (see Georg Waitz, *Deutsche Verfassungsgeschichte,* II, 359, and note 2; IV, 328 and note). Gregory of Tours, a contemporary of Cassiodorus, uses the term three times in his *History of the Franks:* in IV. 16; IX. 18; III. 8. In none of these instances is the title one of political authority, but rather one of social prestige or position and equivalent to "a person of prominence," "a landed magnate," etc. "Vir inluster" under the Merovingians, however, was an authoritative title attributed to the mayor of the palace, while "patricius" was similarly an authoritative title borne by the king. "Magnificus vir" was probably not an official title in Cassiodorus' time, even in Italy, but rather a social appellative meaning "a man of distinction."

[39] § 12 = (Pseudo?)Apuleius, *Perihermenias,* pp. 274–277: Mart. IV. 411–413: (Isid. II. xxviii. 2–22).

There are three forms of the categorical, that is, the predicative, syllogism; in the first form there are nine moods, in the second form four moods, and in the third, six moods.[40]

The moods of the first form are nine in number. The *first* mood is that which concludes, that is, deduces, a universal affirmative directly from universal affirmatives, as in the following: "Everything just is honorable; everything honorable is good; therefore everything just is good." The *second* mood is that which concludes a universal affirmative directly from a universal affirmative and a universal negative, as in the following: "Everything just is honorable; nothing honorable is base; therefore nothing just is base." The *third* mood is that which concludes a particular affirmative directly from a particular affirmative and a universal affirmative, as in the following: "Something just is honorable; everything honorable is useful; therefore something just is useful." The *fourth* mood is that which concludes a particular negative directly from a particular affirmative and a universal negative, as in the following: "Something just is honorable; nothing honorable is base; therefore something just is not base." The *fifth* mood is that which concludes a particular affirmative, by reflection, from universal affirmatives, as in the following: "Everything just is honorable; everything honorable is good; therefore something good is just." The *sixth* mood is that which concludes a universal negative, by reflection, from a universal affirmative and a universal negative, as in the following: "Everything just is honorable; nothing honorable is base; therefore nothing base is just." The *seventh* mood is that which concludes a particular affirmative, by reflection, from a particular affirmative and a universal affirmative, as in the following: "Something just is honorable; everything honorable is useful; therefore something useful is just." The *eighth* mood is that which concludes a particular negative, by reflection, from a universal negative and a universal affirmative; for example: "Nothing base is honorable; everything honorable is just; therefore something just is not base." The *ninth* mood is that which concludes a particular negative, by reflection, from a universal nega-

---

[40] Δ adds: CXHMA ΠΡΩΤΟ (*sic*) EXEI TPOΠOTC ENEA—CXHMA B' EXEI TPOΠOTC Δ'—CXHMA Γ' EXEI TPOΠOTC EΞ H ENTA (*sic*).

tive and a particular affirmative; for example: "Nothing base is honorable; something honorable is just; therefore something just is not base."

The moods of the second form are four in number. The *first* mood is that which concludes a universal negative directly from a universal affirmative and a universal negative, as, for example: "Everything just is honorable; nothing base is honorable; therefore nothing base is just." The *second* mood is that which concludes a universal negative directly from a universal negative and a universal affirmative; for example: "Nothing base is honorable; everything just is honorable; therefore nothing base is just." The *third* mood is that which concludes a particular negative directly from a particular affirmative and a universal negative; for example: "Something just is honorable; nothing base is honorable; therefore something just is not base." The *fourth* mood is that which concludes a particular negative directly from a particular negative and a universal affirmative, as in the following: "Something just is not base; everything bad is base; therefore something just is not bad."

The moods of the third form are six in number. The *first* mood is that which concludes a particular affirmative, both directly and conversely, from universal affirmatives, as in the following: "Everything just is honorable; everything honorable is just;[41] everything just is good; therefore something honorable is good or something good is honorable." The *second* mood is that which concludes a particular affirmative directly from a particular affirmative and a universal affirmative, as in the following: "Something just is honorable; everything just is good; therefore something honorable is good." The *third* mood is that which concludes a particular affirmative directly from a universal affirmative and a particular affirmative, as in the following: "Everything just is honorable; something just is good; therefore something honorable is good." The *fourth* mood is that which concludes a particular negative directly from a universal affirmative and a universal negative, as in the following: "Everything just is honorable; nothing just is bad; therefore something honorable is not bad." The *fifth* mood is that which concludes a

---

[41] Ω and Isid. have this clause; Φ Δ omit it.

particular negative directly from a particular affirmative and a universal negative, as in the following: "Something just is honorable; nothing just is bad; therefore something honorable [42] is not bad." The *sixth* mood is that which concludes a particular negative directly from a universal affirmative and a particular negative, as in the following: "Everything just is honorable; something just is not bad; therefore something honorable is not bad."

Let him who desires to have full knowledge of these forms of categorical syllogism read Apuleius' book entitled *Perihermenias* [43] and he will learn the matters which are very subtly treated. And may the words which are repeated not bore us unduly; for with the Lord's help, when they are properly distinguished and reflected upon, they lead us in profitable fashion to the great highways of understanding. Let us now in turn come to hypothetical syllogisms.

13. The moods [44] of the hypothetical syllogism, which is formed by a connection of ideas, are seven in number. The *first* mood is this: "If it is day, it is light; it is day; therefore it is light." The *second* mood is this: "If it is day, it is light; it is not light; therefore it is not day." The *third* mood is as follows: "It is not day without being light; now it is day; therefore it is light." The *fourth* mood is as follows: "It is either day or night; now it is day; therefore it is not night." The *fifth* mood is as follows: "It is either day or night; now it is not night; therefore it is day." The *sixth* mood is as follows: "It is not day without being light; but it is day; therefore it is not night." The *seventh* mood is as follows: "It is not both day and night; now it is not night; therefore it is day."

If anyone, moreover, desires fuller knowledge of the moods of the hypothetical syllogism, let him read the book by Marius Victorinus which is entitled *On Hypothetical Syllogisms*. One should also know that Tullius Marcellus the Carthaginian [45] has treated

[42] "Honorable": editors, Pseudo-Apuleius, Mart.; "just": *codices* and Isid.

[43] That is, *"On Interpretation."* The ascription of this book to Apuleius (of Madaura), the philosopher and rhetorician of the second century A.D., is doubtful.

[44] The first eight sentences of this section are from Marius Victorinus, *De syllogismis hypotheticis.* (The first nine sentences = Isid. II. xxviii. 23–25.)

[45] Apparently mentioned only by Cassiodorus.

categorical and hypothetical syllogisms, which have been discussed at great length by various philosophers, so carefully and subtly in seven books as to take up the rule for dialectical syllogisms, as he himself says, in the first book, and to complete in the second and third books a brief description of Aristotle's voluminous utterances on categorical syllogisms, and to concentrate in the fourth and fifth books the treatment of hypothetical syllogisms which the Stoics have spread over countless tomes; he has treated mixed syllogisms in the sixth book and composite syllogisms in the seventh. I have left you this codex to read.

14. Let us proceed [46] from this subject to the most excellent types of definition, which are of such surpassing worth that they may be called clear manifestations of utterance and signs of speech.[47] A definition is defined as a short statement of a thing's essential nature which separates it from others of its class by determining its proper significance. This statement is made in many ways and in accordance with many rules. Definitions are divided into the following types: [48] οὐσιώδης, that is, essential; ἐννοηματική, that is, notional; ποιώδης, that is, qualitative; ὑπογραφική, that is, descriptive; κατ' ἀντίλεξιν, that is, substitutional; [49] κατὰ διαφοράν, that is, distinguishing; κατὰ μεταφοράν, that is, metaphorical; κατ' ἀφαίρεσιν τοῦ ἐναντίου, that is, by the negation of the opposite; κατὰ τύπωσιν, that is, by the use of an image; ὡς τύπῳ, that is, by way of example; κατ' ἐλλιπὲς ὁλοκλήρου ὁμογενοῦς, that is, by a statement of what is lacking to bring completeness within the same genus; κατ' ἔπαινον, that is, by way of praise; κατ' ἀναλογίαν, that is, proportional; κατὰ τὸ πρός τι, that is, relational; κατ' αἰτιολογίαν, that is, causational. The *first* type of definition is οὐσιώδης, that is, essential, and it is properly and truly called a definition; an example follows: "Man is a rational and mortal animal capable of understanding and learning." This definition, indeed, comes down through species and differences as far as property and indicates with great completeness what a man is. The *second* type of definition is that which is called ἐννοηματική in Greek and a predication

---

[46] § 14 comes from Marius Victorinus' book *On Definitions*.

[47] This sentence = Isid. II. xxviii. 26; the remainder of § 14 = Isid. II. xxix. 1–16.

[48] Instead of the preceding clause Δ presents here a continuous list of the Greek names of the fifteen types in addition to the single Greek names and their translations cited below.

[49] Literally *adverbium* = "something added to a word (*or* verb)."

in Latin and which, by using a general and not a particular term,[50] we may designate as a notion. This type is always formed in the following way: "Man is the animal which leads all the rest in rational thinking"; it has not, to be sure, said what a man is, but what he does, as if a sign had been evoked to give an idea of the thing. Of course, in the present type of definition and in the remaining types the notion adduced is not the essential notion, as it is in the first type; and, inasmuch as the first type is the essential type, it is to be preferred to all other definitions. The *third* type of definition is that which is called ποιώδης in Greek and qualitative in Latin.[51] By stating characteristics it points out the nature of a thing clearly, as in the following example: "Man is a being who is strong in intellect, rich in arts, and who through his knowledge of affairs either chooses what he ought to do or scornfully rejects what is unprofitable." Man is, indeed, portrayed and defined by these qualities. The *fourth* type of definition is that which is named ὑπογραφική in Greek and descriptive in Latin, and which points out the nature of a thing by employing a roundabout description, as in the following definition of luxurious: "Luxurious is applied to a mode of life desirous of the unnecessary, the costly, and the burdensome; abounding in pleasures, and quick to seek sensual enjoyment." [52] These details and others of the same sort define luxurious; and in view of its diffuseness this type of definition is better suited to orators than to dialecticians. This descriptive definition is used of good things and also of bad things. The *fifth* type of definition is that which we call κατ' ἀντίλεξιν in Greek and substitutional in Latin.[53] This type defines the word whose meaning is sought by substituting another single word, and in a measure states the signification of the desired word by employing another, as in the following example: "To cease speaking is to be silent." This type is likewise used when we call a boundary a limit or when we interpret "destroyed" as being "ruined." The *sixth* type of definition is that which the Greeks call κατὰ διαφοράν and we call distinguishing; in other words, when the distinction between a king and a tyrant is sought, the nature of each is defined by an enumeration of the differences, as in the

---

[50] Cassiodorus' *Comm. Psalt.* chap. 1, near the beginning.
[51] *Ibid.* xxi. 3, and elsewhere.   [52] *Ibid.* lxxix. 13.
[53] *Ibid.* xvi. 14 and often.

following: "A king is moderate and temperate; a tyrant, however, impious and inexorable." The *seventh* type of definition is that which Greek writers call κατὰ μεταφοράν and Latin writers metaphorical, as in the following definition from Cicero's *Topica:* [54] "A shore is a place where the waves cease their rolling." [55] This type can be treated in various ways: at one moment [56] to arouse, as in the statement "The head is the citadel of the body"; at another to blame, as in the statement "Riches are the long purse for short life"; at still another to praise: "Youth is the flower of life." The *eighth* type of definition is that which Greek writers call κατ' ἀφαίρεσιν τοῦ ἐναντίου and Latin writers a definition by the negation of the opposite of what is defined; examples follow: "What is not bad is good; what is not unjust is just"; and the like; the two parts are so naturally bound together that the understanding of one brings the requisite knowledge concerning the other.[57] We should, however, use this type of definition only when the opposite is known, for no one deems as certain that which is derived from the uncertain. A further example of this type follows: "Substance is that which is neither quality nor quantity nor accident." This type of definition may be used in defining God. For, though we are in no way able to comprehend the nature of God, the removal of all existing things, which the Greeks call ὄντα, gives us an idea of God by circumscribing and taking away our knowledge of the known, as if we should say: "God is that which is neither a person nor an element nor an animal nor mind nor feeling nor intellect nor anything which may be derived from the preceding items"—for by getting rid of these items and others like them, God's nature may be defined. The *ninth* type of definition is that which Greek writers call κατὰ τύπωσιν and Latin writers definition by the use of an image, as in the following: "Aeneas is the son of Venus and Anchises." [58] This type always has to do with indivisible

---

[54] A work on "commonplaces" or general arguments which do not grow out of the particular facts of a case, but are applicable to any class of cases.

[55] Cassiodorus' *Comm. Psalt.* xviii. 7. The quotation is from the *Topica* vii. 32.

[56] Isidore and Victorinus read here: "to warn: 'Nobility is the burden of the excellence of ancestors borne by their descendants,' to point out: 'The apex [= cap or crown; Victorinus reads "head"] is the citadel . . .' *etc.*"

[57] *Comm. Psalt.* xxxi. 1, and elsewhere.

[58] *Ibid.,* chap. lxxii, near the beginning.

entities, which the Greeks term ἄτομα; [59] it is likewise used in the
kind of discourse in which the speaker is ashamed or afraid to
say something outright, as in the example to which Cicero refers
in the following remark: "Although it is myself, let me tell you,
that those cut-throats are describing." [60] The *tenth* type of definition is that which Greek writers call ὡς τύπῳ and Latin writers
definition by way of example, so that, if one asks what an animal
is, the answer is "Man." [61] Of course, this statement obviously
is not intended to imply that the only animal is man, since there
are countless other animals, but, when "Man" is mentioned, it
defines animal by means of the example, man, though many things
are comprehended under the name "animal." The aforesaid example has made the point in question clear; it is of course the
property of a definition to explain the nature of the point in
question. The *eleventh* type of definition is that which Greek
writers call κατ' ἐλλιπὲς ὁλοκλήρου ὁμογενοῦς and Latin writers definition by a statement of what is lacking to bring completeness
within the same genus, so that if one asks what a quarter [62] is,
the answer is: "that which lacks three-quarters of being unity." [63]
The *twelfth* type of definition is that which Greek writers call
κατ' ἔπαινον and Latin writers definition by way of praise,[64] as in
the following example from Tully's speech in defense of Cluen-
tius: "Law is the mind and soul and counsel and judgment of the
state"; [65] and in the following example from another speech of
Tully's: "Peace is quiet liberty." [66] This type is also used to define by way of blame, which the Greeks call ψόγος: "Slavery is the

---

[59] "Atoms," but the meaning here is "individuals" (as applied to beings or objects).

[60] *Pro Milone* xviii. 47. The example lies in the fact that the men who were afraid
to name Cicero openly as the inspirer of Milo's murder of Clodius nevertheless
named Cicero by implication by referring to him as "a more important person."
Cicero puts it as follows (*loc. cit.,* just before the passage quoted by Cassiodorus):
"You know, gentlemen, that there were some who, in urging the setting up of this
court, ventured to assert that Milo's hand had done the deed, but that the mind that
prompted it belonged to a more important person." The passage quoted by Cassiodorus differs in several particulars from the versions found in most MSS of
Cicero; as it stands, it is apparently to be connected grammatically with the words
which follow in the text of Cicero—*Iacent suis testibus . . . liberatus sum . . .*
("they are discomfited by their own evidence . . . I have been acquitted.")

[61] *Comm. Psalt.* xlviii. 12.

[62] Φ Δ *Isid.* incorrectly read "a third."

[63] "Unity" = *assis* (a less usual form of the nominative than *as*).

[64] *Comm. Psalt.* xvii. 1, and often.   [65] *Pro Cluentio* liii. 146.

[66] *Philippics,* oration II, chap. xliv, § 113.

worst of all evils, to be repelled not only by war but by death as well." [67] The *thirteenth* type of definition is that which Greek writers call κατ' ἀναλογίαν and Latin writers proportional; this type occurs when a lesser thing is defined in terms of a greater, as in the statement: "Man is a lesser world." [68] Cicero has employed it in the following manner: "An edict is an annual law." [69] The *fourteenth* type of definition is that which Greek writers term κατὰ τὸ πρός τι and Latin writers relational; [70] examples are the statements "A father is one who has a son" and "A master is one who has a slave," and the following definitions from Cicero's *Rhetorical Books:* "A genus is that which embraces several sub-divisions" [71] and "A subdivision is that which is subordinate to a genus." [72] The *fifteenth* type of definition is that which Greek writers call κατ' αἰτιολογίαν and Latin writers causational; an example follows: "Day is the sun above the earth; night is the sun beneath the earth." We ought, moreover, to realize that the above-mentioned types of definition have been justly associated with commonplaces, [73] since these types are employed in some arguments and are mentioned at some points in commonplaces. Let us now come to commonplaces, [74] which are the bases of arguments, the well springs of ideas, and the sources of modes of expression. [75]

15. Commonplaces, [76] or the places from which arguments are derived, are divided into several groups: some are inherent in the question under discussion; others, called affected, [77] are in a

---

[67] *Ibid.*

[68] *Comm. Psalt.* lxxxi. 6.

[69] *Verrines,* oration 1, chap. xlii, § 109. "Edict" here means the public announcement of the praetor, in which he states, on entering upon his office, the rules by which he will be guided in administering justice. Out of such regulations, renewed and made more complete every year, there was gradually formed an important part of the body of Roman law.   [70] *Comm. Psalt.* lxxxviii. 27.

[71] *De inventione* i. 42.   [72] *Ibid.*

[73] "Topica": general forms of argument.

[74] *Comm. Psalt.* cxliv. 21.

[75] At this point Φ and Δ add: "A brief statement ought to be made about them in order that we may recognize both dialectical and rhetorical commonplaces and their varieties. A statement ought to be made first concerning dialectical commonplaces." Here follow excerpts from Boethius' work *De differentiis topicis;* see Mynors, pp. xxv and xxxvii. The version of Cassiodorus' treatment of commonplaces (§§ 15–17, below) found in Φ and Δ is relegated to Appendix A.

[76] §§ 15–16 are possibly from Marius Victorinus' commentary on Cicero's *Topica;* (§§ 15–17 = Isid. II. xxx).

[77] "Effected": Isid.

certain measure produced by additional circumstances; still others are assumed to be extrinsic. The arguments which are inherent in the question under discussion are these: from the whole, from parts, and from etymology. An argument *from the whole* is the employment of a definition for the point to be determined, as in Cicero's statement: "Glory is the praise for deeds well done, and the reputation for great services to the state." [78] An argument *from parts* is either a denial by the defendant that the deed was done or a claim by him that the deed was justly done. An argument *from etymology* is an argument derived from the force of a word, as in the following example from Cicero: "It was a consul, a consul,[79] I say, that I was seeking, but I was unable to find one in that infamous emasculate." [80] Effected [81] arguments are those which are in a certain measure produced by additional circumstances: arguments from cognate words,[82] from genus, from species, from likeness, from difference, from the opposite, from analogy, from anterior circumstances, from posterior circumstances, from contradictory ideas, from causes, from effects, and from comparison (of the greater to the lesser, of the lesser to the greater, and of equal to equal). An argument from *cognate words* occurs when a noun is modified to form a verb, as in Cicero's statement that Verres "swept" the province "clean," [83] or a verb is modified to form a noun, as in "plunderer" from "to plunder," or one noun is modified to form another, as in Terence's remark: "It's a scheme of lunatics, not lovers" [84]—provided the last part of one word is inflected somewhat differently from the corresponding part of the other word. An argument *from genus* is the inferring of an idea concerning a species from the genus to which the species belongs, as in Virgil's words: "A fickle and changeful thing is woman ever." [85] An argument *from*

---

[78] *Pro Marcello* viii. 26.

[79] "Consul" is cognate with "consilium" ("counsel") and "consulo" ("to take counsel").

[80] *In Pisonem* ix. 19.   [81] "Affected": M.

[82] Or, as in the third example presented in the definition below, from similarity of form.

[83] *Verrines,* oration ii. chap. 7, § 19. There is a play on "Verres" and "everrisse" ("swept clean," "plundered"). The exact derivation of Verres is uncertain.

[84] *Andria,* l. 218. There is a play on "amentium" ("lunatics") and "amantium" ("lovers"), which are etymologically unrelated.

[85] *Aeneid* iv. 569; said of Dido in a speech to Aeneas by Mercury.

species is the lending of truth by a particular statement to a general one: "But it was not thus that the Phrygian shepherd entered Lacedaemon." [86] An argument *from likeness* is the discovery of like circumstances in particular things, as in Virgil's lines: "Bring me store of weapons; none of all those that once on Ilium's plains were lodged in bodies of the Greeks shall my hand hurl at Rutulians in vain." [87] An argument *from difference* is the distinguishing of particular things by a citation of their dissimilarities, as in Virgil's statement: "Not Diomede's horses dost thou see, nor Achilles' car." [88] An argument *from the opposite* is a term applied to the juxtaposition of contrary ideas, as in Virgil's question: "Should hulls framed by mortal hand have immortal rights, and should Aeneas in surety traverse unsure perils?" [89] An argument *from posterior* [90] *circumstances* is a statement of something which inevitably follows from a definite assumption, as in Virgil's guarantee: "No such violence is in our hearts; nor have the vanquished such assurance." [91] An argument *from anterior circumstances* is a demonstration that particular things are the results of previous actions, as in the following example from Cicero's speech in defense of Milo: "Since he has not hesitated to disclose what he thought, can you doubt what he did?" [92] An argument *from contradictory ideas* is the destruction of a charge by the opposition of a notion inconsistent with it, as in Cicero's observation: "He, therefore, who not only had been freed from such danger but had been endowed with the greatest public honor would have liked to slay you in his home." [93] An argument *from kindred ideas* [94] is a demonstration, by means

---

[86] *Ibid.* VII. 363; Amata, Lavinia's mother, is here comparing Paris' rape of Helen to the projected marriage of Aeneas and Lavinia, who is already betrothed to Turnus. The usual version of this line appears below in Appendix A.

[87] *Ibid.* X. 333–335; Aeneas addresses his squire Achates.

[88] *Ibid.* X. 581; Liger, a friend of Turnus, addresses Aeneas before combat.

[89] *Ibid.* IX. 95–97; Jupiter is answering his mother's request for a guarantee of the safety of Aeneas and his companions.

[90] In the list near the beginning of § 15 "anterior" precedes "posterior."

[91] *Aeneid* I. 529; Ilioneus assures Dido of the peaceful intentions of the shipwrecked Trojans.

[92] *Pro Milone* xvi. 44.

[93] *Pro rege Deiotaro* v. 15; the observation is, of course, ironical.

[94] *A coniugatis.* One would have expected something like *a coniunctis*, since *a coniugatis* is used above in the sense of an argument *from cognate words* or *similarity of form.* The present argument seems to be the opposite of the argument *from contradictory ideas*, which precedes, and follows naturally after the latter. It is

of a comparison, of the effect which will arise from something: "If they drive us forth, they deem that naught will stay them from laying all Hesperia utterly beneath their yoke." [95] An argument *from causes* is the treatment of something in accordance with a general habit of action, as in Terence's lines: "For some time I have had my fears about you, Davus, that you might follow the run of servants and trick me." [96] An argument *from effects* is a demonstration that something is a result of preceding acts, as in Virgil's saying: " 'T is fear that proves souls base." [97] An argument *from comparison* is the forming of an opinion about something by implication after it has been compared to persons or causes, as in Virgil's words: "Thou hast power to steal Aeneas from the hands of the Greeks; but that we in turn have given some aid to the Rutulians, is that monstrous?" [98]

16. Extrinsic arguments are those which the Greeks term ἄτεχνοι, that is, without art,[99] as in the case of evidence. Evidence rests upon the following: person; the authority of nature; the authority of circumstance, which consists of eight modes (talent, wealth, age, luck, art, experience, necessity, and concourse of fortuitous events); the words and deeds of our ancestors; and torments. *Evidence* is everything which is taken from some external thing to produce credence. Not every *person* is the sort of individual whose evidence carries weight in the producing of credence, but a witness ought to be a person who deserves praise for the excellence of his moral character. The authority of *nature* [100] is the authority which possesses the greatest excellence. There are many modes of evidence [101] which carry weight, to wit: talent, wealth, age, luck, art, experience, necessity, con-

---

probably to be identified with the argument *from analogy* (*ab adiunctis*) cited in the list near the beginning of § 15 before the argument *from anterior circumstances;* cf. Cicero's *Topica* iii. 11 and iv. 18. Cf. Appendix A, No. 7 (*a coniunctis*), below, p. 212 and note 22.   [95] *Aeneid* VIII. 147–148.

[96] *Andria* ll. 582–583.   [97] *Aeneid* IV. 13.

[98] *Aeneid* x. 81 and 84; Juno is angrily addressing Venus during a council of the gods.

[99] "Empirical"; "which require no art on the orator's part." Cicero, *Topica* IV. 24.

[100] That is, "natural endowment." This sentence, then, really means the same as the preceding. In Cicero's *Topica* xix. 23 *persona* is not a separate category.

[101] "Having to do with *circumstance*," apparently omitted by Cassiodorus, is necessary to complete the sense here; cf. Cicero, *Topica* xix. 73: "in tempore autem multa sunt quae adferant auctoritatem."

course of fortuitous events. One seeks to produce credence through the use of *the words and deeds of our ancestors* when he cites the words and deeds of the ancients. Credence is produced by *torments,* after the employment of which no one is thought to have any desire to lie. The matters which are mentioned under *circumstances* [102] do not need defining, since their meaning is clearly indicated by their appellations.

17. One should also store away in his memory the fact that commonplaces furnish arguments alike to orators, dialecticians, poets, and lawyers; but when they demonstrate a particular point they have to do with orators, poets, and lawyers, and when they treat a general question they clearly concern dialecticians.[103] Clearly a remarkable species of achievement—the fact that there could be assembled in a single place everything which the mobility and variety of the human mind has been able to discover in seeking the meaning of various situations! This achievement confines the free and voluntary intellect; for, wherever the human mind turns, whatever thoughts it considers, it refers of necessity to one of the commonplaces named above.

18. We have decided, moreover, to recapitulate briefly a matter that is appropriate—the names of the men by whose labor these things have been transferred to the Latin language, in order that the glory of the authors may not perish and in order that the truth of these things may become fully known to us. The orator [104] Victorinus has translated the *Isagoge;* [105] Boethius, a man of distinction,[106] has published a commentary on

[102] In § 16, sentences 2 and 6, above.

[103] "Philosophers" Φ Δ.

[104] In place of this sentence and the three sentences which follow Φ and Δ have the following version: "The patrician Boethius has translated the *Isagoge,* leaving us his two commentaries (*see note 107, below*). The patrician Boethius has likewise translated the *Categories* [*of Aristotle*] and has also composed a commentary on this work in three books (*sic*). The same patrician Boethius has translated [*Aristotle's*] *Perihermenias* into Latin and has written two commentaries on it [*the first in two books, the second in six*] which contain most minute reasoning. Apuleius of Madaura has written a brief explanation of categorical syllogisms [*in his Perihermenias; cf. § 12, note 43, above*]; the above-mentioned patrician Boethius has treated hypothetical syllogisms with exceptional clarity." On the title "patrician" ("patricius") see § 11 and note 38, above.

[105] Marius Victorinus: Porphyry's *Isagoge,* or introduction to the *Categories* of Aristotle; cf. §§ 3, 8 (*ter*), above.

[106] "Vir magnificus." On this appellative see § 11, last sentence, and note 38, above.

the same work in five books.[107] Victorinus has likewise translated the *Categories* [108] and has also composed a commentary on
the work in eight books. The same Victorinus has translated the
Perihermenias [109] into Latin, and the patrician Boethius has written a commentary on it in six books, which contain most minute
reasoning. Apuleius of Madaura has written a brief explanation
of categorical syllogisms; [110] Victorinus has treated hypothetical
syllogisms; [111] the same Marius Victorinus has also carefully
taught us that there are fifteen types of definition.[112] Cicero has
rendered Aristotle's *Topica* into Latin, and Victorinus, who loves
Latin writers and looks out for their needs, has written a commentary in four books on Cicero's translation.[113] Not unsuitably,
perhaps,[114] have I assembled the translations mentioned above
in a single codex, in order that everything which has to do with
dialectic may be contained within the covers of one volume. And
we have consequently had the commentaries on the different
works written in separate codices, since they are extensive, and,
with the Lord's help, I have left them to you in a single collection.

19. Matters concerning the liberal arts, therefore, insofar as
we have judged them to be profitable to uncultivated individuals,
have been discussed perhaps in order that you may approach the
threshold of the sciences in your eagerness with certain doors,
as it were, already open.[115] For even if certain difficulties attend
the penetration and learning of the sciences, the latter retain the
drudgery of elementary studies only until the nature of their de-

---

[107] (This sentence: Isid. II. xxv. 9.) Boethius published two commentaries—the
first, in two books, based on Marius Victorinus' translation, the second, in five books,
based on his own.

[108] Of Aristotle. V.'s trans. is a possible source of §§ 9–10, above.

[109] Of Aristotle.   [110] Cf. § 12, note 43, above.

[111] Cf. § 13, note 44, above.   [112] § 14, above.

[113] Cf. ii. 14 and iii. 15–16, above. Instead of this sentence Φ and Δ have the two
which follow: "Cicero has translated Aristotle's *Topica* into Latin in one book and
the patrician Boethius, who loves Latin writers and looks out for their needs (Δ
omits this clause), has written a commmentary on Cicero's work in eight books.
And the aforesaid Boethius, the patrician (Δ *omits "aforesaid" and "patrician"*)
has rendered the aforesaid *Topic* of Aristotle into the Latin language in eight books."

[114] This sentence, the rest of this §, and all of § 19, below, are omitted by Φ and Δ.

[115] That is, the (liberal) arts, here restricted to grammar, rhetoric, and dialectic,
are introductions to the four sciences (*disciplinae*)—arithmetic, music, geometry,
and astronomy.

lightfulness is explored; when students have completely achieved their goal, they will all be glad to have endured to the end the annoyance caused by this fatiguing toil. It is now time for us to take up the extremely celebrated divisions of the sciences in the same spirit, a matter not unjustly considered to be expressed better in Greek than in Latin; we shall make our descriptions as brief as those in the Greek in our attempt not so much to explain the divisions as to point them out. For why should that which is found to be expressed distinctly and plainly in the original be discussed at greater length, as if such discussion were superior?

20. We must now, moreover, consider a point upon which we have already touched in the chapter on rhetoric,[116] since opportunity offered, namely, the difference between an art and a science,[117] in order that the distinction between the words may not become confused and confounded. Plato and Aristotle, renowned teachers of secular letters, had the following distinction in mind: an art is an intellectual quality that works with possibles, which can be regarded as other than they are; a science, however, is that which is concerned with what cannot be other than it is. But it has been taken for granted that these definitions were applied to secular letters, for only divine letters are incapable of being other than they are,[118] since they possess the immovable authority of truth. We have also heard that Felix Capella has written a treatise on the sciences,[119] lest simple brothers be left without knowledge of such liberal studies, but we have not yet been able to get possession of this treatise. In view of its unavailability, however, it is better for us not to offer it to you, but rather to make a prompt presentation of our own work, however poor it may be, to you who are anxious to learn. Let us now come to the beginning of mathematics.

On Mathematics

21. Mathematics,[120] which we may term "a theoretical

---

[116] Chap. ii, § 17, sentences 1 and 2. [117] *Disciplina.*

[118] Whereas secular letters, insofar as an *art* is concerned, may be regarded as other than they are. Φ and Δ omit this sentence and the next two. Δ also omits the last sentence of this §.

[119] Really on the seven liberal arts: cf. i. 3, note 25, and ii. 17, note 72, above.

[120] § 21 = Isid. III. *praef.* On this sentence and the next cf. II. pref. 4, last sentence, above.

study" [121] in Latin, is the science which considers abstract quantity.[122] Abstract quantity is that which we separate in the intellect from matter or other accidents, such as being even or odd or other things of this sort, and treat by reasoning alone.[123] It, that is, mathematics, is divided into the following parts: arithmetic, music, geometry, and astronomy. *Arithmetic* is the science of numerable quantity considered in itself.[124] *Music* is the science which treats measure in relation to sound.[125] *Geometry* is the science of stationary magnitude and of figures.[126] *Astronomy* is the science of the movement of heavenly bodies which surveys all their forms and investigates the accustomed state of the stars in relation to themselves and to the earth.[127] We shall describe these sciences at somewhat greater length in the appropriate places, in order that their excellence may be suitably revealed.

22. Let us now discuss the term "science." [128] Sciences, as has already been stated, are studies, free from the snare of opinion, which are never other than they are, and they are so called because they necessarily keep their own rules.[129] They are neither increased by expansion nor diminished by contraction nor modified by any changes, but they abide in their proper nature and observe their own rules with indisputable constancy.[130] When we turn them over in our minds in frequent meditation, they sharpen our understanding and wipe away the mud of ignorance; and, provided we are favored with soundness of mind, they lead us, with the Lord's help, to glorious theoretical contemplation. We ought, moreover, to remember that Josephus, the most learned of the Hebrews, says in the ninth chapter of the first book of his *Antiquities* that Abraham first transmitted arithmetic and astronomy to the Egyptians,[131] and that since they are men of

---

[121] Cf. iii. 6, sentence 3, above.

[122] (This sentence and the next two = Rabanus III. 21.)

[123] Chap. iii, § 6, sentence 4, above, is practically identical.

[124] This sentence and the next three = iii. 6, sentences 6–9, above. (Rabanus III. 22.)

[125] This sentence = v. 4, sentence 2, below.

[126] This sentence = vi. 2, sentence 1, below.

[127] This sentence = essentially vii. 2, sentence 1, below.

[128] Cf. § 20, above, and ii. 17, sentence 2, above.

[129] That is, *disciplina* ("science") = "discipline" in the sense of "subjection to rule."

[130] Boethius, *Arithmetica* I. 1.   [131] (Cf. Isid. III. xxv. 1.)

unusually keen intellect they developed the seeds from these sources until they produced the remaining sciences.[132] With reason do our holy Fathers persuade us that the sciences ought to be perused by those who are fond of learning, for these studies are in large measure instrumental in drawing our desire away from carnal matters and in making us desire things which, with the Lord's aid, we can see with the mind alone. It is therefore time for us to discuss them briefly, one by one.

IV. ON ARITHMETIC

1. Writers of secular letters have meant to convey the idea that arithmetic is the first among the mathematical sciences, inasmuch as music and geometry and astronomy, which follow it, require it for the explanation of their own potentialities.[1] Music, for example, requires it because music deals, among other things, with the relationship between a simple number and its double;[2] geometry likewise requires it, because geometry deals with the triangle, the quadrangle, and the like; astronomy too requires it, because astronomy deals with the reckoning of the changing positions of the heavenly bodies; arithmetic, however, depends for its existence neither upon music nor upon geometry nor upon astronomy. On that account arithmetic is recognized as being the origin and source of the others, and Pythagoras[3] is known to have praised this science to such a degree as to state that all things were created by God on the basis of number and measure, saying that some things were fashioned in motion, and other things at rest, but that all things were fashioned in such a way that nothing had any substance beyond the substratum mentioned above; I believe that this explanation is correct, and I derive my belief in this origin of things, as many philosophers have done, from that prophetic statement which says that God ordered all things *in measure, and number, and weight.*[4]

---

[132] (This sentence and the next = Rabanus III. 22.) On Josephus' *Antiquities* cf. I. xvii. 1, sentence 3, above.

[1] (Isid. III. i. 1.) Cf. Boethius, *Arithmetica* I. 1.

[2] Cf. v. 4, sentence 2, below.

[3] The famous leader (*floruit* 540–510 B.C.) of a philosophical school at Croton, in southern Italy.

[4] Wisdom of Solomon 11:21.

2. The present study, therefore, consists of separate quantity, which produces varieties of number that do not possess a common boundary.[5] For 5 is not united to 10 by any common boundary; nor is 6 thus united to 4; nor 7 to 3. Our study is called arithmetic because it has numbers as its special province.[6] Now a number is a quantity made up of units; for example, 3, 5, 10, 20, and so forth. The purpose of arithmetic is to teach us the nature of abstract number and its accidents; for example, evenness, oddness, and so forth.

3. Number,[7] moreover, is divided into

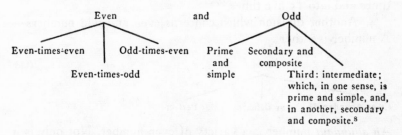

An *even* number is one which can be divided into two equal parts; for example, 2, 4, 6, 8, 10, and so forth. An *unequal* number is one which can in no way be divided into two equal parts; for example, 3, 5, 7, 9, 11, and so forth. An *even-times-even* number is one whose successive divisions into two equal parts can be continued as far as unity; for example, 64, half of which is 32, while half of 32 is 16, half of 16 is 8, half of 8 is 4, half of 4 is 2, and half of 2 is 1. An *even-times-odd* number is one whose similar division into two equal parts can occur but once; for example, 10, whose half is 5; 14, whose half is 7; 18, whose half is 9; and the like. An *odd-times-even* number is one which can be divided twice or more successively into two equal parts without reaching unity as a quotient; for example, 24, which halved equals 12, while 12 halved equals 6, and 6 halved equals 3, a quotient which can no longer be halved. Among the odd numbers a *prime*

---

[5] Cf. iii. 10, sentence 4, above.

[6] ἡ ἀριθμητική = the science which has to do with numbers (ἀριθμοί).

[7] §§ 3–6 are derived from Boethius' Latin translation of the Greek work on arithmetic by Nicomachus.

[8] Φ and Δ set part of the table here, a second part after the next two sentences, and a third part three sentences farther on.

and simple number is one which can be divided by unity alone; [9] for example, 3, 5, 7, 11, 13, 17, and the like. A *secondary and composite* number is one which can be divided not merely by unity but also by some number beyond unity; for example, 9, 15, 21, and the like. An *intermediate* number is one which, in one sense, is prime and incomposite and, in another, secondary and composite; for example, 9, which when compared with 25 is prime and incomposite, since it has no common factor except unity, and when compared with 15 is secondary and composite, since it has a common factor beyond unity, namely, 3, which goes into 9 three times and into 15 five times.[10]

4. Another division which concerns even and odd numbers— A number is either

Even   or   Odd

either Abundant [11]   or Deficient   or Perfect

An *abundant* number is a variety of even number. Not only is it even but it also has factors whose sum is greater than itself; for example, 12, whose half is 6, whose sixth part 2, whose fourth part 3, whose third part 4, and whose twelfth part 1, and whose factors added together make 16. A *deficient* number is also a variety of even number. It has factors whose sum is less than itself; for example, 8, whose half is 4, whose fourth part 2, whose eighth part 1, and whose factors added together make 7. A *perfect* number is likewise a variety of even number. Not only is it even, but it also has factors whose sum is equal to itself; for example, 6, whose half is 3, whose third part 2, whose sixth part 1, and whose factors added together make the number 6 itself.

5. A third division of numbers as a whole [12]— Every number is considered either absolutely or

[9] And of course by itself as well.
[10] (This sentence = Isid. III. v. 8.)
[11] *Superfluus:* literally "superfluous," "overabundant."
[12] (§§ 5–6 = Isid. III. vi–vii.)

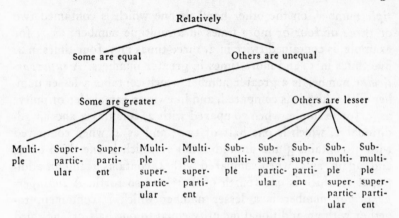

A number considered *absolutely* is one which is said to have no relation to another; for example, 3, 4, 5, 6, and the like. A number considered *relatively* is one which is associated and compared with other numbers; as 4, for example, when compared with 2, and 6 when compared with 3, and 8 when compared with 4, and 10 when compared with 5 are all considered double and multiple; and, again, as 3 when compared with 1, and 6 when compared with 2, and 9 when compared with 3, and so forth, are all triple. *Equal* numbers are those which are equal in quantity; for example, 2 and 2, 3 and 3, 10 and 10, 100 and 100, and so forth. *Unequal* numbers are those which upon comparison with one another show an inequality; for example, 3 and 2, 4 and 3, 5 and 4, 10 and 6; and in general a number of this sort is called unequal whether the comparison be between a greater and a lesser or between a lesser and a greater. A *greater* number is one which contains the lesser number, with which it is compared, and some additional quantity; as, 5, for example, is greater than 3, because 5 contains 3 and two units besides; and so forth. A *lesser* number is one which . . .[13] A *multiple* number is one which contains a lesser number two or three or four or more times; as 2, for example, when compared with 1 is double, 3 compared with 1 triple, 4 compared with 1 quadruple, and so forth. A *submul-*

---

[13] This sentence is omitted by the MSS of Cassiodorus. Some of Isidore's MSS supply the following: "A *lesser* number is one which is contained, together with an additional quantity, in a greater, with which it is compared, as 3, for example, is less than 5; for 3 and two additional units are contained in 5."

tiple number, on the other hand, is one which is contained two
or three or four or more times in a multiple number; as 1, for
example, is contained twice in 2, three times in 3, four times in 4,
five times in 5, and more times in greater numbers. A *superparticular* number is a greater number which contains a lesser number with which it is compared, and likewise a remainder of unity;
as 3, for example, when compared with 2, contains 2 and an additional 1, which is one half of two; and as 4, when compared
with 3, contains 3 and an additional 1, which is one third of 3;
and, again, as 5, when compared with 4, contains 4 and an additional 1, which is one fourth of 4;[14] and so forth. A *subsuper-
particular* number is a lesser number which is contained, together with an additional quantity equal to one half or one third
or one fourth or one fifth, in a greater number; as 2, for example,
when compared with 3, 3 when compared with 4, 4 with 5, and
so forth. A *superpartient* number is one which contains a lesser
number in its entirety with a remainder, of 2 or 3 or 4 or 5 or
more, which is less than the lesser number; as 5, for example,
when compared with 3, contains 3 with a remainder of 2; and as
7, when compared with 4, contains 4 and a remainder of 3; and
as 9, when compared with 5, contains 5 and a remainder of 4.[15]
A *subsuperpartient* number is one which is contained, together
with an additional quantity equal to 2 or 3 or more but less than
the given number, in a superpartient number; as 3, for example,
together with an additional 2, is contained in 5; as 4, together
with an additional 3, is contained in 7;[16] and as 5, together with
an additional 4, is contained in 9. A *multiple superparticular*
number is one which when compared with a lesser number contains the lesser number in its entirety more than once with a
remainder of unity; as 5, for example, when compared with 2,
contains 2 twice, with 1 left over; as 9, when compared with 4,
contains 4 twice, with 1 left over. A *submultiple superparticular*
number is one which when compared with a greater number is
contained more than once, together with an additional 1, in the
greater number; as 2, for example, when compared with 5, is

[14] This clause is omitted by Δ.   [15] This clause is omitted by Δ.
[16] Φ and Δ preserve this clause; otherwise omitted.

contained twice, with an additional 1, in 5. A *multiple superpartient* number is one which when compared with a lesser number contains that lesser number more than once with a remainder greater than unity but less than the lesser number; as 8, for example, when compared with 3, contains 3 twice, with 2 left over; as 14, when compared with 6, contains 6 twice, with 2 left over; [17] as 16, when compared with 7, contains the latter twice, with 2 left over; as 19, when compared with 8, contains 8 twice, with 3 left over. A *submultiple superpartient* number is one which, compared with a greater number, is contained more than once, together with a quantity greater than unity but less than the given number, in the greater number; as 3, for example, is contained twice in 8, with 2 left over; as 4 is contained three times in 15, with 3 left over.

6. A fourth division of numbers as a whole follows—Numbers are either discrete [18] or Continuous

Linear   Superficial   Solid

A *discrete* number is one which consists of separate units; [19] as 3, for example, is separate from 4, and as 5 is separate from 6, and so forth. A *continuous* number is one which consists of connected units; as 3, for example, would be called continuous if it was understood to be the measurement of a magnitude, that is, the measurement of a line or a space or a solid; the same applies to 4 and to 5. A *linear* number is one which starts from unity and continues in a straight line to infinity; [20] for this reason alpha, a letter which among the Greeks signifies unity, is used to designate lines—a a a. A *superficial* number is one which has to do not merely with length but also with width; for example, a triangular number, a quadrate number, a pentagonal number, a circular number, and other numbers which are at all times concerned with

[17] For this clause Δ reads: "as 16, when compared with 6, contains 6 twice and 4 left over."

[18] That is, separate.

[19] Without any application to measurement.

[20] Unity is not included, for a line is the aggregate of two or more points. 2, 3, 4, 5, 6, etc. are linear numbers.

surfaces. An example of a triangular number follows [21]—

An example of a quadrate number follows [22]—

An example of a pentagonal number follows [23]—

A *circular* number is one which, when multiplied by itself, both starts from itself and returns to itself; [24] as 5 times 5, for example, is 25, as the following diagram indicates:

[And likewise, if we consider the number 6, 6 times 6 equals 36, and 6 times 36 equals 236.] [25] A *solid* number is one which has to do with length and width and depth. Examples follow: pyramids, which rise like a flame, as in the following diagram:

[21] A triangular number is properly the sum of any group of successive numbers which begin with 1; it is a number which, when analyzed into units, shapes into triangular form the equilateral placement of its parts in a plane; examples are 3, 6, 10, 15, etc. Thus, 6 (illustrated above) is the sum of 1 (a), 2 (aa), and 3 (aaa), and its units, arranged equilaterally, form a triangle. (The formula may be expressed as half the product of any two successive numbers: $\frac{n\ (n+1),\ )}{2}$.

[22] A quadrate number is properly the sum of the series of odd numbers from 1 to $2n + 1$; it is a square, the advance in the sides of which progresses with the natural numbers and the side consists of as many units as there are numbers taken into the sum to produce it; e.g., $1 + 3 + 5 = 3^2$ or 9 (illustrated above).

[23] A pentagonal number is properly a number formed by the sum of the terms of an arithmetical progression beginning from 1 with a common difference of 3 which, when resolved into units and depicted as a plane figure, assumes the geometrical form of an equilateral five-angled figure (here a square with a triangle on top) each side of which consists of as many units as there are numbers taken into the sum to produce it; e.g., $1 + 4 = 5$ (illustrated above); the formula is $n^2 + \frac{1}{2}n\ (n-1)$.

[24] That is, a number whose powers terminate in the same digit as the number itself; e.g., 5, 6, 11.

[25] This sentence appears inside the circle in Δ, but is omitted by Φ, Ω, and Isid.

cubes such as dice, for instance, as in the following diagram:

spheres, which have an even roundness in every part, as in the following diagram:

A *spherical* number, moreover, is one which when multiplied by a circular number both starts from itself and returns to itself;[26] 5 times 5, for example, is 25, and this circular number when multiplied by the original number makes a spherical number: that is, 5 times 25 is 125.

7. Since these matters have been carefully treated, do you therefore bear in mind that this science takes precedence over the rest for the reason stated above,[27] namely, that it depends for its existence upon no other science, whereas the others which follow after depend for their being and existence upon the science of arithmetic, as the quality of its excellence has already shown. Among the Greeks, Nicomachus [28] has written a diligent explanation of this science. The first scholar to give the Romans a Latin translation of this work to read was Apuleius·of Madaura;[29] the second, Boethius, a man of distinction;[30] and if, as the saying goes, one makes frequent use of these translations, one will, within human limitations, undoubtedly be imbued with an exceptionally clear understanding. We have, moreover, been allowed to live in great part under the sway of this very science; when we learn the hours through its agency, when we reckon the course of the months, when we discern the circuit of the revolving year, it is through number [31] that we are instructed, lest we become confused.[32] Take it away from the generation of those

---

[26] That is, a number whose third power terminates in the same digit as the number itself.   [27] § 1, sentences 1 and 2, above.

[28] Nicomachus of Gerasa (*floruit ca.* A.D. 150) wrote a work on arithmetic ('Αριθμητικὴ εἰσαγωγή) and another work on music ('Εγχειρίδιον ἁρμονικῆς).

[29] See chap. iii. 12, and note 43, and § 18, both above.

[30] See iii. 11, last sentence, and note 38, above.

[31] That is, arithmetic.   [32] This sentence and the next = Isid. III. iv. 3.

who now possess it, and blind ignorance will encompass all things; he who does not understand reckoning cannot be distinguished from the other animals. It is, moreover, as glorious a thing as our life requires; for through its agency our worldly goods are reckoned with the greatest certainty and the amount of our expenses is disbursed only after proper computation. Number it is which disposes all things; through it we learn what we ought to do first and what we ought to do second.

8. If you should examine the cause of this important fact minutely, not even the miracles of the Lord are foreign to the power of number.[33] The number one pertains to the single God, as we read, for example, in the Pentateuch:[34] "Hear, O Israel, the Lord thy God is one Lord."[35] Two pertains to the two Testaments, since it says in Kings:[36] "And within the oracle he made two cherubims, each ten cubits high." And, finally, the sweetest fruit of all our hope is stored up in the Holy Trinity, not because the Holy Trinity is subject to number, but because it shows the usefulness of number through the power of its majesty. In substance the Divinity is understood to be one; in his personal manifestations, however, three; for one reads in the epistle of John: "And there are three that bear witness: the water, and the blood, and the spirit."[37] And one also reads in Ezekiel concerning the four gospels: "And in the midst thereof the likeness of four living creatures."[38] The number five is known to pertain to the five books of Moses, as one reads in the Apostle:[39] "In the church I had rather speak five words that are understood." It was on the sixth day, however, that the Lord made "man in [his] image and likeness."[40] On the other hand, we say and believe that the Holy Ghost is sevenfold—and we

---

[33] This sentence and all the rest in this § except the last are omitted by Φ and Δ. At the end of this chapter Δ adds "Breviarium ex libro arithmeticae disciplinae cum capitulis suis," made up with some abbreviation from Boethius' *De institutione arithmetica* I. i–iii, vi–xi, xiii–xviii; cf. Mynors, p. xxxvii.

[34] Deuteronomy 6:4.

[35] This sentence and the next six = Eucherius (*floruit ca.* A.D. 434), *Formulae spiritalis intellegentiae* (a collection of Biblical allegories and pictures).

[36] III Kings 6:23 (I Kings 6:23). Apparently, the two Testaments of the Scriptures, revealed by God in the holy of holies (= the oracle) within the temple, are symbolized by the two cherubim.

[37] I John 5:8.   [38] Ezekiel 1:5.
[39] That is, Paul.—I Corinthians 14:19.   [40] Genesis 1:26.

need number for the understanding of the highest and most mighty [41] conceptions. Let us now come to music, which is delightful in name and in function.

V. ON MUSIC [1]

1. A certain Gaudentius, writing on music, says [2] that Pythagoras discovered its beginnings in the sounds of hammers and the striking upon taut strings.[3] And Mutianus, a most facile writer,[4] has translated Gaudentius into Latin in order that the nature of the work undertaken may disclose his talents. Clement, the priest of Alexandria,[5] on the other hand, says in his book *Against the Pagans* [6] that music began with the Muses and carefully sets forth the reason why the Muses themselves were invented. For the Muses themselves received their name from the word *maso*,[7] that is, "to seek," since through their agency, according to the ancients, the power of song and the harmony of the voice were sought. We have also come upon Censorinus,[8] who has written a work addressed to Quintus Caerellius which is called *On His Birthday*, a work in which the former has treated musical science and another division of learning which ought not to be neglected; [9] for it is profitable to read this book, in order

---

[41] Literally, "most almighty."

[1] *O* has an interpolated version of this chapter; cf. Mynors, pp. xxi, xxvi.

[2] In his *Isagoge*, chap. xi. Gaudentius wrote in Greek, at some time during the first three centuries after Christ.

[3] This sentence = Isid. III. xvi. 1.

[4] Cf. his translation of Chrysostom, mentioned in I. viii. 3, above. According to van de Vyver, *Vivarium*, p. 88, note 2, it seems likely that Mutianus eventually left Cassiodorus, who in the β MSS suppresses the *amicus noster* of the α MSS (Mynors 142.15) and who even omits Mutianus' name (Mynors 149.17), which appears in the α MSS.

[5] Cf. above, I. pref. 4, sentence 1, and I. viii. 4, sentence 1.

[6] That is, Προτρεπτικὸς λόγος πρὸς ῞Ελληνας (an introduction to Christianity addressed to the Greeks), § 31.

[7] *apo tu maso* Σ and (apparently) Isid.—*to masu* B M U.—τοῦ μῶσθαι (*from Plato's Cratylas* 406 A) or μάσαι *editors of Isidore.*—ΑΠΟ ΤΟΤ ΜΑϹΤΟΤΕΙΝ (*i.e.,* μαστεύειν) Δ.—The exact form of the Greek word here causes difficulty, though it is obviously some part of * μάω ("to seek after").

[8] Cf. i. 1, sentence 5, above.

[9] Cf. Teuffel, § 379.4–6. Censorinus' book *On His Birthday* (written in the third century A.D.) has three parts: an introduction (chaps. i–iii), and sections on the origin of the human race (chaps. iv–xiv) and on time (*de temporibus;* chaps. xvi–xxiv). To this work is appended the so-called "fragment of Censorinus," an encyclopedic discourse written by an anonymous author who lived after Lucan

that the contents may be stored away in the innermost recesses of the mind through frequent meditation.

2. Musical science,[10] then, is diffused through all the acts of our life if we before all else obey the commands of the Creator and observe with pure hearts the rules which he has established. For whatever we say or whatever inward effect is caused by the beating of our pulse is joined by musical rhythms to the power of harmony. Music is indeed the science of proper modulation; and if we observe the good way of life we are always associated with this excellent science. When we sin, however, we no longer have music. The sky and the earth and everything which is accomplished in them by the supernal stewardship are not without the science of music; for Pythagoras is witness to the fact that this world was founded through the instrumentality of music and can be governed by it.[11] 3. Music also freely permeates religion itself: witness the ten-stringed instrument of the Decalogue, the reverberations of the harp, timbrels, the melody of the organ, the sound of cymbals. There is no doubt, moreover, that the Psalter itself was named after a musical instrument [12] because it contains the exceedingly pleasant and agreeable modulation of the heavenly virtues.

4. Let us now proceed with our discussion of the divisions of music as they have been handed down by our ancestors. The science of music is the branch of knowledge which treats numbers in relation to sound; such numbers, for example, as double, triple, quadruple, and others of the same sort which are said to be related to sound.[13] 5. The divisions [14] of music are three in number: harmonics, rhythmics, and metrics. *Harmonics* is the division of musical knowledge which distinguishes treble sounds from bass. *Rhythmics* is the division which seeks to know, when

---

(A.D. 39–65) on the nature of the earth, the sky, and the stars, on geometry, and on music. Cassiodorus apparently refers to the anonymous discourse here as if it were an integral part of Censorinus' work.

[10] (§ 2 = Rabanus III. 24.)

[11] Censorinus, *De natali eius die,* xiii. 1.

[12] *Psalterium* (= ψαλτήριον) means a "psaltery" (a stringed instrument of the lute kind).

[13] Cf. *Comm. Psalt.* lxxx. 3; xcvii, toward the end.

[14] (This § = Isid. III. xviii; Aurelianus Reomensis [*floruit ca.* A.D. 850], *De musica disciplina,* chap. iv.)

words are brought together,[15] whether the sound is agreeable or disagreeable. *Metrics* is the division which investigates, in a manner deserving of approbation, the measure of the various poetical verses, such as the heroic, the iambic, the elegiac, and so forth. 6. The types of musical instrument are three in number: percussion instruments, stringed instruments, and wind instruments. *Percussion instruments* are bronze and silver bells [16] and other objects which when struck by a rigid piece of metal return a pleasant ringing sound.[17] *Stringed instruments* are artfully fastened cords, which when struck by the application of a plectrum agreeably delight the hearing; among their number are the various forms of harp.[18] *Wind instruments* are objects which are blown full of breath to produce a sound; for example, trumpets, pipes, organs, pandores,[19] and other instruments of this sort.[20]

7. It now remains for us to speak of consonances. A *consonance* is a proper mixing—productive of euphony in a stringed, wind, or percussion instrument—of a bass sound with a treble or of a treble sound with a bass. There are, moreover, six consonant intervals: first, the diatessaron; second, the diapente; third, the diapason; fourth, the diapason and diatessaron taken together; fifth, the diapason and the diapente taken together; sixth, the disdiapason.[21] I. The interval of the diatessaron is that which is arranged in the ratio of 4 to 3 and is produced through four sounds, whence it receives its name.[22] II. The interval of the diapente is that which is arranged in the ratio of 3 to 2 and is produced by five sounds.[23] III. The interval of the diapason is that which is also called the octave. It is arranged in a double ratio, that is, the ratio of 2 to 1; it is produced, moreover,

---

[15] I translate the reading of Φ and Δ: "in concursione." Mynors' text reads: "incursionem."

[16] "Acitabula": cup-shaped musical instruments struck with a small metal, spade-like hammer.

[17] (Isid. III. xxii. 1.)   [18] Literally "cithara."

[19] "Pandores" or "bandores" (pandoria) are classified in the lexica as stringed instruments similar to lutes (cf. T. Reinach, *La Musique grecque* [1926], p. 127), but Ennis cites evidence to show that Cassiodorus and others believe that they are wind instruments.

[20] (Isid. III. xxi. 1.)   [21] (Aurelianus Reomensis, chap. vii.)

[22] διὰ τεσσάρων (*sc.* χορδῶν): "through four strings"; *i.e.,* a musical fourth.

[23] διὰ πέντε (*sc.* χορδῶν): "through five strings"; *i.e.,* a musical fifth.

through eight sounds, whence it receives the name of octave [or diapason],[24] since among the ancients harps [25] used to consist of eight strings; being produced, as it were, through all the sounds, it is accordingly called a diapason.[26] IV. The interval of the diapason and the diatessaron taken together is that which is arranged in the ratio of 24 to 8; it is produced, moreover, through eleven sounds.[27] V. The interval of the diapason and the diapente taken together is that which is arranged in the ratio of 3 to 1; it is produced, moreover, through twelve sounds.[28] VI. The interval of the disdiapason, that is, the double diapason, is that which is arranged in the ratio of 4 to 1; it is produced, moreover, through fifteen sounds.[29]

8. A tone,[30] that is, a pitch or dominant sound, is the distinguishing quantity in the entire musical structure.[31] There are fifteen tones: [32] Hypodorian, Hypoionian, Hypophrygian, Hypoaeolian, Hypolydian, Dorian, Ionian, Phrygian, Aeolian, Lydian, Hyperdorian, Hyperionian, Hyperphrygian, Hyperaeolian, Hyperlydian.[33] I. The Hypodorian tone is the deepest of all in sound and is therefore called the lowest.[34] II. The Hypoionian [35] is a half step higher than the Hypodorian. III. The Hypophrygian [36] is a half step higher than the Hypoionian and a whole step higher than the Hypodorian. IV. The Hypoaeolian [37] is a half step higher than the Hypophrygian, a whole step higher than

---

[24] The words bracketed are obviously an interpolation, though not so marked in Mynors' text.

[25] Literally "citharas."

[26] διὰ πασῶν (*sc.* χορδῶν): "through all the strings."

[27] A compound musical fourth. The ratio is not 24 to 8 (= 3 to 1, the interval of a compound *fifth*), but actually 24 to 9 (= 8 to 3).

[28] A compound musical fifth.   [29] A double octave.

[30] See Ennis, p. 129, note 251: a tone here is a pitch-key having no connection with the octave-species. In addition to the literature cited by Ennis on the difficult word see O. J. Gombosi, *Tonarten und Stimmungen der antiken Musik* (Munksgaard: Copenhagen, 1939) and Curt Sachs' review in *Classical Weekly*, XXXIII (1940), 267. Cf. also K. Schlesinger, *The Greek Aulos* (Methuen: London, 1939), and Spyros Stamos, "A History of Greek Music," *Athene*, VI (Chicago, 1945), 43–45 especially.

[31] Aurelianus Reomensis, chap. viii.

[32] That is, systems of keys based on difference of pitch.

[33] The remainder of this §, except for the last sentence, = Aurelianus Reomensis, chap. vi.

[34] An arrangement of intervals in an octave-system at a pitch of *E*.

[35] An arrangement at a pitch of *F*.   [36] An arrangement at a pitch of *F♯*.

[37] An arrangement at a pitch of *G*.

the Hypoionian, and a step and a half higher than the Hypodorian. V. The Hypolydian [38] is a half step higher than the Hypoaeolian, a whole step higher than the Hypophrygian, a step and a half higher than the Hypoionian, and two steps higher than the Hypodorian. VI. The Dorian [39] is a half step higher than the Hypolydian, a whole step higher than the Hypoaeolian, a step and a half higher than the Hypophrygian, two steps higher than the Hypoionian, and two and a half steps (that is, the interval of the diatessaron) higher than the Hypodorian. VII. The Ionian [40] is a half step higher than the Dorian, a whole step higher than the Hypolydian, a step and a half higher than the Hypoaeolian, two steps higher than the Hypophrygian, two steps and a half (that is, the interval of the diatessaron) higher than the Hypoionian, and three steps higher than the Hypodorian. VIII. The Phrygian [41] is a half step higher than the Ionian, a whole step higher than the Dorian, a step and a half higher than the Hypolydian, two steps higher than the Hypoaeolian, two and a half steps (that is, the interval of the diatessaron) higher than the Hypophrygian, three steps higher than the Hypoionian, and three and a half steps (that is, the interval of the diapente) higher than the Hypodorian. IX. The Aeolian [42] is a half step higher than the Phrygian, a whole step higher than the Ionian, a step and a half higher than the Dorian, two steps higher than the Hypolydian, two and a half steps (that is, the interval of the diatessaron) higher than the Hypoaeolian, three steps higher than the Hypophrygian, three and a half steps (that is, the interval of the diapente) higher than the Hypoionian, and four steps higher than the Hypodorian. X. The Lydian [43] is a half step higher than the Aeolian, a whole step higher than the Phrygian, a step and a half higher than the Ionian, two steps higher than the Dorian, two and a half steps (that is, the interval of the diatessaron) higher than the Hypolydian, three steps higher than the Hypoaeolian, three and a half steps (that is, the interval of the diapente) higher than the Hypophrygian, four steps higher than the Hypoionian, and four and a half steps

---

[38] An arrangement at a pitch of *G*♯.   [39] An arrangement at a pitch of *a*.
[40] An arrangement at a pitch of *a*♯.   [41] An arrangement at a pitch of *b*.
[42] An arrangement at a pitch of *c*.   [43] An arrangement at a pitch of *c*♯.

higher than the Hypodorian. XI. The Hyperdorian [44] is a half step higher than the Lydian, a whole step higher than the Aeolian, a step and a half higher than the Phrygian, two steps higher than the Ionian, two and a half steps (that is, the interval of the diatessaron) higher than the Dorian, three steps higher than the Hypolydian, three and a half steps (that is, the interval of the diapente) higher than the Hypoaeolian, four steps higher than the Hypophrygian, four and a half steps higher than the Hypoionian, and five steps higher than the Hypodorian. XII. The Hyperionian [45] is a half step higher than the Hyperdorian, a whole step higher than the Lydian, a step and a half higher than the Aeolian, two steps higher than the Phrygian, two and a half steps (that is, the interval of the diatessaron) higher than the Ionian, three steps higher than the Dorian, three and a half steps (that is, the interval of the diapente) higher than the Hypolydian, four steps higher than the Hypoaeolian, four and a half steps higher than the Hypophrygian, five steps higher than the Hypoionian, and five and a half steps higher than the Hypodorian. XIII. The Hyperphrygian [46] is a half step higher than the Hyperionian, a whole step higher than the Hyperdorian, a step and a half higher than the Lydian, two steps higher than the Aeolian, two and a half steps (that is, the interval of the diatessaron) higher than the Phrygian, three steps higher than the Ionian, three and a half steps (that is, the interval of the diapente) higher than the Dorian, four steps higher than the Hypolydian, four and a half steps higher than the Hypoaeolian, five steps higher than the Hypophrygian, five and a half steps higher than the Hypoionian, and six steps (that is, the interval of the diapason) higher than the Hypodorian. XIV. The Hyperaeolian [47] is a half step higher than the Hyperphrygian, a whole step higher than the Hyperionian, a step and a half higher than the Hyperdorian, two steps higher than the Lydian, two and a half steps (that is, the interval of the diatessaron) higher than the Aeolian, three steps higher than the Phrygian, three and a half steps (that is, the interval of the diapente) higher than the Ionian, four steps higher than the Dorian, four and a half steps

---

[44] An arrangement at a pitch of *d*.
[45] An arrangement at a pitch of *d♯*.
[46] An arrangement at a pitch of *e*.
[47] An arrangement at a pitch of *f*.

higher than the Hypolydian, five steps higher than the Hypoaeolian, five and a half steps higher than the Hypophrygian, six
steps (that is, the interval of the diapason) higher than the
Hypoionian, and six and a half steps higher than the Hypodorian. XV. The Hyperlydian [48] is the last and highest of all, a
half step higher than the Hyperaeolian, a whole step higher than
the Hyperphrygian, a step and a half higher than the Hyperionian, two steps higher than the Hyperdorian, two and a half
steps (that is, the interval of the diatessaron) higher than the
Lydian, three steps higher than the Aeolian, three and a half
steps (that is, the interval of the diapente) higher than the
Phrygian, four steps higher than the Ionian, four and a half
steps higher than the Dorian, five steps higher than the Hypolydian, five and a half steps higher than the Hypoaeolian, six
steps (that is, the interval of the diapason) higher than the
Hypophrygian, six and a half steps higher than the Hypoionian, and seven steps higher than the Hypodorian. Whence it is
clear that the Hyperlydian tone, the highest of all, is seven steps
higher than the Hypodorian, the lowest of all. These tones, as
Varro has pointed out, have been shown to possess such great
usefulness that they calm excited minds and cause even wild animals and serpents and birds and dolphins to approach and listen
to their harmony. [49]

9. [50] For, if we do not speak of Orpheus' lyre and the song
of the Sirens on the ground that they are fabulous, what shall
we say of David, who delivered Saul from the unclean spirit by
means of his redeeming melody and who by this unusual method,
namely, having the King listen, brought him the health which
doctors were unable to bring through the power of herbs? [51]
Asclepiades [52] too, a most learned physician according to the
testimony of our ancestors, is said to have restored a certain
madman to his original sanity through the use of music. Many

---

[48] An arrangement at a pitch of f♯.   [49] (Isid. III. xvii. 3.)

[50] On this § cf. Var. II. 40; Censorinus *De accentibus* xii. 4; (Isid. IV. xiii. 3 and
III. xvii. 1).

[51] I Kings 16: 14–23 (I Samuel 16: 14–23).

[52] The name of several physicians, derived from the god Asclepius. The most
distinguished was a native of Prusa in Bithynia who came to Rome in the middle
of the first century B.C., where he acquired a great reputation for his successful
cures.

indeed are the miracles said to have been performed upon suffering men through the agency of this science. The sky itself, as we have stated above,[53] is said to revolve with delightful harmony;[54] and, to state the whole matter succinctly, whatever heavenly or earthly occurrence takes place in a manner consistent with the ordering of its Author is said not to be exempt from this science.

10. Most pleasant and useful, then, is the branch of learning which leads our understanding to heavenly things and soothes our ears with sweet harmony. Among Greek writers Alypius,[55] Euclid,[56] Ptolemy,[57] and others have instructed us in it with excellent elementary treatises; among Latin writers Albinus,[58] a man of distinction, has written a compendious work on this subject, which we recall having had in the library at Rome and having read carefully. If perchance this work has been destroyed by the barbarian assault, you still have Gaudentius;[59] and if you read him punctiliously, he will open the entrance halls of this science to you. Apuleius of Madaura [60] is also said to have written an elementary treatise on this subject in Latin. Father Augustine too has written a work in six books entitled *On Music,* in which he has pointed out that the human voice can by reason of its nature utter rhythmical sounds and melodious harmony in long and short syllables. Censorinus [61] too has discussed accents, which are most necessary to our voice, in subtle fashion, and he states that they have to do with musical science; I have left you a copy of his work among others.

---

[53] § 2, sentence 5.

[54] According to the Pythagoreans the transparent spherical shells in which stars, sun, planets, and moon are supposed to be set, are separated by intervals corresponding to the relative lengths of strings which produce harmonious tones; as the shells revolve, they produce "the music of the spheres." Cf. Cicero *Somnium Scipionis* § 5 (10).

[55] Lived presumably at some time during the first three centuries after Christ.

[56] The elementary treatise on music which bears the name of Euclid (the famous geometrician of the third century B.C.) is really the work of a pupil of Aristoxenus (who lived in the preceding century).

[57] Claudius Ptolemaeus, the Alexandrian geographer and astronomer of the second century A.D., wrote a theoretical work on harmony.

[58] Of the fourth century A.D. Cf. Boethius *De institutione musica* I. xii and xxvi. Cf. Teuffel § 407.5. The title "man of distinction" (*vir magnificus*) is applied to no one else in the *Inst.* except Boethius (4 times).

[59] Cf. v. 1 and I. viii. 3, both above.

[60] Cf. iii. 12, and note 43, and iii. 18, both above.

[61] Cf. § 1, sentence 5, and chap. i, § 1, sentence 5, both above.

11.[62] Let us now come to geometry, which is the theoretical description of figures [63] and also the visible [64] proof possessed by philosophers; who, in order to exalt it by their utterances, assert that their Jupiter uses the methods of geometry in his own works. I am uncertain whether geometry is praised or blamed when they falsely declare that Jupiter fashions in the sky what they represent in colored sand. But if it be associated, to one's salvation, with the true Creator and the omnipotent Lord, this idea may perhaps be consistent with the truth—for, if one be permitted to say so, the Holy Trinity employs geometry when it grants various species and forms to its creatures which it has even now caused to exist; when with venerable power it apportions the courses of the stars and causes those which are movable to pass swiftly along established paths and sets in a definite position those which are fixed. Whatever is well ordered and complete can be attributed to the properties of this science.

VI. ON GEOMETRY

1. Geometry [1] is rendered into Latin as the measuring of the earth, because, according to some, Egypt was at first divided among its own lords by means of the various forms of this science; [2] and those who taught it used to be called measurers. But Varro, the greatest of Latin writers in practical knowledge, explains the origin of the name as follows: at first, when the existing boundaries were unsettled and conflicting, measuring of the earth brought the people the benefits of tranquillity; thereafter, the circle of the entire year was divided by the number of the months and consequently the months themselves, [3] so called because they measure the year, were established. But after these things were discovered, learned men, incited to learn about intangible objects, [4] began to seek the distance between the moon and the earth, and between the sun itself and the moon, and the distance to the very top of the sky; he relates that the most skill-

---

[62] (§ 11 = Rabanus III. xxiii.)

[63] That is, solids, surfaces, lines, and angles, all in space.

[64] That is, "worldly" as contrasted with "spiritual."

[1] The first two sentences of this section = [Boethius] *De geometria*. (The first two sentences and the first clause of the fourth = [Boethius] *Demonstratio artis geometria*, edited by Lachmann, I, 353.) (All of § 1 except the last sentence = Rabanus III. xxiii.) [2] Var. III. lii.

[3] *Menses* ("months") = "measures." [4] (Isid. III. x. 2.)

ful geometers arrived at these facts. He then gives an excellent account of the measuring of the entire earth; and it was for this reason that this science happened to be called geometry, a name which it has guarded for many generations. And consequently Censorinus has carefully described the size of the circumferences of heaven and earth in stades [5] in the book which he has written and dedicated to Quintus Cerellius; [6] and if anyone desires to examine this book, he will not read long before learning many secrets of the philosophers.

2.[7] Geometry is the science of immovable magnitude and of figures. Geometry has the following divisions: plane figures, numerable magnitude, rational and irrational magnitude, and solid figures. *Plane figures* are those which possess length and breadth. A *numerable magnitude* is one which can be divided arithmetically.[8] *Rational and irrational magnitudes* are, respectively, commensurable and incommensurable. *Solid figures* are those which possess length, breadth, and thickness.

3. The science of geometry is treated in its entirety in these parts and divisions and the multiplicity of figures which exists in earthly and heavenly objects is comprehended in the above description. Among the Greeks Euclid,[9] Apollonius,[10] Archimedes,[11] and other excellent writers have been conspicuous for their books on this science; the work of one of these men, Euclid, has been translated into Latin by the previously mentioned [12] Boethius, a man of distinction.[13] If this work be read carefully, the matter which has been set forth in the divisions mentioned above will be distinctly and clearly understood.[14]

[5] A "stade" is a unit of linear measure which equals a little less than ⅛ of an English mile.   [6] *De die natali,* chap. xiii.

[7] (§ 2 = Isid. III. xi–xii. 1.)   [8] That is, can be expressed in numbers.

[9] Taught at Alexandria *ca.* 300 B.C. His *Elements* (Στοιχεῖα) has long been synonymous with geometry. (Cf. Var. VII. v. 3.)

[10] Of Perga; lived in Alexandria and Pergamum *ca.* 200 B.C. He is the author of the famous work on conic sections in eight books (the first four of which exist in the Greek original with the commentary by Eutocius and the last three of which have come down to us in an Arabic translation).

[11] The famous Syracusan mathematician who lived from 287 to 212 B.C. He wrote numerous works on geometry, mechanics, and mathematics—among them works on the measurement of the circle, the calculation of cones and cylinders, etc.

[12] Last mentioned above in iv. 11, sentence 2.

[13] On this title (*vir magnificus*) see iii. 11, note 38, above.

[14] At this point Δ adds *Principles of the science of geometry;* see Appendix C, below.

4. Astronomy remains; [15] if we seek to learn it with piety and moderation, it too will imbue our understanding, as the ancients say, with great clarity. What a priceless experience it is to approach the heavens with the mind and to investigate the entire construction of the sky, and in some measure to deduce by sublime mental contemplation that which secrets of such great magnitude have concealed! For the world itself, according to some, is supposed to be spherical in form in order that it may embrace the various forms of objects with its circumferential boundary. Seneca [16] has therefore composed a book entitled *On the Shape of the World,* with an argument suited to philosophers; we have left you this book also to read.

VII. ON ASTRONOMY

1. Astronomy,[1] accordingly, is rendered into Latin as the law of the stars (the literal meaning of the word), inasmuch as the stars can neither remain fixed nor move in any way other than that in which they have been arranged by their Creator; [2] except perchance when they are changed at the will of the Divinity on the occasion of some miracle, as Joshua is said to have obtained his request that the sun stand still upon Gibeon,[3] and as a star announcing to the world the coming of the Lord for its salvation is said to have been shown to the three wise men; [4] and in the passion of the Lord Christ as well the sun was darkened for three hours; [5] and so forth. These events are called miracles [6] because they concern unexpected matters that deserve wonder. For according to the astronomers the stars which are fixed in the sky are supported without motion; [7] the planets, however, that

[15] (All except the last clause of this § = [Boethius'] *Demonstratio artis geometriae,* p. 394.) (§ 4 = Rabanus III. xxv.)

[16] The younger Lucius Annaeus Seneca (*ca.* 4 B.C.–A.D. 65).

[1] (§ 1–§ 2, sentence 1 = Rabanus III. xxv.) The reader should note that "stars" in this sentence and occasionally elsewhere in this chapter means "any heavenly bodies."

[2] (Isid. III. xxiv.)   [3] Or "Gabaon." For the story see Joshua 10: 12.

[4] Matthew 2: 2. Instead of the clause "and as a star . . . wise men" Δ reads: "and in the time of King Hezekiah it was moved backward *ten degrees*" (IV Kings 20: 11).

[5] Luke 23: 44.   [6] Literally, "wonders."

[7] That is, the fixed stars do not move, within long periods, in relation to other astral bodies. Cf. § 2, sentence 12 (*status stellarum*), below (Isid. III. lxiii).

is, "the wanderers," do move, though the boundaries of the courses which they traverse are fixed.

2. Astronomy, then, as has already been stated,[8] is the science which surveys the movements of heavenly bodies and all their forms and investigates the accustomed state of the stars in relation to themselves and to the earth. The divisions of astronomy are as follows: spherical position; spherical motion; the East; the West; the North; the South; the hemisphere above the earth; the hemisphere beneath the earth; the orbital number of the stars; the forward movement or progression of the stars; the backward movement or retrogression of the stars; the pause of the stars; the correction of a computation by addition; the correction of a computation by subtraction; the magnitude of the sun, moon, and earth; the eclipse; and other phases which occur in these bodies. The *spherical position* is the means by which one learns the nature of a sphere's situation.[9] The *spherical motion* is the means by which a sphere moves spherically.[10] *The East* is the place from which some stars rise.[11] *The West* is the place in which some stars set insofar as we are concerned. *The North* is the place at which the sun arrives when the days are longer than the nights. *The South* is the place at which the sun arrives when the nights are longer than the days. *The hemisphere above the earth* is the part of the sky which is seen in its entirety by us. *The hemisphere beneath the earth* is that which cannot be seen as long as it remains beneath the earth. *The orbital number of the stars* [12] is the measurement of longitude [13] and latitude [14] by

---

[8] Chap. iii. 6, last sentence, and iii. 21, last sentence, both above. These two definitions differ slightly in that they say "science of the movement of heavenly bodies which surveys. . . ." *Comm. Psalt.* chap. cxlviii, near the end.

[9] *Sphere* here seems to mean "heavenly body," rather than "celestial sphere." The spherical position, then, is the position of a heavenly body ("sphere") on the celestial sphere (apparent surface of the sky) defined with reference to imaginary circles on the sphere by the coördinates: *latitude* and *longitude,* when the fundamental plane is the ecliptic (position of the body with reference to the sun); *declination* (*latitude* among the ancients) and *right ascension* (*longitude* among the ancients) when the fundamental plane is the celestial equator (position of a body as seen from the earth).

[10] In other words, either (1) orbital motion, the apparent motion of the heavenly bodies within their orbits in the celestial sphere from east to west; or (2) the real motion of the bodies in their revolution around their suns; or (3) their revolution on their own axes.

[11] (On this sentence and the next four cf. Isid. iii. xlii. 1 and xliii.)

[12] (*Ibid.* lxvi. 1.)   [13] That is, right ascension.

[14] That is, declination.

which one is said to learn the time required by each star to complete its orbit. *The forward movement, or progression, of the stars,* which the Greeks call προποδισμόν, occurs when a star, though apparently carrying out its usual motion, advances somewhat beyond its accustomed course.[15] *The backward movement, or retrogression, of the stars,* which the Greeks call ὑποποδισμόν or ἀναποδισμόν, occurs when a star, though carrying out its regular motion, seems at the same time to move backward.[16] *The pause of the stars,* which the Greeks call στηριγμόν, occurs when a star, though constantly in motion, nevertheless seems in some positions to be motionless;[17] for Varro points out, in his book *On Astronomy,* that "star" is so called from standing still.[18] *The correction of a computation by addition* takes place whenever astronomers, in accordance with astronomical rules, add a second computation to one already made.[19] *The correction of a computation by subtraction* takes place whenever astronomers, reckoning in accordance with astronomical rules, decide that a second computation ought to be subtracted from one already made.[20] *The magnitude of the sun, moon, and earth* denotes a demonstration of the amount by which the sun's magnitude is greater than that of the earth and the amount by which the earth's is greater than that of the moon.[21] *An eclipse* of the sun occurs whenever the moon itself appears to us on the thirtieth day[22] of its synodic period and the sun is thereby hidden from us; an eclipse of the moon occurs whenever the moon falls into the earth's shadow.[23]

3. Books have been written on the science of astronomy in

[15] (On this sentence, the first which follows, and the first half of the second which follows cf. Isid. III. lxviii–lxx.) *Progression* is a direct movement through the signs of the zodiac from west to east.

[16] That is, from east to west (contrary in direction to that of the general planetary courses).

[17] The period between direct and retrograde motion of a heavenly body in its apparent path on the celestial sphere when the body and the earth are in opposition and for a brief time the body seems to be without motion.

[18] *Stella* ("star") from *stare* ("to stand"). The ordinary derivation, however, thinks of *stella* ("star") as representing * *sterula* (cf. Sanskrit *staras,* Greek ἀστήρ), perhaps from the root *ster-* of *sterno* ("to spread"; cf. Greek στορέννυμι, "to spread").

[19] To allow for inclination of the earth, planet, etc., or to correct a fundamental fact by comparison of two distant observations.

[20] *Idem.*

[21] (Isid. III. xlviii.)

[22] "Luna tricesima," the interlunar period between the old and the new moon, when the moon is in conjunction with the sun and the moon is normally invisible.

[23] (Isid. III. lix.)

both Greek and Latin by various authors,[24] among whom Ptolemy,[25] who has published two works on this subject—one called *The Lesser Astronomer*,[26] the other *The Greater Astronomer*,[27] is considered the outstanding writer among the Greeks. He has also drawn up *Canons*,[28] in order that the courses of the stars may thereby be discovered; and, lest the untutored be in some way confused, it is in my opinion not unwise to use these *Canons* as a means of learning the latitudes,[29] perhaps, and of perceiving the measure of the hours, and of observing the nature of the moon's course (in order to determine the date of Easter) and of a solar eclipse. The latitudes have been described as seven lines, as it were, drawn from the East to the West—lines on which are found different kinds of human beings and certain unusually varied animals;[30] the latitudes are named after certain famous places, the first being Meroe,[31] the second Syene,[32] the third the coast [33] (of Africa), the fourth Rhodes, the fifth the Hellespont, the sixth the Black Sea,[34] and the seventh the Borysthenes.[35] Moreover, clocks on which the hours are indicated by the bright sunlight [36] remain faithfully adjusted to the individual regions of the latitudes in accordance with certain definite rules; it is generally agreed that this useful principle was investigated through the diligence of earlier writers, particularly Ptolemy.

4. There is another advantage arising from studies of this

---

[24] (Isid. III. xxvi.)

[25] Claudius Ptolomaeus of the second century A.D., who wrote a work on cosmography (see above, I. xxv. 2), and a work on harmony (see above, II. v. 10, sentence 2).

[26] Perhaps the Φάσεις ἀπλανῶν ἀστέρων or the Ὑποθέσεις τῶν πλανωμένων. Two other short works of his, the Περὶ ἀναλήμματος and the Ἁπλωσις ἐπιφανείας σφαίρας, have come to us only by way of later Arabic translations. A Τετράβιβλος (σύνταξις) in 4 books is falsely attributed to Ptolemy.

[27] Μεγάλη σύνταξις τῆς ἀστρονομίας in 13 books.

[28] Πρόχειροι κανόνες, tables of computations and observations.

[29] That is, the lines which bound the various regions of the heavens, regions which are divided in various ways by mathematicians.

[30] The celestial latitudes are apparently a mere extension of the terrestrial latitudes here described.

[31] A city located on the upper Nile, north of Khartum.

[32] A town at the southern extremity of Upper Egypt; now Essouan.

[33] "Catochoras" = κάτω χώρας ("on the coast"). Alexandria is meant.

[34] "Mesopontum": obviously the Black Sea. Eratosthenes, Strabo, and Ptolemy, however, omit this. E. and S. add "Cinnamomifera" (south of Meroe) and P. adds "Thule" (north of Borysthenes).

[35] The Dnieper River. (For this entire sentence: Isid. III. xliii. 4.)

[36] That is, sun-dials.

sort, which is not to be despised, if we learn from them the proper season for sailing, the time for ploughing, the date of the summer's heat and of the autumn's suspected rains. For to every one of us, his creatures, God has given some power whose existence we may in each case recognize without harm. Other powers which pertain to an acquaintance with the stars—that is, a knowledge of fate—and which without doubt are contrary to our faith deserve to be ignored in such manner that they may seem not to have been mentioned by writers.[37] The most learned father Basil,[38] moreover, has treated this subject with extreme care and diligence in the sixth book of the work which he has termed *The Six Days of the Creation*,[39] cutting off worries of this sort from men's minds in a most pious disquisition; and we have cited him for your reading in the very first place in our chapter on the Octateuch.[40] Father Augustine has also written on this subject in the second book of his work *On Christian Learning*,[41] saying "that astronomical knowledge is adapted to the pernicious error of those who foolishly prophesy fate"; and that therefore, if such a belief is not understood, "it is more suitably and more properly despised."—Moreover, Varro, a most diligent writer, has in his *Geometry* compared the world's shape to an elliptical roundness, representing its form to be like that of an egg, which is circular from side to side, but elliptical from end to end.—For us, however, it is enough in this connection to know only as much as one reads in the Holy Scriptures,[42] since it is absurd beyond measure to follow human opinion in a matter in which, insofar as it is expedient for us, we are known to have divine learning.[43]

In the course of this brief treatment of secular studies, then, it becomes clear that these studies possess no little utility in bringing about an understanding of the divine law—a fact which has been pointed out by certain holy Fathers as well.

---

[37] (For this entire sentence: Isid. III. lxxi. 38.)

[38] See above, I. i. I, sentence 2; § 2, sentence 2; § 4, sentence 2; cf. Preface, § 4, sentence I.

[39] *Homiliae in Hexaëmeron.*

[40] Bk. I. i. I, sentence 2.

[41] Bk. II. xxix. 46. The *quia* which means "because" in Augustine has been changed to mean "that" in Cassiodorus.

[42] Δ adds *EXPLICIT · AMEN* and omits the rest of this §.

[43] Φ ends here, omitting the rest of the §.

CONCLUSION

1. Since, then, our promises have, we believe, been fulfilled with the Lord's aid according to the measure of our ability, we shall consider the reason why this regular succession of sciences has been extended as far as the stars;[1] clearly, in order to lead from earthly affairs minds which have been devoted to secular wisdom and have been purified by training in the sciences and to place these minds in laudable fashion in the celestial regions created by God.[2]

2. But some men, enticed by the beauty of the heavenly bodies and by the brilliance of their luster, seeking the causes of their own perdition most eagerly, have rushed hastily to the courses of the stars with blinded minds in such fashion as to be confident that they could know the outcome of actions beforehand through pernicious computations which are called astrology. Plato, Aristotle, and other men of outstanding ability, not to mention writers in our own language, have been disturbed by the true state of these very matters and have unanimously condemned these individuals, saying that nothing but a confusion in affairs was generated by such a belief; for if the human race were urged on to its various acts by the inevitable circumstances of birth, why should good morals merit praise or bad ones incur the punishment assigned by the laws?[3] And though the writers mentioned above were not devoted to heavenly wisdom, nevertheless, by the testimony of the truth they justly destroyed the delusions of these men, of whom the Apostle says:[4]

Ye observe days and months; I am afraid of you, lest I have bestowed upon you labour in vain.[5]

And on this point the Lord gives fuller indication of his desire in Deuteronomy:[6]

Neither let there be found among you anyone that shall expiate[7] his son or daughter, nor that useth divination by fire, nor that observeth birds;

---

[1] That is, to include astronomy.   [2] (Isid. III. lxxi. 41.)
[3] Cf. *Comm. Psalt.* chap. lxx, near the end.
[4] (All of this section up to this point = Isid. III. lxxi. 39–40.)
[5] Galatians 4: 10–11.
[6] Deuteronomy 18: 10–12. The text quoted below by Cassiodorus differs in several particulars from the texts now established.
[7] That is, "seek to atone for by means of a propitiatory offering."

neither let there be any wizard that observeth omens, nor ventriloquist that useth magic spells, nor fortune teller,[8] nor necromancer; for all that do these things are an abomination unto the Lord thy God.

3. But let us who sincerely long to enter heaven through intellectual exertions believe that God disposes all things in accordance with his will, and let us, as stated in Book I,[9] reject and condemn the vanities of the present life and carefully investigate the books of the Divine Scriptures in their normal order, so that by referring all things to the glory of the Creator we may profitably assign to the celestial mysteries that which those men have seemed to seek vainly for the sake of mortal praise. And therefore, as the blessed Augustine [10] and other very learned Fathers say, secular writings should not be spurned. It is proper, however, as the Scripture states,[11] to "meditate in the (divine) law day and night," for, though a worthy knowledge of some matters is occasionally obtained from secular writings, this law is the source of eternal life.

4. If anyone, fired with heavenly love and freed from earthly desires, really longs to gaze upon the celestial virtues, let him read the Apocalypse of St. John and as he contemplates this work intently he will perceive that the Lord Christ, who has devised such great and such marvellous works with the aid of providence, who has arranged them with his understanding, and who has perfected them with his excellence, now supports them with the divine Spirit, holds them in awe with his power, and governs them with his piety—incomprehensible, ineffable, and fully known to no one except himself. The reader will also perceive that Christ, seated on his majestic throne, admonishes the churches through the holy angels, threatens the evil with punishment, promises rewards to the good, and is venerated in suppliant fashion with the greatest dread by all the elders,[12] the archangels, and the entire heavenly host; and that their particular and sole concern is to celebrate eternally with indefatigable devotion the glory of the Holy Trinity. The reader will also understand that

---

[8] Literally, "viewer of prodigies" (or of "omens").
[9] Of the present work.
[10] *De doctrina Christiana.*
[11] Psalms 1:2; cf. Joshua 1:8.
[12] Or *ancients.* Revelation 4:10.

this world is ruled by Christ's command and that at its end, when Christ wishes, it will be changed for the better. Then, as angels sound their trumpets, the dead will rise, and the human race, long buried,[13] will be restored to a new life. Christ himself too, inspiring awe and dread, preceded by thunder and lightning, will destroy the son of iniquity [14] and come to judge the world, disclosing his virtues, which through God's provident order he determined not to show indiscriminately during his first coming. And after that the reader will understand how great are the toils and troubles from which the church must be freed before it will rejoice eternally in the Lord and with what justice those who follow the devil's biddings perish with him; and then truly will the reader be thoroughly imbued with a great exultation when he has contemplated these matters to the full. Moreover, according to the Scriptures, after these things of the present there will be "a new heaven and a new earth"; [15] and if we but believe this immutably and inviolably, through Christ's bounty we shall succeed in surveying that glory.

5. But if, moreover, we desire to be filled with greater light, so that the future life may become sweet to us even in this world, let us contemplate with very great dread and wonder, only as far as the human mind reaches soberly, how the Holy Trinity, distinct in its persons, yet by nature inseparably joined together and consubstantial, frequenting and permeating its creatures, is omnipresent in its entirety; let us contemplate next how it is caused by evil to appear absent, though it does not cease to be present; in the third place, let us contemplate how, despite the fact that its substance is brighter than all light and its brilliance singular, it cannot be fully surveyed by any of its creatures just as it is, as the Apostle, for example, says: "We shall see him as he is"; [16] and, in the fourth place, let us contemplate the nature of the piety of Christ the King, which caused the Lord of angels not to disdain to assume man's nature and which caused the Life [17] of all to choose to bear the cross. For in order that death might be vanquished by the human race, he who cannot die did

---

[13] That is, spiritually buried.
[15] Revelation 21:1.
[17] That is, the Lord.

[14] That is, the devil.
[16] I John 3:2.

so in the assumption of the flesh; and concerning this matter there are other things truly proclaimed by various Fathers, filled with the divine Spirit.

6. In these matters and others like them all wonder is inadequate, all human investigation fails, and yet these are the delights of Christians; this is the great consolation of those who sorrow, since so long as we ponder such things reverently and intently, through Christ's bounty we put the devil and his works to flight. These things, however, should be regarded with such admiration as to cause them to be believed immovably and indisputably; they should be admitted to be beyond our understanding in such a way that they may remain wholly fixed in our minds. For our senses may retire from such contemplations; our faith, however, is not permitted to waver and hesitate at all. But nevertheless, that which we cannot attain on this earth (although we have seen the Lord through his own indulgence) we unhesitatingly recognize, insofar as he has granted us the power and insofar as our slight ability allows; just as the Apostle says "Now we see through a glass, darkly,[18] but then face to face." [19]

7. But what of the fact that the face of God is promised to the blessed, although he is not fashioned of separate parts? Without doubt the face of God is the venerable awareness of his excellence, the holy manifestation of the divine light, the extraordinary grandeur of his omnipotence, the purity of justice so great that all equity becomes vile in comparison, the immutable intrepidity of truth, the balanced moderation of patience, the unfailing fullness of piety, the amazing dispensation of understanding, the wonderful glory, the matchless clemency. O great happiness of the faithful, to whom is promised the sight of the Lord "as he is" [20] and who in their pious belief in him are already filled with a great hope of blessedness! [21] How extraordinary, I ask, will be the sight of him who has already conferred such favors in return for our belief? Indeed, it is an inestimable gift to behold the Creator, the source of life for all things endowed with life, the source of knowledge for all existing things, the ruler of

---

[18] Literally, *in a riddle*.   [19] I Corinthians 13:12.
[20] I John 3:2.   [21] That is, salvation.

all things created, the restorer of all things which arise renewed and improved, the source of all things by means of which this world itself is vanquished. But though the Righteous Judge sustains all things, though he governs all things in an inexpressible manner, these are, however, gifts of exceeding sweetness, since the most merciful Redeemer will deign to appear before our eyes. These things and similar things that can be conceived about his majesty are in my opinion what the Apostle calls the face of God.

8. Vouchsafe us, we beg thee, O Lord, the most glorious holiness of this vision, so that thou mayest not suffer those in whom thou hast aroused such a great desire to be deprived of this blessing. May we see thee who wilt live forever, though thou hast deigned to die for us; may we see the glory of thy majesty, though thou didst desire to appear humble in our flesh. Even in this world thou mayest gaze benevolently upon thy servants; in this world they, however, may not look fully and clearly at thy face. Vouchsafe, O Lord, to bestow upon those who believe in thee that in which thou dost include all benefits.

9. And accordingly, dearest brothers, Father Augustine, who is usually profitable to the faithful, has discussed this point in very full and marvellous fashion in his book which is dedicated to Paulina and entitled *On Seeing God;* [22] and at the end of the book there is a clear and brief description of the manner in which God is seen. Therefore, trusting not in our merits but rather in God's grace, may we continually request the granting of that sight, since he munificently reminds his needy flock with the following threefold promise: "Ask and ye shall receive, seek and ye shall find, knock and it shall be opened unto you." [23] Hence, dearest brothers, as it happens, we truly deserve to enter heaven because of the Lord's bounty and not because of merit, on account of which the pagans erroneously thought that they were building something for the celestial workshop.[24] We may perhaps seem to have exceeded the normal length of a book; but if one considers

[22] *De videndo Deo ad Paulinam* (Epistula 147).
[23] Matthew 7:7; Luke 11:9. Instead of "ye shall receive" (*accipietis*) the Douai-Rheims and the King James versions read: "it shall be given you" (*dabitur vobis*).
[24] That is, heaven.

the extent of Genesis and Exodus and other books, those which we have previously judged to be rather long begin to be short.[25]

[25] At this point U adds: *The two books of Cassiodorus Senator's An Introduction to divine and human readings have ended auspiciously;* B adds the foregoing and also: THE ARCHETYPAL MANUSCRIPT AGAINST COPIES OF WHICH OTHER MANUSCRIPTS OUGHT TO BE CORRECTED. M reads merely: *Here ends the book of secular letters from Cassiodorus Senator's Introduction;* p: *Cassiodorus Senator's book on secular disciplines is finished;* and Σ: *Here ends the book on human readings from Cassiodorus Senator's Introduction.* B also adds the following: *After the two books of the Introduction which briefly comprise divine and human letters have been comprehended and carefully discussed, it is time in my opinion for us to read the edifying rules of the ancients (that is, the introductory book) which introduces us in excellent and profitable fashion to sacred letters.* (Here follows Mallius Theodorus *de Metris*.)

Appendix

A. *Commonplaces which are found in* Φ *and* Δ *(see Mynors, pp. xxv and xxxvii); words which have been added to the commonplaces of Cassiodorus and in some cases passages which have been rephrased* (Bk. II, chap. 3, §§ 14, last sentence—17, above) *are printed in italics below (but the reader should consult the Latin text to discover the exact additions).*

Commonplaces are the bases of arguments, the wellsprings of ideas, the sources of modes of expression. *And therefore a general topic* [1] *may be defined as the basis of an argument, and an argument as a reason which makes something doubtful seem credible.*[2] *And arguments exist* in the question under discussion, *or they are drawn from matters which are in some way related to this question* and are produced by additional circumstances, *or* they are assumed to be really extrinsic. *Now three types of argument* are inherent in the *question* under discussion, namely, from the whole, from parts, and from etymology. And, to go on, an argument from the whole is the employment of a definition for the point to be determined, as in Cicero's statement [3] "Glory is the praise for deeds well [4] done, and the reputation [5] for great services to the state." *Behold! since glory is the whole, he points out what it is by the use of a definition.* An argument from parts *is illustrated by the following:* "If the eye sees, the entire body does not therefore see." [6] Moreover, an argument from derivation, *which is called etymology in Greek, is fashioned as follows:* "If a consul is one who takes counsel for the state, what else did Tully effect when he affected the conspirators with punishment?" [7] *Now, arguments are also drawn from matters* which *are* in some way *related to the question under discussion* and are produced by additional circumstances; and these arguments have thirteen types: [8] from cognate words; [9] from genus; from a particular type of the genus, *that is, from species;* from likeness; from difference; from the opposite; from a

---

[1] "Locus" (= commonplace).

[2] Boethius *De differentiis topicis* I (Migne, *Pat. Lat.*, LXIV, 1174 and 1180C). Mart. v. 474.

[3] *Pro Marcello* viii. 26.

[4] I have changed the "certe" ("surely") to "recte" ("well"). The latter, found in II. iii. 15, sentence 3, above, seems to be the correct reading.

[5] "The reputation" ("fama") is omitted by Δ.

[6] Mart. v. 481.   [7] *Ibid.*, § 483.   [8] Cf. Mart. v. 474.

[9] Or similarity of form; cf. II. iii. 15, sentence 6, note 82, above. This item and each of the twelve which follow is preceded by *alia* (*i.e.*, literally "Some arguments are from cognate words, others from genus," etc.).

combination of circumstances; from anterior circumstances; from posterior circumstances; from contradictory ideas; from causes; from effects; and from comparison of *lesser, greater, or equal things. In the first place, then, an argument is fashioned from cognate words.* 1.[10] *Cognate words are said to occur* when a noun is modified to form a verb, as in Cicero's statement that Verres "swept" the province "clean";[11] or a verb is modified to form a noun, as "plunderer" from "to plunder"; *or* one noun is modified to form another, *as* in Terence's remark "It's a scheme of lunatics, not lovers."[12] 2. An argument from genus is a *descent*[13] *from a genus to some species, as in Virgil's famous dictum:* "A fickle and changeful thing is woman ever"[14]—*for since Dido is a species, she might have been fickle and changeful; or as in Cicero's famous remark,*[15] *which formed an argument that descends from genus to species:* "For not only ought you to make a careful computation for all the provinces and all our allies, but, gentlemen of the jury, an especially careful computation in the case of Sicily." 3. *The fashioning* of an argument from species requires the lending of truth by a particular statement to a general one, *as in Virgil's well-known words "Or was it not thus that the Phrygian shepherd entered Lacedaemon?"*[16] *Inasmuch as "the Phrygian shepherd" is a species, if this single person acted thus, then other individuals belonging to the Trojan genus could also act thus.* 4. An argument from likeness is the discovery of like circumstances in particular things, as in Virgil's lines: "Bring me store of weapons; none of all those that once on Ilium's plains were lodged in bodies of the Greeks shall my hand hurl at Rutulians in vain."[17] 5. An argument from difference *is formed* when *particular things*[18] are distinguished by a citation of their dissimilarities, *as* in Virgil's statement "Not Diomedes' horses dost thou see, nor[19] Achilles' car."[20] 6. An argument from the opposite *is formed* when contrary ideas are juxtaposed, *as in Terence's question "For if you scold a man who has helped to save a life, what will you do to one who has brought you loss or harm?"*[21] 7. *Credence in an argument from a combination of circumstances*[22] *is sought when items which are individually weak take on the strength of truth when combined, as, for example:* "But, in addition to this, what if you happened*[23]* to be poor before the deed? What if you were greedy? What if you were bold? What if you were an

---

[10] Φ omits this number and all of those which follow.

[11] *Verrines*, oration II, chap. vii, § 19.

[12] *Andria*, l. 218. There is a play on *amentium* ("lunatics") and *amantium* ("lovers").

[13] Most of this sentence = Mart. v. 485.

[14] *Aeneid* IV. 569.

[15] *Verrines*, oration II, chap. i, § 2.

[16] *Aeneid* VII. 363.

[17] *Ibid.* X. 333–335.

[18] *Aliquae res* (Bk. II. iii. 15: *aliqua*).

[19] *non* instead of *nec*.

[20] *Aeneid* X. 581.

[21] Mart. v. 488; Terence *Andria*, l. 142.

[22] *A coniunctis*. This commonplace seems to be different from that designated "from kindred ideas" (*a coniugatis; = ab adiunctis?*) in II. iii. 15, above.

[23] Instead of Mynors' "Quid accedit" I translate the "Quid si accedit" of Mart. and of Cicero himself.

enemy of the man who was killed?" [24] *Since these items are individually insufficient, they are therefore combined in order that something may be proved from the combination of many of them.* 8. An argument from anterior circumstances is a demonstration that particular things are the results of previous actions, *as* in the following example from Cicero's speech in defense of Milo: "Since he has not hesitated to disclose what he thought, can you doubt what he did?" [25] *For first comes a premise, in which the argument consists, and the result follows.* 9. An argument from posterior circumstances, however, is a statement of something which inevitably follows from a definite assumption, *as in the statement: "If a woman has given birth to a child, she has lain with a man."* [26] 10. An argument from contradictory ideas is the destruction of a charge by the opposition of a notion inconsistent with it, as in Cicero's *words: "It is* therefore *shown* that he who not only had been freed from such danger but had *even* been endowed with the greatest public honor *by you* would have liked to slay you in *his* home." [27] 11. An argument from causes is the *proof* that the matter *under* consideration *could have happened in* accordance with a general habit of action, *as in* Terence's lines "For some time I have had my fears about you, Davus, that you might follow the run of servants and trick me." [28] 12. An argument from effects *is formed* when something is a result of preceding acts, as *in* Virgil's saying "'T is fear that proves souls base." [29] *For fear is the reason why the soul is base, because baseness is the effect of fear.* 13. An argument from comparison is *said to be* the *confirmation* of an opinion about something after it has been compared to persons or causes.[30] *And an argument from comparison of the greater to the lesser is illustrated by Virgil's line "You can arm brothers of one soul to war against one another,"* [31]—*therefore, since you can do this to brothers, how much more you can accomplish in the case of others! An argument from comparison of the lesser to the greater is exemplified by the sentence "Publius Scipio, a private citizen, slew Tiberius Gracchus, pontifex maximus, though the latter was only slightly undermining the condition of the state."* [32] *An argument from comparison of equal to equal drawn from Cicero's speech against Piso follows: "It makes no difference whether the consul harasses the state with reprobate speeches and dangerous laws or allows others to do so."* [33] Extrinsic arguments, *however, are considered* to be *those which the Greeks*

---

[24] Mart., § 489: Cicero *Pro Sexto Roscio Amerino* xxxi. 86.

[25] Mart., § 490: Cicero *Pro Milone* xvi. 44.

[26] Mart., § 491, from Cicero *De inventione* i. 44.

[27] Mart., § 492: Cicero *Pro rege Deiotaro* v. 15.

[28] *Andria,* ll. 582–583. [29] *Aeneid* IV. 13.

[30] Mart., § 494.

[31] Mart., § 495: *Aeneid* vii. 335.

[32] Mart., § 496: Cicero *In Catilinam,* oration I, chap. i, § 3. The words *pontifex maximus* (not strictly a political office) actually apply to Scipio in Cicero's text, which Cassiodorus quotes incorrectly.

[33] Mart., § 497; Cicero *In Pisonem,* chap. v, § 10.

term ἄτεχνοι, that is, *not according to the rules of art,*[34] *because* one draws *by way of evidence* from some external thing to produce credence.[35] *And first,* evidence *from* a person is such that the person whose evidence carries weight in the producing of credence is not anyone without exception, but one who deserves praise for the excellence of his moral character. Evidence *from* nature is the evidence which possesses the greatest excellence. *And* there are modes of evidence *having to do with circumstance* which carry weight, to wit: talent, wealth, age, luck, art, experience, necessity, concourse of fortuitous events. *And* one seeks to produce credence through the use of the words and deeds of our ancestors. *And* credence is produced by torments, after the employment of which no one is thought to have any desire to lie.

Here follows again in Φ, but not in Δ, Bk. II, chap. iii, § 17, above: "One should also store away in his memory (*Memoriae quoque*) . . . the human mind of necessity refers to one of the commonplaces named above (*cadat ingenium*)."

B. An excerpt concerning the four elements, which Δ adds to our text without title (see Mynors, p. xxx; Mynors does not know its source).

And now behold how the intermediate bodies of the world, that is, water and air, have, as we have shown, taken their force and character from numbers. For just as in the upper world each of the two intermediate bodies receives two collateral characteristics from the adjacent extreme element and a third characteristic from the remaining elements, even in this world fire and the remaining element [1] produce intermediate bodies if the characteristics are mixed in proper proportion. Let us, then, consider the elements of which we are speaking, that is, fire and earth, and let us carefully investigate their peculiar properties which cannot be mixed with other qualities. We surely see that earth is immovable, corporeal, and blunt. Fire, on the other hand, can certainly prove that it is movable, incorporeal, and sharp. These characteristics are so conflicting and opposed that the elements arrogate to themselves substances from the adjacent elements and obtain a relationship with true nature by a sort of family tree. Water, of course, is the element next to earth, and air is then placed above water. Now air has fire as its upper limit, since these afore-mentioned intermediate bodies of the world consist in each instance of two characteristics drawn from the nearest element [2] and a third characteristic drawn from an element farther removed.[3] For if we are right in saying that earth is corporeal, blunt, and

---

[34] See II. iii. 16, sentence 1, and note 99, above.
[35] Mart., § 474.
[1] Earth.
[2] The nearest element, either extreme or intermediate.
[3] The phrase "from the remaining elements" in sentence 2, above, really equals in

immovable, we shall be right in saying that water is movable, corporeal, and blunt; if careful thought finds that fire is sharp, incorporeal, and movable, air will be correctly judged to be incorporeal, movable and blunt. And therefore insofar as water is movable, it is fire; its qualities of corporeality and bluntness have been adopted from the mass of its stationary neighbor.[4] Air's quality of bluntness, in turn, comes from the lower elements; the third element [5] gets its incorporeality and mobility from the upper air,[6] to which it is most closely related. We shall observe these facts more easily by consulting the lines of the diagram below.[7]

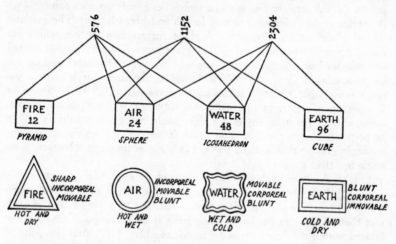

The unequal oblique lines at the top, brought together at equal intervals, are not encumbered with the full descriptions of the figures at the very bottom of the diagram; hence it is through combinations more obvious than they would otherwise have been that these lines not only indicate substances of an interdependent type but also join themselves together despite the intervention of their differences.[8] This is the cord which ties the world's

---

effect the phrase in the present sentence: "drawn from an element further removed." Thus, in the second sentence below this point, water receives one characteristic, mobility, from fire, but water might just as well be said to have received this characteristic from air.

[4] Earth.

[5] Air.

[6] *Aether.* Presumably to be identified here with *fire.*

[7] Mynors (p. 168) notes that the diagram should be placed after the third sentence of this §, but the words *quae subsunt* ("below") seem to indicate clearly that it should be placed either after the present sentence or at the end of the §.

[8] My translation represents merely an attempt to guess the meaning of this sentence. The Latin text follows: Earum a summo dispar obliquitas paribus conserta dispendiis sic in adversorum plenitudinem deficit, ut per obvios coetus vicissim et alterni generis substantias pariant et insertis in se diversitatibus congregentur.

covenant together; this is the relationship which binds the elements together.

C. An excerpt concerning geometry which Δ adds to the text after Bk. *II, chap. vi,* § 3.

PRINCIPLES OF THE SCIENCE OF GEOMETRY

[*Euclid, Bk. I, Definitions*] [1] (1.) A point [2] is that which has no part. (2.) A line is length without breadth. (3.) The extremities of a line are points. (4.) A straight line is a line which lies evenly upon its points. [3] (5.) A surface is that which has merely length and breadth. (6.) The extremities of a surface are lines. (7.) A plane surface is a surface which lies evenly upon its straight lines. [4] (8.) A plane angle is the inclination toward one another [5] of two lines in a plane which touch one another and do not lie in a straight line. (9.) When, however, the lines which contain the angle are straight, the angle is then called rectilinear. (10.) When a straight line set upon a straight line makes the adjacent angles equal to one another, each of the equal angles is a right angle, and the upper line is said to be perpendicular to the line upon which it rests. (11.) An obtuse angle is an angle greater than a right angle. (12.) An acute angle, however, is an angle less than a right angle.

(14.) [6] A figure is that which is enclosed by some boundary or boundaries. (13.) A boundary, in turn, is that which is an extremity of something. (15.) A circle is a plane figure enclosed by a single line of such sort that all the straight lines falling upon it from one point among those located within the figure are equal to one another. [7] (16.) And this point is called the center of the circle. (17.) A diameter of the circle is any straight line drawn through the center and terminated in both directions by the circumference of the circle, and such a straight line divides the circle into two equal parts. (18.) A semicircle is a plane figure enclosed by the diam-

---

[1] This paragraph and the three which follow (containing the 23 definitions, the 5 *petitiones*, and the *communes animi conceptiones*) = Boethius' *Euclid* (K. Lachmann, *Gromatici veteres*, Berlin, 1848, pp. 377–379): cf. Boethius' *Geometry* (ed. by J. G. Friedlein, *Boethius, De institutione arithmetica . . . accedit geometria*, Leipzig, 1867), pp. 374–378: other versions occur in Mart., Bk. VI, and Censorinus (*ed.* Hultsch, Leipzig, 1867), pp. 60–63. On the first six definitions cf. Isid. III. xii. 7.

[2] Cf. Cassiodorus, *Comm. Psalt.*, on Psalms 96:4.

[3] The exact meaning is obscure. For a discussion of Euclid's somewhat different definition see Heath, I, 165–169: "A straight line is a line which lies evenly with the straight lines on itself."

[4] Euclid's definition, which follows exactly his definition of a straight line, is: "A plane surface is a surface which lies evenly with the straight lines on itself." See Heath, I, 171–176.

[5] "Ad alterutram conclusio." Cf. Heath, I, 176–181.

[6] Note that 14 precedes 13 here.

[7] Cf. Cassiodorus, *Comm. Psalt.*, on Psalms 96:4.

eter and that part of the circumference which the diameter cuts off. (19.)
Rectilinear figures are those bounded by straight lines: a trilateral figure, by
three; a quadrilateral, by four;[8] a multilateral, by more than four.[9] (20.)[10]
An equilateral triangle, then, is that which is enclosed by three equal sides;
an isosceles triangle that which has only two of its sides equal; and a scalene
triangle that which has[11] its three sides unequal. (21.) Moreover, of the
trilateral figures the orthogonal, that is, a right-angled triangle, is the figure which has a right angle; the amblygonal, or obtuse-angled triangle, is
that in which there is an obtuse angle; the oxygonal, which means acute-
angled triangle, is that in which the three angles are acute. (22.) Of the
quadrilateral figures that which is equilateral and right-angled is called a
square; that which is right-angled but not equilateral is an oblong;[12] that
which is equilateral but not right-angled is a rhombus; that, moreover, in
which the opposite sides and angles are equal is a rhomboid—it is, however, neither right-angled nor equilateral. All quadrilateral figures other
than these are called[13] trapezia, that is, "little tables."[14] (23.) Straight
lines which, being in the same plane surface and being prolonged[15] in both
directions, meet in neither direction are called parallel, that is, "alongside
one another."[16]

[*Postulates 1-5.*] There are five postulates, as follows: that a straight
line can be drawn from any point to any point; and likewise that a finite
straight line can be prolonged continuously in a straight line; and likewise
that a circle can be described with any center and distance;[17] and that all
right angles are equal to one another; and that, if a straight line falling on
two straight lines make the two interior angles on the same side less than
two right angles, the two straight lines, if prolonged indefinitely, meet on
the side on which are situated the angles less than two right angles.

[*Common notions.*][18] The common notions are as follows. (1.) Things
which are equal to the same thing are also equal to one another. (3.)[19]

---

[8] Literally, "by four sides" (*lateribus*).   [9] Literally, "four sides" (*lateribus*).
[10] Euclid's phrase "Of trilateral figures" is omitted at the beginning of this
definition. It appears properly, however, at the beginning of the next.
[11] Literally, "will have" (*possidebit*).
[12] Literally "longer on one side than on the other" (*parte vero altera longius*).
[13] Euclid has: "let all . . . be called."
[14] "Mensulae." The term "trapezium," though applied here to all quadrilaterals
other than squares, oblongs, rhombi, and rhomboids, is properly restricted to a
quadrilateral with only two sides parallel and the word is apparently used in this
restricted sense by Euclid in his book Περὶ διαιρέσεων (on divisions of figures). All
other quadrilaterals are properly denoted by the term "trapezoid."
[15] Euclid adds "indefinitely" (εἰς ἄπειρον).
[16] "Alternae."   [17] "Distance": radius.
[18] That is, axioms.
[19] (3.) precedes (2.) here. There are four additional axioms (of the same type
as 1-3) which occur in the MSS and editions: (4.) If equals be added to unequals,
the sums are unequal. (5.) If equals be subtracted from unequals, the remainders
are unequal. (6.) Things which are doubles of the same thing are equal to one

And if equals be subtracted from equals, the remainders are equal. (2.) And if equals be added to equals, the sums are also equal. (8.) [20] And things which coincide with one another are equal.[21]

[*Bk. II*, *definition 2.*] In any parallelogrammic area any one whatever of the V-shaped figures [22] about its [23] diameter with the two complements is a gnomon.[24]

[*Bk. V, Definitions.*] (1.) A lesser magnitude is a part [25] of a greater magnitude when the lesser measures the greater. (2.) A greater magnitude is a multiple of a lesser magnitude whenever the greater is measured [26] by the lesser. (3.) A ratio is a relation arising from a comparison of two related magnitudes with one another: [27] (4.) Magnitudes are said to have a ratio to one another which are capable, when multiplied, of exceeding one another. (5.) Magnitudes are said to be in the same ratio, the first to the second and the third to the fourth, when if any equimultiples whatever be taken of the first and third and any equimultiples whatever of the second and fourth, the former equimultiples exceed, or fall short of, or are equal to the latter equimultiples, respectively, taken in corresponding order. (6.) Let magnitudes which have the same ratio be called proportional. (7.) When, of the equimultiples, the multiple of the first magnitude exceeds the multiple of the second, but the multiple of the third does not exceed the multiple of the fourth, then the first is said to have a greater ratio to the second than the third has to the fourth. (8.) A proportion in three terms is the least possible. (11.) [28] The term "corresponding magnitudes" is used of antecedents in relation to antecedents and of consequents in relation to consequents. (9.) When three magnitudes are proportionally related, the first is then said to have to the third the duplicate ratio of that which it has to the second. (10.) When four magnitudes are proportionally related,[29] the first is then said to have to the fourth the triplicate ratio of that

---

another. (7.) Things which are halves of the same thing are equal to one another. Cf. Heath, I, p. 223.   [20] (7.) in Mynors.

[21] On a fifth additional axiom (= No. 9: The whole is greater than the part) see Heath, I, 232.

[22] In Euclid "parallelograms" appears here instead of "V-shaped figures." The gnomon is, however, V-shaped. See Heath, I, 370–372.

[23] "Its": Mynors' "eandem" should be "eiusdem."

[24] Cf. Lachmann, *op. cit.*, p. 385; Friedlein, *op. cit.*, p. 378.

[25] "Part" has the restricted sense of *submultiple* here, as distinct from the more general sense in which it is used in common notion 9 (see note 21 above).

[26] "Is measured": "integra dimensione suppletur."

[27] On the meaning of this definition cf. Heath, II, 116–119.

[28] (11.) here precedes (9.) and (10.). The text, which is defective, reads: "cum proportionales idem eiusdem magnitudines † proportiones esse dicuntur praecedentes praecedentibus et consequentibus consequentes." Mynors suggests that "cum" and "proportiones" be bracketed. Even then there are difficulties: "proportionales" seems to be used instead of "homologae" (Euclid's ὁμόλογα), and the sense of "idem eiusdem" is uncertain. I do not attempt to translate this defective text, but give instead a translation of Euclid's Greek.

[29] That is, continuously proportional.

which it has to the second.[30] (13.) [31] Inverse ratio means taking the consequent as antecedent in relation to the antecedent as consequent.[32] (12.) Alternate ratio means taking the antecedent in relation to the antecedent and likewise the consequent in relation to the consequent. (14.) Composition of a ratio means taking the antecedent together with the consequent as one in relation to the consequent by itself. (15.) Separation of a ratio means taking the excess by which the antecedent exceeds the consequent in relation to the consequent by itself.[33] (16.) Conversion of a ratio means taking the antecedent in relation to the excess by which the antecedent exceeds the consequent.[34] (18.) [35] A perturbed proportion arises when, < there being three magnitudes and another set equal to them in multitude > as antecedent is to consequent < among the first magnitudes >, so is antecedent to consequent [36] < among the second magnitudes >, while, as the consequent is to a third < among the first magnitudes >, so is a third to the antecedent < among the second magnitudes.> (17.) a ratio *ex aequali* is the taking of the extreme terms by virtue of the removal of the intermediate terms.[37]

---

[30] Euclid adds: "and so on continually, whatever be the proportion."

[31] (13.) precedes (12.) here.—Definitions 12–16 here probably refer to *ratios* rather than *proportions of four terms:* cf. Heath, II, 134.

[32] I translate Euclid's Greek. The text of Cassiodorus seems to mean: "Inverse ratio means taking the consequent in relation to the antecedent, and likewise the consequent in relation to the antecedent" (*sic!*). This seems to make no sense.

[33] In my translation I omit the last half of the text ("ita se habere . . . consequitur."), which merely repeats the first half.

[34] As above, I omit the last half of the text ("ita se habere . . . quod consequens"), which repeats the first half.

[35] (18.) precedes (17.) here. The additional words which are supplied from Euclid's Greek are enclosed in brackets: < . . . >.

[36] The text mistakenly reads: "so is consequent to antecedent."

[37] Euclid's definition is longer; see Heath, II, 115 and 136. It seems to mean a *proportion* here rather than a ratio as in definitions 12–16 above. The meaning is clearly as follows. If a, b, c, d . . . be one set of magnitudes, and A, B, C, D . . . another set, such that a is to b as A is to B, and b is to c as B is to C, and so on, the last proportion being, e.g., k is to l, as K is to L, then the inference *ex aequali* is that a is to l as A is to L.

HERE THROUGH GOD'S GRACE THIS SECTION ENDS.

Bibliography

A LIST of abbreviations for the books and articles cited most frequently in this volume appears on page xiii. Below is printed an additional list of important bibliographical items not cited in this volume. Even if the works in both lists be combined with the numerous other works whose titles are cited in full in the notes, the combination will not of course constitute a full bibliography of the subject treated. For a fairly complete list of items on the history of the period in which Cassiodorus lived see Konrad Bursian's *Jahresberichte über die Fortschritte der klassischen Altertumswissenschaft* (Leipzig), CLXXXIV (1920), 1–90, and CCXIII (1927), 41–167; and the later general works noted in van de Vyver, p. 244, n. 1.

Bardenhewer, Otto. Patrologie. 3d ed. Freiburg, 1910. § 120.

Capelli, Luigi Mario. "I fonti delle 'Institutiones humanarum rerum' di Cassiodoro," *Rendiconti del Istituto Lombardo,* XXXI (1898).

Cessi, Roberto. Preface to his edition of the Anonymous Valesianus in L. Muratori's *Rerum Italicarum scriptores,* 2d ed. by G. Carducci and V. Fiorini, Vol. XXIV, Part 4 (fasc. 114–115), Bologna, 1913.

Church, Richard William. "Cassiodorus," in his *Miscellaneous Essays* (London, 1888), pp. 155–204.

Ciampi, Ignazio. I Cassiodori nel V e nel VI secolo. Rome, 1877.

Corrsen, P. "Die Bibeln des Cassiodorus und der Codex Amiatinus," in *Jahrbuch protestanter Theologie,* IX (1883), 619 ff.

Delehaye, Hippolyte. "Saint Cassiodore," in *Mélanges Paul Fabre:* étude d'histoire du moyen âge (Paris, 1902), pp. 40–50.

Duckett, Eleanor Shipley. The Gateway to the Middle Ages. New York, 1938. Chap. ii: "The Gothic Rule in Italy: Cassiodorus, Secretary of Theodoric the Great."

Hartmann, Ludwig Moritz. Geschichte Italiens im Mittelalter. 4 vols. Leipzig, 1897–1915. Vol. I: Das italienische Königreich, 2d ed. Gotha, 1923.

Hodgkin, Thomas. Italy and Her Invaders. 2d ed. Oxford, 1896.

—— Theodoric the Goth. 2d ed. London, 1923. Chap. ix.

Körbs, O. Untersuchungen zur ostgotischen Geschichte. Eisenberg, 1913. Dissertation.

Lowe, Elias Avery. "An Uncial MS. of Mutianus," in *Journal of Theological Studies,* XXIX (1927–1928), 129–133.

Mierow, Charles Christopher, trans. Jordanes, Origin and Deeds of the Goths. 2d ed. Princeton, 1915.

Milkau, S. "Zu Cassiodorus," in *Von Büchern und Bibliotheken: Festschrift Kuhnert* (Berlin, 1928), pp. 40 ff.

Mommsen, Theodor. "Ostgotische Studien," in *Neues Archiv der Gesellschaft für ältere deutsche Geschichtskunde,* XIV (1889), 223–249, 455–544; XV (1890), 181–188. Gesammelte Schriften, III [1910], 362–484.

Morin, G. "L'Ordre des heures canoniales dans les monastères de Cassiodore," *Revue bénédictine,* XLIII (1931), 145–152.

Mortet, Victor. Notes sur la texte des Institutiones de Cassiodore, d'après divers manuscrits; recherches critiques sur la tradition des arts libéraux de l'antiquité au moyen âge. Paris, 1904. In part a reprint from *Revue de Philologie,* 1900–1904.

Nickstadt, Helmut Friedrich Alexander. De digressionibus quibus in Variis usus est Cassiodorus. Marburg, 1921. Dissertation.

Olleris, Alexandre. Cassiodore: conservateur des livres de l'antiquité latine. Paris, 1841.

Overbeck, F. Vorgeschichte und Jugend der mittelalterlichen Scholastik: eine kirchenhistorische Vorlesung. Basel, 1917.

Schmidt, K. W. Quaestiones de musicis scriptoribus Romanis imprimis de Cassiodoro et Isidoro. Giessen, 1899. Dissertation.

Schneider, Fedor Heinrich Gustav Hermann. Rom und der Romgedanke im Mittelalter. Munich, 1926.

van de Vyver, A. "Les étapes de développement philosophique du haut-moyen-âge," in *Revue belge de philologie et d'histoire,* VIII (1929), 425–452.

Wattenbach, Wilhelm. Deutschlands Geschichtsquellen im Mittelalter bis zur Mitte des dreizehnten Jahrhunderts. 6th ed., 2 vols. Berlin, 1893–1894. Vol. I in 7th ed., by E. Dümmler; Stuttgart and Berlin, 1904.

Weinberger, Wilhelm. "Hss. von Vivarium," in *Miscellanea Franz Ehrle* (Rome, 1924), IV, 75–88.

Index